AF897683

HANDBOOK OF REVIVALS

Handbook of Revivals

Henry C Fish

CountedFaithful

HANDBOOK OF REVIVALS
First published in 1874

COUNTED FAITHFUL
2 Drakewood Road
London SW16 5DT

Website: http://www.countedfaithful.org

ISBN
Book: 978-1-78872-117-2
ePub: 978-1-78872-118-9
Kindle: 978-1-78872-119-6

Contents

Preface

THERE are three factors which have led to the preparation of this volume.

1. The obvious need of a fresh work on Revivals of religion.
2. A deep and earnest conviction of the momentous importance of the subject discussed.
3. The wish to furnish, both for inspiration and guidance, such facts, examples, arguments, directions and suggestions, touching the whole matter of revivals, as might lead to their greater appreciation and promotion.

Indebtedness is here acknowledged to the following authorities:

- Stevens' *History of Methodism;*
- Tracy's *Great Awakening;*
- Barnes' *Lectures on Revivals;*
- Sprague's *Lectures on Revivals;*
- Finney's *Lectures on Revivals;*
- Humphrey's *Revival Manual;*
- Headley's *Harvest Work of the Spirit;*
- Earle's *Bringing in Sheaves;*
- Alexander's *Revival and its Lessons;*
- *Narratives and Revival Incidents,* by William C Conant;
- Newcomb's *Harvest and Reapers;*
- *Lectures on Revivals,* by Ministers of Scotland;
- *Revivals of the 18th Century;*
- Humphrey's *Letters to his Son in the Ministry;*

- *Memoir of Nettleton;*
- *Edwards on Revivals;*
- *Revival Miscellanies,* by Caughey;
- Porter's *Letters on Revivals;*
- Tyler's *Prayer for Colleges;*
- Prime's *Power of Prayer;*
- Chambers' *Noon-Day Prayer-Meeting;*
- Hovey's *Life and Times of Isaac Backus;*
- Gibson's *Year of Grace;*
- Hawes' *Tribute to the Pilgrims;*
- *The New England Memorial;*
- Martin Moore's *Boston Revival in 1842;*
- *Autobiography of Lyman Beecher;*
- *Revival in Plymouth Church;*
- Bushnell's and Skinner's *Christian Spectator Articles;*
- *History of Revivals in the British Isles.*

This general reference must suffice, instead of encumbering the pages of the work with numerous particular citations.

Thanks are especially due to Rev Drs Stephen H Tyng, Richard Fuller, E S Atwood, E P Goodwin, E B Webb, S D Burchard, and S S Cutting, for their valuable contributions on *Child-Piety*, and the *Training of Converts*.

Grateful for the privilege of making this slight contribution to the cause of genuine religious awakenings, it is humbly committed to the Divine favour.

Henry C Fish
Newark, New Jersey;
December 1873

1
What is a Revival?

MUCH of existing indifference and opposition to revivals comes from a confusion of terms. There attaches to the word revival what does not belong to it. Exception is not so much taken to that which is inherent and essential, as to that which is accidental and contingent.

This shows the importance of having a clear conception of the thing meant. We must carefully separate the revival from its adjuncts and accessories. We must distinguish it from false and dangerous excitements, which have usurped its name; for, common and almost technical as the word revival has become, it is often understood by those who oppose all earnestness in religion, and all true religion itself, to denote every species of religious extravagance. Even the wildest outbreakings of fanaticism and superstition are dignified by the name of revivals.

And yet the term is properly used with some latitude of meaning. Words often become broadened in their signification. It is so with the word *revive*. Strictly speaking, it means to bring again to life, to re-animate. While, then, we may speak of Christians as being revived, it could not be said of the unregenerate. As they are "*dead* in trespasses and sins," there could be no *re*-viving. That which has never lived could not be *re*-animated.

In popular use, however, the word revival embraces the idea of the conversion of sinners as well as the awakening of saints. And perhaps no better word could be employed. Certainly it is not improperly used; for it is applicable alike to the quickening of the individual soul, and the community. Indeed, where Christians are revived, there will always be the conversion of men.

Hence the word has a two-fold meaning: implying the renewal of spirituality and vigour among Christians, and the conversion of sinners in considerable numbers to God. The terms "reformation," "awakening," and so on, mean the same thing.

Dr Hetherington, of Scotland, gives the following very just criticism upon the term revival. "The word itself, (in some of its forms), is often used in Scripture; and, as so used, it generally implies the reproduction of a spiritual life which had almost died away. It is not, however, strictly synonymous with the term *conversion;* for while *revival* implies the renewal of a life which had almost died away, *conversion* strictly means the conferring of a spiritual life not before existing. In truth, it so happens that revivals and conversions commonly accompany each other; so that, where *conversions* are frequent and striking, many will be re-quickened or *revived*."

Revivals, then, are seasons when Christians are awoken to a more spiritual frame, to more fervent prayer, and to more earnest endeavours to promote the cause of Christ and redemption; and consequent upon this, seasons when the impenitent are aroused to the concerns of the soul and the work of personal religion. They are times when the Spirit of the Lord again moves on the face of the waters, and the freshness and beauty of the new creature come forth. Nature itself seems more full of God; the very words of Scripture seem thereby invested with a new light and glory and fulness and meaning. As Edwards says: "All things abroad, the sun, moon, and stars, the heavens and the earth, appear as it were with a cast of divine glory and sweetness upon them."

The most prominent idea generally associated with the word revival is the regeneration of many souls. Multiplied conversions is the great outstanding characteristic of a time of revival. Multitudes, lying dead in the valley of vision, find that it becomes to them the valley of decision. Mr Barnes says, take the case of a single true conversion to God, and extend it to a community – to many individuals passing through that change, and you have all the theory of a revival of religion. It is bringing together many conversions; arresting simultaneously many minds; perhaps condensing into a single place, and into a few weeks, the ordinary work of many places and many years.

It hardly need be added, that this true view of revivals is to be disassociated from the idea of *means* and *measures*. These have nothing whatever to do with the pure signification of the term; and confusion here should be avoided.

Revivals may be either false or genuine. Under the former are to be classed mere religious excitements, extemporised by human agency, and subsiding without permanent results. There may be a whirlwind of agitation and no real revival.

And these spurious movements have done much to harm the cause of true revivals. Artifices to catch attention; devices to entrap the careless; representations to create impressions; an exaggerated style of preaching to produce alarm and shake suspicious hopes, and to raise a *furore*, no matter of what kind, these have in some cases been put into requisition, over which truth, and reverence, and humility must weep, and which have done more to injure revivals than all opposition and unbelief on the part of those making no professions of piety.

Genuine revivals are the fruit of the Holy Spirit. "Until the Spirit be poured out from on high," saints are neither quickened nor sinners saved. The effective cause in all true revivals is the life-giving, light-imparting, quickening, regenerating and sanctifying energy of the Holy Spirit, converting the hardened sinner and reclaiming the backslidden and dormant believer. The quaint old Thomas Adams says: "No *means* on earth can soften the heart; whether you anoint it with the supple balms of entreaties, or thunder against it the bolts of menaces, or beat it with the hammer of mortal blows. Behold, God showers his rain from heaven, and it is suddenly softened. One sermon may prick to the heart. One drop of a Saviour's blood, distilled on it by the Spirit, in the preaching of the Word, melts it like wax. The drunkard is made sober, the adulterer chaste, Zacchaeus merciful, and raging Paul as tame as a lamb."

Again, diversities of aspect attach to revivals. "The principle should not be forgotten," says Dr J W Alexander, "that while the great laws of the divine government and the dispensation of grace remain the same, the Supreme Giver varies his modes of bounty with reference to differences of country and period." Apostolic awakenings were in some things unlike those of the Reformation day. The quiet, spring-like renewal of vital godliness, under Spener, Francke, and the Pietists, bore little external resemblance to the prodigious revolution under the Wesleys, Whitefield, Edwards, the Tennents and the Blairs. The very remarkable awakenings in which Dr Nettleton and his friends were instrumental, differ again from the times of refreshing in which we live.

Revivals are unlike in their beginnings. Some particular sermon; some sickness or death in the community; some appalling Providence; some awakening near by; the visit of some pastor or evangelist, and the like, may be the apparent cause of a revival. Or it may come mysteriously. A deep and widespread solemnity may suddenly seize a congregation or community, and the manifestation of an increased interest may spring up, as without cause, in the Sunday School, the prayer-meeting, the factory, or the school district.

So do revivals differ in their phenomena. The subjects of them are variously wrought upon. In some cases they readily and gently yield to the sweet pleadings of love; in others there are resistance and marked outward manifestations.

In some cases, too, the work may progress quietly; in others it comes with observation. Dr Griffin says of a work in his day in Newark, New Jersey: "In point of power and stillness, it exceeds all that I have ever seen. While it bears down everything with irresistible force and seems almost to dispense with human instrumentality, it moves with so much silence, that unless we attentively observe its effects, we are tempted at times to doubt whether anything uncommon is taking place." But revivals were progressing at that very time, in different localities, with marked peculiarities of just the contrary character. "It was no uncommon thing in the days of the Tennents," says Tracy, "to see persons, in the time of hearing, sobbing as if their hearts would break, but without any public outcry: and some have been carried out of the assembly, (being overcome), as if they had been dead." Gillies mentions faintings, so that a number were carried out in a state of insensibility, under the preaching of Rowland, in a Baptist church, probably at Philadelphia; but he gives no date. Gilbert Tennent was present; and at his suggestion, Rowland changed the style of his discourse, and the faintings ceased. In Finley's Nottingham sermon, "Christ triumphing and Satan raging – wherein is proved that the kingdom of God is come unto us at this day," which was printed at Philadelphia, Boston, and London, in 1741, we are told that opposers of the revival, "without observing the deep concern that souls seem to be under, only ask about the fits and convulsions that their sorrow throws them into."

The nervous excitements connected with the revivals under the Wesleys and Tennents, and Whitefield, and Edwards, and those of later days, are well known. Persons often involuntarily fell down, fainted and went into convulsions.

Among the most remarkable of these cases of physical manifestations were those in the "Kentucky Revival," which commenced in 1800. Accounts were given by learned men, physicians, divines, and others, who were eye-witnesses and careful observers; but the most graphic and instructive seems to be that of the shrewd, though eccentric, Lorenzo Dow. He preached in the Court-house at Knoxville, Tennessee, in 1805, when about one hundred and fifty of his hearers were exercised with "the jerks;" that is, with violent spasmodic contractions of the muscles, which sometimes turned the head quickly from right to left and back again; and sometimes threw the person on the ground, where he rolled about strangely. He says, "I have seen all denominations of religion exercised with the jerks, gentleman and lady, black and white, young and old, without exception. I have passed a meeting-house where I observed the undergrowth had been cut for a camp-meeting, and from fifty to a hundred saplings were left, breast high, on purpose for the people who were jerked to hold on by. I observed, where they had held on, they had kicked up the earth as a horse stamping flies. A Presbyterian minister told me that while preaching the day before some had the jerks. I believe it does not affect those naturalists, who wish and try to get it to philosophise upon it; and rarely those who are the most pious; but the lukewarm, lazy professor is subject to it. The wicked fear it, and are subject to it; but the persecutors are more subject to it than any, and they have sometimes cursed and swore and damned it, while jerking."

Dr Robertson, an eye-witness, says, in his Inaugural Essay before the Medical Faculty at Philadelphia: "It attacks both sexes, and every constitution; but evidently more readily those who are enthusiasts in religion." Dr Alexander says that the phenomena "were common to all ages and sexes, and to all sorts of characters." Dow says that "persecutors" had it, without relaxing their open hatred of religion. Others testify that they have been thrown into "the jerks" by hearing a description of the jerking of others, and without any religious impression, either attending or following the attack. Cartwright mentions one fatal case of the "jerks." "This large man cursed the jerks and all religion. Shortly afterward he took the jerks and started to run, but he jerked so powerfully he could not get away. He halted among some saplings, and although he was violently agitated, he took out his bottle of whisky, and swore he would drink the jerks to death; but he jerked at such a rate that he could not get the bottle to his mouth, though he tried hard. At length he fetched a sudden jerk, and the bottle struck a sapling and was broken to pieces, and spilled his whisky on the ground. He became very much enraged and cursed and swore very profanely, his jerks still increasing. At length he fetched a very violent jerk, snapped his neck, fell, and soon expired, with his mouth full of cursing and bitterness." [1]

John Wesley looked upon these physical agitations as proofs of the divine presence. Charles Wesley suspected and discouraged them. Whitefield was incredulous. Edwards puts in an apology for them. But very few ministers favoured them. Finding by careful examination that they were often accompanied with rational conviction and sound conversion, they treated them gently, but did not ascribe them to divine influence, nor hold them to be parts of a revival. It were better, no doubt, had there been a more decided discouragement of them. Even with the aids of science in its present advanced state, it is not possible to account for these physical effects; nor is it important. Agitations quite as marked have occurred when in no way connected with religion, and also with fanatical heresies. A writer is probably correct in defining them to be "a catalepsy, or a suspension, more or less, of the functions of the cerebrum, attended by an abnormal activity of those of the cerebellum. The rational powers – the will, judgment or reason – are thus temporarily put in abeyance, and the involuntary susceptibilities left subject to the prevailing impression or influence."

As to these and other aspects attendant upon revivals, it is not for us to limit the Holy One of Israel. There are diversities of operations

1. This subject is ably illustrated in an *Essay upon the Influence of the Imagination on the Nervous System*, contributing to a False Hope in Religion, by Rev Grant Powers; Andover, Flagg & Gould, 1828. Also in *Religious Catalepsy*, by Rev Silas Comfort, in *Methodist Quarterly Review* for April, 1859. Also, Gibson's *Year of Grace*, page 380. The account given by the Rev Dr Alexander may be found in the *Connecticut Evan. Mag.* Volume 2, page 354.

by the same Spirit, suited to differences of country and time. The awakenings of the past were in some things unlike those of the present. And it may please God to change still further the modes of his bounty in the days to come. Nevertheless, true religion is the same in all times and places, and genuine revivals, in their essential features, are the same. To show his sovereignty and fulfil his plans, and from other causes, the Most High may in one case bestow the Spirit gently like the falling dew; and in another, amid thunderings and quakings. In one case he may bring in hundreds and thousands, and in others only a few. In one case the revival takes in persons of all classes, and in another it reaches one or two classes, leaving the rest as it found them. In one case it pervades the whole town, while in another it is confined mainly to the centre, or the out-districts. In one case it begins among the higher classes, and another among the lower; in one with the young men, in another with the young women, and in another with one or both sexes in middle life. But wherever and however, it is the same Holy Spirit "turning men from darkness to light and from the power of Satan unto God."

Nor is it difficult to designate the essential features of a genuine revival of religion. For one thing, we may be sure that "*the truth as it is in Jesus*" accompanies a real work of grace. To borrow an example, suppose there were to be a powerful excitement on the subject of religion produced by means which are at war with the spirit of the gospel – suppose doctrines were to be preached which the gospel does not recognise, and doctrines omitted which the gospel regards fundamental – suppose that for the simple, and honest, and faithful use of the sword of the Spirit, there should be substituted a mass of machinery designed to produce its effect on the animal passions – suppose the substance of religion, instead of being made to consist in repentance, and faith, and holiness, should consist of falling, and groaning, and shouting – we should say unhesitatingly that that could not be a genuine work of divine grace; or, if there were some pure wheat, there must be a vast amount of chaff and stubble.

On the other hand, where there is an attention to religion excited by the plain and faithful preaching of God's truth in all its length and breadth, and by the use of those simple and honest means which God's Word either directly prescribes or fairly sanctions, we cannot reasonably doubt that there is a genuine work of the Holy Spirit.

Again, there will not be simple *excitement of feeling* in a true work of grace, but *knowledge and reflection*, as well. Truth enters the heart through the understanding, and if the feelings manifested, whether of peace or distress, be the effect of an enlightened apprehension, and intelligent conviction, there is reason to hope that God's Spirit is really at work. But where the mind is in a great degree blind and passive while yet the sensibilities are wrought to a high pitch, there is reason to doubt the genuineness of the supposed conversions, and that which claims to be a revival is pretty surely not a genuine but a spurious one.

Again, the genuineness of a work is to be suspected unless the *holiness, zeal and devotedness of Christians* are increased. Where they awake to a sense of neglected obligations, and mourn over and confess them; where they in earnestness implore the descent of the Holy Spirit, taking heed, themselves, lest they grieve and quench that Spirit; where their conversation becomes spiritual and they put each other in remembrance of the covenant vows; where they tenderly speak to the unrenewed, beseeching them to be reconciled to God; and where, as the result, conviction seizes upon the careless, and multitudes are inquiring what they shall do to be saved, there is no room to doubt that a true work of grace is in progress.

In the absence of all this, no matter by what name a work is called, it is not a real revival of religion.

Further; where the work is genuine there will be *abiding results*. If an excitement on the subject of religion, no matter how great it may have been, passes away and leaves behind little or no substantial and enduring good; if most of those who profess to have been converted return speedily or gradually to the world, living a careless and godless life, then we may know that a revival had in it little more than the name. On the other hand, let religion be acted out in the life; let those professing a change illustrate, daily, the Christian virtues and graces, and one need not ask for further evidence of the agency of the Spirit of God.

It is not difficult to see in President Edwards' description of Northampton, at the time of the great awakening there, the marks of a genuine work of grace: "This work soon made a glorious alteration in the town; so that in the spring and summer following, it seemed to be full of the presence of God; it never was so full of love, nor so full of joy, and yet so full of distress as it was then. There were remarkable tokens of God's presence in almost every house. It was a time of joy in families on account of salvation being brought to them; parents rejoicing over their children as new born, and husbands over their wives, and wives over their husbands. The goings of God were then seen in his sanctuary. God's day was a delight, and his tabernacles were amiable. Our public assemblies were then beautiful; the congregation was alive in God's service, everyone earnestly intent on the public worship, every hearer eager to drink in the words of the minister as they came from his mouth. The assembly in general were, from time to time, in tears while the Word was preached; some weeping with sorrow and distress, others with joy and love, others with pity and concern for the souls of their neighbours."

"O Lord, Revive Thy Work!"

2
Historical View of Revivals

THE history of revivals is the history of religion. If we consult the Bible we shall find awakenings from the earliest times. Thus in the days of Samuel, when the people had done evil a long time, serving Baalim, it is said, "Israel lamented after the Lord," and Samuel said, "If ye do return unto the Lord with all your hearts, and serve him only, he will deliver you." Upon doing it the blessing came. Drawing near to battle, "the Lord thundered with a great thunder on that day upon the Philistines and discomfited them, and they were smitten before Israel." Then they came together and "drew water, and poured it out before the Lord;" – an emblem, perhaps, of the fulness of their penitent sorrow, and of the felt blessings of the Most High. The narrative is short; but there was here an effective revival. (*1 Samuel 7:1-14*).

Often in the succeeding ages hope almost expired; but "a remnant was left of those that feared the Lord;" and in the reigns of David, and Solomon, and Asa and Jehoshaphat, and Hezekiah and Josiah, seasons of recovery and refreshing were not withheld.

Soon after the return from the captivity there was a great reformation. The people gathered themselves together in Jerusalem as one man, and called upon Ezra to bring out the book of the law of Moses which the Lord had commanded to Israel; and he read therein from morning till midday; "and the ears of all the people were attentive unto the book of the law." (*Nehemiah 8:3*). For when he opened the book in the sight of all the people, they all stood up. And when he blessed the Lord, the great God, "all the people answered, Amen, amen, lifting up their hands, and worshipping the Lord with their faces on the ground." (*Nehemiah 8:6*). And they proved their sincerity by hastening to do works meet for repentance. For they restored the worship of God which had fallen into disuse, and separated themselves from heathen alliances, and contributed regularly to the support of the temple services.

Dark days came on. From the time of Malachi we hear of no true prophets to warn the people; and corruption spread "from the sole of the foot even unto the head."

Then came John the Baptist preaching in the wilderness of Judea, and saying, "Repent ye, for the kingdom of heaven is at hand." He was no ordinary preacher. The truth was searching, arousing, pungent. The spirit of Elijah burned in his breast and thundered in his voice. And a powerful revival ensued. For "there went out to him Jerusalem and all Judea, and all the region round about Jordan, and were baptised in Jordan, confessing their sins." (*Matthew 3:1-5*).

Exalted at the right hand of the Father, the Redeemer was to vouchsafe his grand coronation gift. It came. The star-light falling upon a solitary people became the splendour of the all-warming, all-vivifying sun. The narrow pent-up stream became the majestic river, rolling health and gladness through all the lands. Brief and pregnant is the record: "And when the day of Pentecost was fully come, they were all with one accord in one place. And suddenly there came a sound from heaven as of a rushing mighty wind, and it filled all the house where they were sitting. And there appeared unto them cloven tongues like as of fire, and it sat upon each of them. And they were all filled with the Holy Ghost, and began to speak with other tongues, as the Spirit gave them utterance. And there were dwelling at Jerusalem Jews, devout men, out of every nation under heaven. Now when this was noised abroad, the multitude came together, and were confounded, because that every man heard them speak in his own language. And they were all amazed, and marvelled, saying one to another, Behold, are not all these which speak Galileans? And how hear we every man in our own tongue, wherein we were born? Parthians, and Medes, and Elamites, and the dwellers in Mesopotamia, and in Judea, and Cappadocia, in Pontus, and Asia, Phrygia, and Pamphylia, in Egypt, and in the parts of Libya about Cyrene, and strangers of Rome, Jews and proselytes, Cretes, and Arabians, we do hear them speak in our tongues the wonderful works of God. And they were all amazed, and were in doubt saying one to another, What meaneth this? Others mocking said, These men are full of new wine." (*Acts 2:1-13*).

Peter explained the strange phenomena, pointing to the prediction here fulfilled, that God would "pour out his Spirit upon all flesh," (*Acts 2:17*), and likewise charged home upon his hearers their awful guilt in rejecting and crucifying the Lord. "Now when they heard this, they were pricked in their heart, and said unto Peter, and to the rest of the Apostles, Men and brethren, what shall we do? Then Peter said unto them, Repent, and be baptised every one of you in the name of Jesus Christ ... Then they that gladly received his word were baptised: and the same day there were added unto them about three thousand souls." (*Acts 2:37-41*).

Now, although the effects of this stupendous manifestation of Messiah's kingly power and munificence were beyond comparison grand and glorious, the scene was strictly of the nature of a revival. In all its essential features it was nothing more. Says Rev Albert Barnes, "I am aware that some have supposed that that whole scene was miraculous, and that it cannot be expected again to occur, since the days of miracles have ceased. But I am ignorant of the arguments which demonstrate that there was anything of miracle in this, except in the power of speaking in foreign languages, conferred on the apostles – a power which of itself converted not one of the three thousand who on that day gave their hearts to the Saviour. The power of speaking foreign languages had but two effects, one was to furnish evidence that the religion was from God; the other to enable them to make known its truths in the ears of the multitude assembled from different parts of the world. It was by the proper influence of *truth* that the multitudes were alarmed and awakened. And why should not the same truth produce the same effect now? It was indeed by the power of God. But that same power is expected in the conversion of every sinner; and why may it not now be employed in converting many simultaneously? It was indeed by the Holy Ghost; but no sinner is awakened or converted now without his power; and why may not that be exerted still on many as well as on one? The great fact in the case was, that several thousands were converted under the preaching of the truth by the influence of the Holy Ghost. Miracles change no one. The laws of mind were violated in the case of no one. No effect was produced which the *truth* was not adapted to produce. And why should not the same effect be again produced by the preaching of the same truth, and by the power of the same sacred Spirit?"

With tongues and hearts of heavenly fire, the chosen heralds went forth from the scene, everywhere to publish peace. And multitudes laid hold of the hope set before them. For we are told that the Lord added to the church daily such as should be saved; and again, the number of the men was about five thousand; and again, multitudes of believers, both men and women, were added to the Lord; the number of the disciples was multiplied at Jerusalem greatly; and a great company of the priests were obedient to the faith. All this took place within two years of the descent of the Spirit. Eight years more had not elapsed before the gospel was preached with saving power to the Gentiles at Caesarea, and at Antioch, where much people were added to the Lord. With what rapidity its triumphs were multiplied, both among them and the Jews scattered abroad, the following testimonies relating to the next eight years of the new dispensation are witness. At Iconium, a great multitude both of Jews and also of the Greeks believed; the converts of Antioch, Syria, and Cilicia were confirmed in the faith, and increased in number daily. In Thessalonica some of the Jews believed, and of the devout Greeks a great multitude, and of the chief women not a few. At Berea, many of the Jews believed, also of honourable women which were Greeks, and of men not a few. Many at Corinth believed and were baptised. The word of God grew mightily at Ephesus and prevailed. At Athens, certain men clave unto Paul, and Demetrius complained that throughout *all Asia* Paul had preached and turned away much people. What a series of glorious revivals we have here recorded!

And it is interesting to observe that this blessed work continued on through the post-apostolic age. It was by a succession of marvellous revivals, as we should call them, rather than by the gradual addition of a few souls at a time, that the churches during the first few centuries made their triumphant onsets upon the powers of darkness. Hence the amazing progress of which the early writers speak.

Pliny the younger, who was some time governor of Bithynia under the bloody emperor Trajan, earnestly dissuaded him from persisting in his persecuting edicts against the Christians in that province, not only by assuring him that they were a harmless people, chargeable with no crime, "meeting together to sing hymns and worship Christ as God," but that they were *very numerous all over the province*, and that the more they were punished the more they increased. And Tertullian, who lived a century later, and died in AD 216, writing to the Roman government in vindication of the new religion, as it was called, says, "Though we are strangers of no long standing, yet we have filled all places of your dominions, cities, islands, corporations, councils, armies, tribes, the senate, the palace, the courts of judicature. If the Christians had a mind to revenge themselves, their numbers are abundant, for they have a party, not in this or that province only, but in all quarters of the world. Nay, if they were to combine and forsake the Roman empire, how vast would be the loss! The world would be amazed at the solitude which would ensue."

Such an extension of Christianity, as a historian has remarked, presupposes a progress of the work of conversion immensely more rapid than what we now observe. The very persecutions also prove this. There must have been a great amount of fuel to support such fires. Even in regions of Africa, which are now a desolation, there were cities and provinces of Christians. The writer just cited, in an appeal to the persecuting governor of Africa, says, "If you persevere in your persecution, what will you do with these many thousands, both men and women, of every rank and every age, who will promptly offer themselves? Carthage itself must be decimated." And again, enumerating the nations who have believed in Christ, he declares that the gospel has penetrated to regions which were inaccessible even to the eagles of imperial Rome, and that the church had already spread itself more widely than the four great monarchies. "Excellent governors," says Tertullian, "you may torment, afflict, and vex us; your wickedness puts our meekness to the test; but your cruelty is of no avail. It is but a stronger invitation to bring others to our persuasion. The more we are mowed down, the more we spring up again. 'The blood of the Christians is seed of the Church.'"

Here we have proof of the spread of Christianity by extensive and powerful reformations – the turning of multitudes, on a vast scale, almost simultaneously, from sin and Satan unto God. In no other way could the work have progressed as it did.

How superstition arose, and the "Man of Sin" gained the ascendancy, and true piety languished during the long succeeding centuries, it is not our province here to depict. All this time God had a true people; but their history is almost illegible.

In sketching the modern revivals, it will be convenient to speak of them under several epochs. The periods may be designated thus:

1st, The great Reformation, properly beginning in the *fourteenth* century, and extending into the *sixteenth* century in the days of Luther, who died 1546.

2nd, The work of God of the *seventeenth* century, in the days of Owen, Leighton, Bunyan, Baxter, Flavel; the last of whom died in 1691.

3rd, The Great Awakening in the *eighteenth* century, about 1740, in the days of Whitefield, Wesley, Edwards, Brainerd, and the Tennents.

4th, The revival of the nineteenth century, beginning about 1790, and extending, say, to the year 1840.

5th, The revival of 1857 to 1860.

First Revival Period: 1310–1560 – We find traces of God's gracious work even throughout that long and horrible night when Popery was holding almost universal empire. There arose, at intervals, within her pale, individuals protesting against her monstrous abominations. Doubtless, too, beyond her pale there existed an unbroken succession of faithful and incorruptible witnesses for the truth: so that when scornfully asked where was the religion of Protestants before Luther, we may answer, "In the Bible," and, "In the valleys of Piedmont."

In the fourteenth century there must have been great revivals; for in Bohemia alone, where the gospel had won its way, there were reckoned, in 1315, no less than 80,000 witnesses for the religion of Jesus.

So, again, in the same century, John Wycliffe, "the morning-star of the Reformation," heralded the day-spring, and many turned to the Lord. He died in 1384; but John Huss, (born 1376), was converted by his writings; and after exerting a mighty influence for the truth, sealed his testimony amid the flames of martyrdom in 1415. Jerome of Prague embraced the doctrines of Huss, (his friend and master), and also died at the stake, a year later.

Born in 1483, Martin Luther, with his coadjutors, shook the papal throne to its foundations. And that most remarkable work was, strictly speaking, a *revival of religion*. Says Dr J W Alexander, with the greatest propriety, "It is a deplorable error to consider this moral convulsion as a mere change of speculative tenets or a mere struggle for liberty of conscience. Both these it did involve, undoubtedly; but beneath these, vivifying and nerving these, was the sense of spiritual things, the experience of conviction, conversion, holy awe, and holy joy, the gracious affections of the new creature, which pervaded countries and traversed a whole continent. It was the personal interest of souls in agony about escape from the wrath to come, which gave interest to the great questions between Popery and Reform. The sudden unveiling of the long-hidden Bible before the laity was like the return of the sun upon a Greenland night. The entrance of the ray gave understanding to the simple; and in thousands of instances, the rejection of Pelagian error and the acceptance of Christ were contemporaneous and indistinguishable exercises. Never certainly since the days of the early Christians was there so wide-spread a concern about religion; never were there so many conversions. The published correspondence of the reformers, and particularly of Martin Luther and John Calvin, shows that a large part of their time was employed in giving counsel and consolation to inquiring, convinced, and tempted individuals; and of their published works considerable portions are wholly employed in discussing those very points which have paramount interest in a season of general awakening in our day."

Such was the progress of this amazing revival, that in face of the united opposition of the church and the empire, against all proscription, in spite of rack and faggot, the principles of evangelical religion soon overspread Germany, France, Switzerland, Holland and the British Isles. First came Lefevre, Farel, Briçonnet, Chatelain, and their friends, in France; then Zwingli, in Switzerland, and almost at the same moment the giant of the Reformation, Martin Luther, in Germany – each attended by a host of zealous and able coadjutors, both in church and state – Œcolampadius, Melanchthon, Calvin – preachers, scholars, princes, and nobles. Soon came Tyndale, with his printed English Testament in England; Patrick Hamilton, George Wishart, and John Knox, in Scotland; John Taussen, in Denmark; John Laski, in Poland; Olaus Petri and Laurentius in

Sweden, and humbler names without number, in every quarter. All these arose at once, or within little more than a quarter of a century, by the mysterious Spirit and providence of God, and triumphantly established the truth of the gospel in the countries now Protestant.

In Scotland, says Kirkton, "The whole nation was converted by lump. Lo! here a nation born in one day; yea, moulded into one congregation, and sealed as a fountain with a solemn oath and covenant." To the same purpose are the following reflections of Fleming, in his *Fulfilling of Scripture:* "It is astonishing, and should be a matter of wonder and praise for after ages, to consider that solemn time of the Reformation, (in Scotland), when the Lord began to visit his church. What a swift course the spreading of the kingdom of Christ had; and how professors of the truth thronged in amidst the greatest threatenings of those on whose side authority and power then was." The testimony of Knox is not less decisive: "Our very enemies can witness in how great purity God did establish his true religion among us."

In Holland the work was with power, especially in connection, with some of the Baptist Reformers. Admitting the presence of errors and excesses, many of the men of this class were "full of faith and of the Holy Ghost," and much people were by them "added unto the Lord." Leonard Bouwens, an eminent Baptist minister in Holland, who died in 1578, left in writing a list of upwards of ten thousand persons whom he had baptised. Menno Simon, and other labourers, introduced to the churches great multitudes of disciples, thousands of whom, after being unjustly reviled and persecuted, became martyrs in attestation of the truth. And thus everywhere the doctrine of justification without works "grew mightily and prevailed."

It is to be said, however, that this work to a great extent receded. The Reformation itself needed reforming; and inhering remnants of the papacy brought forth their legitimate fruits. Persecution also acted a painful part. The fires of martyrdom were frequently lighted in France, Holland and Switzerland; while in England the severity of Elizabeth's government was so great that the separatists of all classes were scattered, and forced to hold their meetings in the utmost privacy. James I, though affecting zeal for Presbyterianism while in Scotland, was as bigoted and despotic as Elizabeth. "I will make them conform," said he, (of the Puritans), "or I will hurry them out of the land, or else worse." And they either fled or kept themselves quiet, hoping almost against hope for the better times to come.

How truly God remembered his cause, and again revived the work which had thus suffered a partial decline, we shall see in the next revival period.

Second Revival Period: 1600–1688 – Two years previous to this first date, (1598), the famous Edict of Nantes by Henry IV, was promulgated, securing religious liberty to the French Protestants. Within these two dates fall the active lives of Richard Baxter, Robert Leighton, John Milton, John Owen, John Flavel, John Bunyan, John Howe, John Tillotson, and Philip James Spener, founder of the sect of the Pietists of Halle. With the latter laboured the devoted Augustus Franke; and there was a great and rapid spread of religion in some parts of the continent through their efforts.

During this period also falls the working of the *Act of Uniformity*, passed in 1662, and in force about 25 years. By it some *two thousand* ministers were ejected from their pulpits. In 1664 the *Conventicle Act* was passed; and the next year the *Five Mile Act*. These inhuman decrees but testify to the zeal and piety of the men against whom they were intended to operate. Because they were "burning and shining lights," whose influence in converting the people to Christ was so great, these measures were instigated by the enemy of all good.

The remarkable condition of things among our American ancestors was the simple consequence of the works of grace prevalent during this period. These men came out from amid *great awakenings;* and after the first plantations, every arrival from the old country brought them news of the revivals which took place under the Bunyans and Baxters of England. It is worth mentioning that Richard Baxter was born in 1616, John Owen in 1616, John Bunyan in 1628, and John Howe in 1630; while the landing of the Pilgrims on our shore occurred in 1620. The connection between the great facts here referred to is not less obvious than instructive.

Pursuing the work still in the old world, it is refreshing indeed to read the annals of God's grace in connection with the persecutions of the saints, especially in Scotland, in the attempts to enforce the *Uniformity Act.* The holy fire burning in the breast of Knox in the preceding century was rekindled, and its heat and light could not be hid. Thus in Stewarton, in 1625, a revival spread, called by the profane rabble, *Stewarton Sickness*, of which Fleming said, "Truly this great spring tide, as I may call it, of the gospel, was not of a short time, but of some years' continuance; yea, thus, like a spreading moor-burn, the power of godliness did advance from one place to another, which put a marvellous lustre on those parts of the country, the savour whereof brought many from other parts of the land to see its truth. Another token for good to the suffering church of Scotland, occurred in the year 1628. At a meeting of the Synod of Edinburgh, in the spring of that year, it had been agreed to apply to his majesty that a general fast might be held all over the kingdom."

A great blessing followed – most marked, perhaps, in the *Kirk of Shotts*, in June 1630, under the preaching of John Livingston, when a Convocation of ministers and people, for several days, was being held. Towards the close of the sermon, the congregation and even the preacher himself, were affected with a deep, unusual awe, melting their hearts and subduing their minds, stripping off inveterate prejudices, awaking the impenitent, producing conviction in the hardened, bowing down the stubborn, and imparting to many an enlightened Christian a large increase of grace and spirituality. "It was known," says Fleming, "as I can speak on sure ground, that nearly *five hundred* that time had a discernible change wrought on them, of whom most proved lively Christians afterwards. It was the sowing of a seed through Clydesdale, so that many of the most eminent Christians of that country could date their conversion, or some remarkable confirmation of their case, from that day."

In 1625, there was also a remarkable revival in the north of Ireland. It took place under the labours of a band of faithful ministers, most of whom went over from Scotland – Brice, Glendenning, Ridge, Blair and others; beginning in the province of *Ulster*, which has ever since been the brightest spot on the map of Ireland. These preachers went forth in companies, labouring with apostolic zeal to evangelise the land – and the Lord wrought through them mightily. This revival in the north of Ireland may with propriety be said to have been one of the most remarkable outpourings of the Spirit upon record. Says Stewart, "These religious agitations continued for a considerable time. The ministers were indefatigable in improving the favourable opportunities thus offered for extending the knowledge and influence of the gospel. The people awakened and inquiring, many of them desponding and alarmed, both desired and needed guidance and instruction. The judicious exhibition of evangelical doctrines and promises by these faithful men, was in due time productive of those happy and tranquilising effects which were early predicted as the characteristics of gospel times. Adopting the beautiful imagery of the prophets, the broken-hearted were bound up and comforted, the spirit of bondage and of fear gave way to a spirit of freedom and of love, the oil of joy was poured forth instead of mourning, and the spirit of heaviness exchanged for the garments of praise and thankfulness."

It would be gratifying to dwell upon God's revival work in England, while his Spirit was being thus poured out in Ireland and Scotland. How much like a description of some of our blessed modern revivals does the pen-picture of Baxter's work in Kidderminster seem, as drawn in his writings. He tells of preaching twice on the Lord's Day, and on Thursday evening at his own private house, besides occasional sermons; of "resolving the doubts" of inquirers; of praying with the awakened in little companies; of a "three hour" prayer-meeting with the young; of the converts holding a Saturday evening prayer-meeting for the success of the Word on the following day; of once in a few weeks having a day of humiliation; of going through the parish, (with the help of his brethren), and visiting all the people, and instructing them in the Scriptures, and urging them, "with all possible engaging reason and vehemence to answerable affection and practice." He spent an hour with a family – occupying "all the afternoon of Mondays and Tuesdays in this way."

As to *results* let him give his own story. "The congregation was usually full, so that we were led to build five galleries after my coming hither, the church itself being very capacious, the most commodious and convenient that ever I was in. Our private meetings also were full. On the Lord's day, there was no disorder to be seen in the streets, but you might hear a hundred families singing psalms and repeating sermons as you passed through the streets. In a word, when I came thither first, there was about one family in a street that worshipped God and called on His name; and when I came away, there were some streets where there was not more than one family in the side of a street that did not so, and that did not, in professing serious godliness, give us hopes of their sincerity. And of those families which were the worst, being inns and ale-houses, usually some persons in each did seem to be religious. Though our administration of the Lord's Supper was so orderly as displeased many, and the far greater part kept themselves away, yet we had six hundred that were communicants, of whom there were not twelve that I had not good hopes of as to their sincerity; and those few that came to our communion and yet lived scandalously, were excommunicated afterwards."

We cannot further sketch the refreshings from God's presence during this second period.

Third Revival Period: 1730–1750 – John Wesley and Jonathan Edwards were born the same year, (1703), Charles Wesley was born two years after, (1705), and George Whitefield nine years still later, (1714).

The appearance of these names on the scroll of history marks a revival period of wonderful interest.

To go back a little, and accept the *resumé* of another, the English church had been "reformed" by act of Parliament under Edward VI, counter-reformed in the same way under Queen Mary, and re-reformed by Queen Elizabeth – the great body of the clergy holding fast their benefices with unscrupulous tenacity throughout these vicissitudes. Nineteen-twentieths of Queen Mary's clergy became Queen Elizabeth's clergy without compunction, and certainly without conversion. It is not surprising, therefore, that generally speaking both religious knowledge and morals, among people and clergy, remained at the lowest ebb; and that the church establishment, after being purged of the most of its piety and learning by the *Act of Uniformity*, continued to descend in the moral scale, carrying the people with it, until, after the accession of the House of Hanover, the scandalous condition of the country was perhaps unequalled in Europe. Bishop Burnet says that candidates for ordination were commonly quite unacquainted with the Bible and unable even to give an account of the statements in the church catechism. When they re-appeared before him to obtain institution to a living, it was still apparent in many that they had not "read the Scriptures nor any other good book since they were ordained." "Of all the ministers of religion he had seen in the course of his extensive travels – Papists,

Lutherans, Calvinists, and Dissenters – they were the most remiss in their labours, and the least severe in their lives."

The infidel works of Hobbes, Tindal, Collins, Shaftesbury, and Chubb, were in full circulation, and were re-enforced by the appearance of the three greatest giants in the cause of sceptical error which modern times have produced – Bolingbroke, Hume and Gibbon. The Encyclopaedists had attempted the design of eradicating from the circle of the sciences every trace of Christian truth; and the polite writers of France, headed by Voltaire and Rousseau, had decked the corrupt doctrines of the day with the attractions of eloquence and poetry, humour and satire, until they swept over the nation like a sirocco, withering not only the sentiments of religion, but the instincts of humanity, and subverting at last, in common ruin, the altar, the throne, and the moral protections of domestic life.

Lady Mary Wortley wrote in 1710, that there were "more atheists among the fine ladies than among the loosest sort of rakes." Ignorance and drunkenness, it is stated, were the predominant qualities of the working classes; licentiousness and infidelity of the higher. Montesquieu, who visited England in 1729-31, protested that the English had no religion at all. "If anyone," he said, "spoke of it, everybody laughed." Low as religion had sunk in France, he confessed that he himself had not enough of it to satisfy his countrymen; and yet he found that he had too much to suit English society.

Rev Mr Ryle, of the Church of England, says: "These times were the darkest age that England has passed through in the last three hundred years. Anything more deplorable than the condition of the country, as to religion, morality, and high principle, it is very difficult to conceive. As to preaching the gospel, the distinguishing doctrines of Christianity – the atonement, the work and office of Christ and the Spirit – were comparatively lost sight of. The vast majority of sermons were miserable moral essays, utterly devoid of anything calculated to awaken, convert, sanctify, or save souls."

And Isaac Taylor, in his history of Methodism, says that when Wesley appeared, "the Anglican church was an ecclesiastical system under which the people of England had lapsed into heathenism, or a state hardly to be distinguished from it."

In America the religious condition was not much better. The primitive standard of morals and piety among the colonies of New England had sadly declined. From the first, isolated revivals had been enjoyed; but there prevailed at this time a lamentable ignorance of the essentials of practical religion.

Dr Increase Mather, in a book entitled, *The Glory Departing from New England*, printed in 1702, says, "We are the posterity of the good old Puritan Non-conformists in England, who were a strict and holy people. Such were our fathers who followed the Lord into this wilderness. Oh New England, New England, look to it that the glory be not removed from thee, for it begins to go. Oh, degenerate New England, what art thou come to at this day! How are those sins become common in thee that once were not so much as heard of in this land!"

In a public lecture printed in 1706, Dr Cotton Mather says, "It is confessed by all who know anything of the matter – and Oh, why not with rivers of tears bewailed? – that there is a general and a horrible decay of Christianity among the professors of it." And Rev Samuel Blair, speaking of the state of things in Pennsylvania previous to 1740, declares that, "Religion lay a-dying and ready to expire its last breath of life."

The causes of this degeneracy are but too apparent. They are well told by Rev Joseph Tracy, in his excellent and standard *History of the Great Awakening*. He says:

"The New England churches had receded from the original standard. The Synod of 1663 had decided that persons baptised in infancy, understanding the doctrine of faith, and publicly professing their assent thereunto, not scandalous in life, and solemnly owning the covenant before the church wherein they give up themselves and their children to the Lord, and subject themselves to the government of Christ in the church – their children are to be baptised, though the parent, thus owning the covenant, be avowedly yet unregenerate, and as such excluded from the Lord's Supper. This practice was immediately adopted by many churches, and, after a violent controversy, became general. This was very naturally followed by a still further innovation. In 1707, 'the venerable Stoddard,' of Northampton, published a sermon in which he maintained 'that sanctification is not a necessary qualification to partaking of the Lord's Supper,' and 'that the Lord's Supper is a converting ordinance.' To this Dr Increase Mather replied the next year; and in 1709, Mr Stoddard published his 'Appeal to the Learned; being a Vindication of the

Right of Visible Saints to the Lord's Supper, though they be destitute of a Saving Work of God's Spirit on their Hearts.' The third book of the Appeal contains 'Arguments to prove, that sanctifying grace is not necessary in order to a lawful partaking of the Lord's Supper.' Mr Stoddard, in his sermon, enforced his arguments with the assertion, 'that no other country does neglect this ordinance as we in New England; and that in our own nation at home, (England), so in Scotland, Holland, Denmark, Sweedland, Germany and France, they do generally celebrate the memorials of Christ's death.' There had been strong tendencies towards such a practice for many years, and probably some instances of its virtual adoption; but it now, for the first time, found an open and able advocate. It was strenuously opposed; but the desire to enjoy the credit and advantages of church membership, aided by Mr Stoddard's influence, carried the day at Northampton, and the practice soon spread extensively in other parts of New England."

Thus, also, Mr Williams, a defender of the Half Way Covenant, in opposition to Jonathan Edwards, mentions two ends contemplated by Christ in appointing the communion: "That such as have grace already should be under proper advantages to gain more, *and that those who have none should be under proper advantages to attain grace.*" And Edwards himself, who utterly repudiated this view, was forced to lament, that "*owning the covenant,* as it is called, has in New England, it is to be feared, too much degenerated into a matter of mere form and ceremony; it being visibly a prevailing custom for persons to neglect this until they come to be married, and then to do it for their credit's sake, and that their children may be baptised." In a word, it was held that the Christian church is but a continuation of the Jewish, the terms of admission remaining unchanged. The position laid down by Mr Stoddard was practically maintained: "That if unsanctified persons might lawfully come to the Passover, then such may lawfully come to the Lord's Supper – and they who convey to their children a right to baptism, have a right themselves to the Lord's Supper, provided they carry on, (that is, behave), inoffensively."

One obvious tendency of this practice was to destroy church discipline; for unconverted members, generally, would not be strict in calling others to account for errors of doctrine or practice. And in his reply to Mr Fish, Isaac Backus testifies, "that it is a *professed rule* with many ministers, not to deal with any person in the church for moral evil till he is *convicted in the state.*"

It is easy to see that this system favoured the entrance of unconverted men into the ministry. If one was fit to be a member of the church; if he was actually a member in good standing, why should he be excluded from the ministry? It could not be. The form of examining candidates as to their piety was still retained, but the spirit of it was dying away; and Mr Stoddard, in his "Appeal to the Learned," argued from the fact which he took for granted, that "unconverted ministers have certain official duties which they may lawfully perform."

Amid scenes of such moral desolation in the old world and the new, it pleased God suddenly to appear in great mercy. And it is worthy of remark, that the blessing came *almost simultaneously on America and Europe.*

First in the order of time there was a revival of considerable power in Freehold, New Jersey, in 1730, and in the three following years, under the labours of the Tennents.

Next commenced the wonderful work in Northampton, Massachusetts, under Edwards, in the autumn of 1734. "Then," says Edwards, "the Spirit of God began extraordinarily to set in and wonderfully to work among us; and there were very suddenly, one after another, five or six persons, who were, to all appearance, savingly converted, and some of them wrought upon in a very remarkable manner." The news spread "like a flash of lightning" and there was a general concern in all parts of the town; and "souls did come, as it were, by flocks to Jesus Christ." The report of the state of things at Northampton spread into other towns, where many "seemed not to know what to make of it." Many ridiculed, "and some compared what we call conversion to certain distempers." Great numbers, however, who came to Northampton and saw for themselves, were differently affected, and not a few of them, from various places, were awakened and apparently brought to repentance. In March, 1735, the revival began to be general in South Hadley, and about the same time in Suffield. It next appeared in Sunderland, Deerfield, and Hatfield; and afterwards at West Springfield, Long Meadow, and Enfield; and then in Hadley Old Town, and in Northfield. In Connecticut the work commenced in the first parish in Windsor, about the same time as at Northampton. It was remarkable at East Windsor, and "wonderful" at Coventry. Similar scenes were witnessed at Lebanon, Durham, Stratford, Ripton, New Haven, Guilford, Mansfield, Tolland, Hebron, Bolton, Preston, Groton, and Woodbury.

Edwards hoped that more than 300 in his parish were converted in the space of half a year.

About the month of May, 1735, the work began sensibly to decline; although for months after, frequent conversions continued. This awakening excited a lively interest among the friends of vital piety at a distance. Dr Colman, of Boston, wrote to Mr Edwards for an account of it. Having obtained one, he published it, and forwarded it to Dr Watts and Dr Guise in London, where its publication exerted a strong influence for good.

A longing existed in many places for similar awakenings; and in the next few succeeding years they began to multiply in different parts of the country. Thus in 1739, in Newark, New Jersey, "the whole town in general was brought under an uncommon concern about their eternal interests." In Harvard, Massachusetts, the same year, a revival much like that at Northampton, (only not so extensive), occurred, resulting in "near a hundred" hopeful conversions.

About the same time the work re-appeared in Northampton; and gentle refreshings were experienced in Pennsylvania, (particularly at Londonderry), and in New Brunswick, New Jersey, and some other places.

Such, properly speaking, was the commencement of the "Great Awakening." But it did not assume its peculiar power until George Whitefield arrived in Philadelphia in the early part of November, 1739.

In that city, and in New York and New Jersey, where he at once began preaching, as well as in Georgia and South Carolina, thousands flocked together, anxious about their souls, and multitudes were added unto the Lord.

In September, 1740, Whitefield visited New England, whither his fame had spread; and here all the people were anxious to hear him. Arriving at Newport, Rhode Island, he began immediately his usual course of incessant preaching. His sermons on his way to Boston spread his reputation, and when within ten miles distance, he was met by the governor's son and a train of the clergy and chief citizens, who escorted him into the city. Belcher, the governor, received him heartily, and became his warm friend. He was denied "King's Chapel," the English Church; but Webb, Foxcroft, Prince, Sewall, and all the other Puritan divines, welcomed him. His preaching had its usual effect. "It was Puritanism revived," said old Mr Walter, the successor of Eliot, the apostle to the Indians. "It was the happiest day I ever saw in my life," exclaimed Colman, after his first sermon. He "itinerated," says one who traced his course, northward from Boston, travelling one hundred and seventy miles, and preaching sixteen times in about a week. On his return the whole city seemed moved. High and low, clergymen and municipal officers, professors and students from the neighbouring college of Cambridge, and people from the country towns, thronged to hear him, and appeared ready to "pluck out their eyes for him." Twenty thousand hearers crowded around him when he delivered his farewell discourse under the trees of the large Common. "Such a power and presence of God with a preacher," wrote one who heard him, "I never saw before. Our governor has carried him from place to place in his coach, and could not help following him fifty miles out of town."

He directed his course westward to Northampton, where he met a congenial spirit in Jonathan Edwards. Pulpits were open to him on all the route, and a "divine unction" attended his preaching. From Northampton he passed down to New Haven, addressing as he journeyed vast and deeply affected congregations. He arrived there October 23, when the Colonial Legislature was in session, and on the Sabbath preached before them and an immense throng, some of whom had come twenty miles to hear him. The aged governor was so deeply affected that he could speak but few words. With tears trickling down his cheeks like drops of rain, he exclaimed: "Thanks be to God for such refreshings on our way to heaven!"

By November 8th he was again in Philadelphia, preaching in a house which had been erected for him during his absence. On the 14th of December he reached the Orphan House, near Savannah. In seventy-five days he had preached a hundred and seventy-five sermons. "Never," he writes, "did I see such a continuance of the divine presence in the congregations to which I have preached."

On the 16th of January, 1741, he again embarked at Charleston for England.

Of course it is impossible to trace the progress of the revivals that sprang up in these years, all through New England and the Middle and Southern States. A large number of pastors in Eastern Massachusetts, in 1745, printed and sent out a *Testimony* to its blessed effects. It was estimated that at that time the population of all the colonies was about 2,000,000; and it was believed that the number of converts amounted to not less than *fifty thousand.* If so, they bore as great a proportion to the whole number of inhabitants, and would as much change the relative proportion of the religious and irreligious, as the conversion of *six or eight hundred thousand* would now. As one result, not less than 150 new Congregational churches were established in twenty years. The increase of Baptist churches was still more wonderful, rising from a few to upwards of 400 in number, with a total of 30,000 members. The increase of the Presbyterians and other denominations in the Middle States appears to be less distinctly marked, but it was very great.

Particularly towards the close of the above period, there were most objectionable outbreaks of animal excitement, and also of untempered religious controversy, marring the gracious fruitage: but making every reasonable abatement, the awakening was a most merciful visitation from the Lord in its immediate and lasting influence upon the young colonies of America.

In England the work began in 1739. On February 17th of that year, Mr Whitefield preached his first field sermon, at a place called Rose Green. He held open air meetings there and at Kingswood for several days, and was listened to by thousands and tens of thousands of astonished hearers. The first evidence he observed of having made any impression on his rude auditors, was their deep silence; the next, and still more convincing, was his observation of the *white gutters* made by the tears which fell plentifully down their cheeks, black and unwashed from the coal-pits. John Wesley, (by whom, on his going to America, Whitefield was succeeded in this most interesting field of labour), speaking of the harvest which it yielded in return to their conjoint prayers and labours, says, "Few persons have lived long in the west of England, who have not heard of the colliers of Kingswood as those neither fearing God nor regarding man. But now we see that in the middle of *February*, Kingswood was a wilderness, and that when the month of *June* arrived, it was already blossoming like the rose."

After a short visit to the north of Wales, where he fell in with that wonderful Welsh preacher Howell Harris, who had been for three years ringing out the gospel notes from "tables, wells and hillocks," Whitefield traversed a great portion of England, preaching in bowling-greens, at market-crosses and on the highways; thus preparing the way for those remarkable field operations of the Wesleys, in connection with whom the arm of the Lord was so mightily revealed in the founding of Methodism.

During the years 1740 and 1741 Wesley traversed many parts of the kingdom, preaching almost daily, and sometimes four sermons on the Sabbath. Ingham, his companion in America, was abroad also, itinerating in Yorkshire, where he formed many societies. Howell Harris pursued his labours successfully in Wales, and John Bennet preached extensively in Derbyshire and its surrounding counties. David Taylor, a man of signal usefulness, also began to travel and preach about this time.

As to Whitefield, he thirteen times crossed the Atlantic; and many thousands hung upon his lips, whether he was in London or other parts of England; in Wales, Scotland, or Ireland; in Georgia, or New Hampshire; in Charleston, Philadelphia, New York, or Boston, or the country intervening. In some cases ten, and in others even twenty thousand, listened to his impassioned appeals; and fruits unto eternal life were gathered all along his course; until "he was not, for God took him."

Of the gracious work of God in Scotland, (particularly at Cambuslang), in 1742, when the Lord sent plenteous rains upon many of the parishes, the annals of those times give most interesting narratives.

In reading the *History of Revivals in the British Isles*, (by Mrs Duncan of Ruthwell), and the lives of Whitefield, Wesley, Lady Huntingdon, and so on, one will see how truly upon those who sat in the shadow of death, the light suddenly arose, and "the thirsty land became springs of water."

Fourth Revival Period: 1790–1842 – It has very properly been said that the year 1790 ushered in a new era, particularly for the

United States. In the old country the fearful inroads of French infidelity had sapped the foundations of faith and hope in God, and, combined with other untoward influences, had made the hearts of the faithful fail them for fear. The overspreading gloom about 1790 aroused Hannah More, Bishop Porteus, Drs Bogue, Andrew Fuller, Burder, and Rowland Hill, and kindred spirits in England, to noble evangelical efforts which greatly blessed the world. There was also a simultaneous work in Scotland, connected with the Haldanes and others. This was the direct cause of the formation of the Religious Tract Society, the British and Foreign Bible Society, the London Missionary, and the Church Missionary (local) Societies. Also the first society for evangelising the heathen – the Baptist Foreign Missionary Society. All these, and other kindred movements, were the fruits of the revivals about 1790 to 1792.

The names of the two brothers referred to above, Robert and James Alexander Haldane, of Scotland, will be had in everlasting remembrance for their burning zeal and untiring labours in the service of Christ, and for the cheerfulness with which they consecrated their wealth, time and talents, in building churches – tabernacles they were called – for the poor, and providing in every practicable way for their religious instruction.

In the north of Wales, under the labours of Charles of Bala, "the apostle of North Wales," a "great revival" occurred in the beginning of 1791.

In America the vast extent of the revival blessings of this period can only be appreciated by considering the deplorable condition into which we had fallen. It is true there were occasional "streams in the desert" during the previous half century. But the Half Way Covenant still lingered in many of the Congregational churches, and Unitarianism had spread so generally that "at the beginning of the nineteenth century all the Congregational churches in Boston, with a single exception, had renounced the faith of the Puritans."[1]

It must be remembered, too, that the political condition of the country was such as constantly to agitate the public mind, and divert attention from spiritual things. A war between France and Spain and England lasted from 1744 to 1748. Soon after this, the controversy commenced between the colonies and the mother country, and

1. *History of Evangelical Churches in Boston*, by Martin Moore.

continued until it finally broke out into open war in 1776. During the eight years of the revolutionary war every nerve of the country was strained to maintain the national conflict. Thus from 1744 to 1783, during a period of almost 40 years, the public mind was continually agitated by political questions. These successive wars did much to break down the sanctity of the Sabbath, and corrupt the morals of the community.

In the meantime, as might have been expected, *French Infidelity*, aided by Paine's *Age of Reason*, Voltaire's assaults upon Christianity, Volney's *Ruins*, and other blasphemous publications, had spread rapidly, especially among the upper classes. The *Illuminati*, so called, of France and Germany, who were secretly associated for the overthrow of all existing religious institutions, had their affiliated societies in this country, enrolling not a few men of high social and political standing and influence. "It became fashionable, in high places and low places, flippantly to prate against the Bible, and sneer at things sacred and divine. Instead of the Scriptures, French philosophy claimed to be the rule of faith and life, and ignoring all the rights of God, was to usher in the glorious millennium of the rights of man."

But when the enemy was thus coming in like a flood, the Lord lifted up a standard against him. About 1790 there were quite extensive works of grace in Western Pennsylvania and Southern and Western Virginia; and a little later the work began in the Eastern States. In these times we meet with the names of Bellamy, Griffin, the younger Edwards, Backus, Robbins, Mills, Perkins, Strong, Porter, Hooker, Williams, Hawley, Manning, Dwight, Hyde, Emmons, Baldwin, Mason, Stillman, Livingston, Furman, Marshall, Nettleton, Lyman Beecher, and many others, who did not shun to declare all the counsel of God.

In 1790 the First Baptist Church in Boston was graciously revived, and two hundred were added in the course of a few years.[2] In 1792, "or the year before," says Dr Griffin, "began the unbroken series of American revivals. There was a revival in North Yarmouth, Maine, in 1791. In the summer of 1792 one appeared in Lee, in the county of

2. Moore, in his *History*, says: "The revival in the First and Second Baptist churches was the first in that series of revivals wherewith God blessed Boston in the present generation. The tide of error with which this city had been for half a century flooded then began to turn."

Berkshire. The following November the first that I had the privilege of witnessing showed itself on the borders of East Haddam and Lyme, Connecticut, which apparently brought to Christ a hundred souls. I saw a continued succession of heavenly sprinklings at New Salem, Farmington, Middlebury, and New Hartford, (all in Connecticut), until, in 1799, I could stand at my door in New Hartford, Litchfield county, and number fifty or sixty congregations laid down in one field of divine wonders, and as many more in different parts of New England." By 1802 remarkable revivals had spread through most of the western and southern States. And Dr Nettleton says, "during a period of four or five years, commencing with 1798, not less than one hundred and fifty churches in New England were favoured with the special effusions of the Holy Spirit; and thousands of souls, in the judgment of charity, were translated from the kingdom of Satan into the kingdom of God's dear Son."

Distinct mention should here be made of that honoured instrument in revivals just mentioned. Certainly no other man did so much, under God, to promote them as Asahel Nettleton; who began to preach as an evangelist in 1812, and continued his labours for upwards of twenty years. To him not inaptly apply Pollok's lines:

> A skilful workman he,
> In God's great moral vineyard: what to prune
> With cautious hand he knew, what to uproot;
> What were mere weeds, and what celestial plants
> Which had immortal vigour in them, knew.
> Oh, who can speak his praise! great humble man!
> He in the current of destruction stood,
> And warned the sinner of his woe; led on
> Immanuel's soldiers in the evil day.
> And with the everlasting arms embracing
> Him around, stood in the dreadful front
> Of battle high, and warred victoriously
> With death and hell.

How wondrously the Lord carried forward his work during almost the whole period now under review, it is not in language to describe. There are extant particular narratives of local revivals in nearly all the States, even a sample of which cannot here be given. Dr Porter examined, in the preparation of his *Letters on Revivals*, the written or printed accounts of over one hundred and seventeen churches; while some of these accounts speak of other places that were revived – one says in fifty or sixty adjacent towns – of which, of course, no particulars are given. And still greater numbers were never reported at all. No part of the country, in proportion to its extent, shared so largely in these "times of refreshing from the presence of the Lord," as Connecticut; but other parts of New England enjoyed precious showers of grace; and during the same period powerful revivals prevailed, more or less extensively, in New York, New Jersey, Pennsylvania, Ohio, Kentucky, Tennessee, the two Carolinas, and Georgia.

Dr Griffin tells of a revival in Newark, New Jersey, in 1803, under his ministry, when "twenty contiguous congregations experienced the mighty power of God." In 1807 he says he was all the while going from house to house; but felt that he was only "holding a torch to the tinder which God had prepared."

Dr Robbins says of Norfolk, Connecticut, in 1799, "The marvellous displays of divine power and grace were conspicuous beyond anything of the kind we had ever witnessed. A universal solemnity spread over the town, and seized the minds of almost all, both old and young. Great numbers were bowed with a sense of the presence of the Lord; some rejoicing and praising God, others crying out in anguish of soul, 'What must we do?' "

A writer from New Hampshire in 1791 speaks of "a glorious revival" there "which began a year ago last spring, and has extended through several towns. The Rev Samuel Shephard has baptised more than a hundred and fifty, and the work still goes on. There have been also very considerable revivals in many churches of other denominations."

Dr Hyde says of Lee, Massachusetts, that in 1792, a marvellous work was begun, and it bore the decisive marks of being God's work. "So great was the excitement, though not yet known abroad, that into whatever section of the town I now went, the people in that immediate neighbourhood would leave their worldly employments at any hour of the day, and soon fill a large room. Before I was aware, and without any previous appointment, I found myself in the midst of a solemn and anxious assembly."

In Boscawen, New Hampshire, Halifax and Rutland and Rupert, Vermont, and other towns, "surprising manifestations of the Lord" were reported about the same time.

Drs Dewitt and Mason, of New York, with others, tell of gracious works in that city in their charges; and, says Harlan Page, under date of January 24th 1831: "The Lord appears now to be coming down on all parts of this great city, to arouse His children and to awaken sinners. Thousands of Christians here are, I think, praying as they never prayed before. Public general meetings commenced yesterday afternoon, and are to be continued through the week. Conversions are occurring in all parts of the city. Churches are daily crowded to overflowing, and a most fixed and solemn attention is given to the dispensation of the truth."

That year the old Chatham Street Theatre, (a haunt of obscenity, blasphemy, and vice), was purchased by a committee for purposes of worship. Two gentlemen called on the lessee of the theatre and proposed to buy his lease. "What for?" said he. "For a church." The astonished man broke into tears, and exclaimed, "You may have it, and I will give $1,000 towards it." The arrangement was completed. At the close of a morning rehearsal, the beautiful hymn, "The Voice of Free Grace," was sung, and Mr Tappan announced to the actors that that evening there would be preaching *on that stage*. A pulpit was placed on the spot where dying agonies had often been counterfeited in tragic mockery; and in front of the footlights of the stage were seats for the inquirers.

The first prayer-meeting in the theatre was attended by 800 persons. On the 6th of May the house was dedicated to the service of God. Mr Finney preached from the text, "Who is on the Lord's side?" For seventy successive nights he preached there to immense audiences. The *bar-room* was changed into a *prayer-room*, and the first man who knelt there poured forth these words, "O Lord, forgive my sin's: the last time I was here thou knowest I was a wicked actor on this stage; O Lord, have mercy on me!" For three years this building was used for revival meetings.

That revival brought into the churches of New York 2,000 souls, many of whom became prominent in great benevolent movements.

Passing to other localities, we find Dr Furman of South Carolina, telling of revivals there in the early part of the century. Rev Mr Stevenson describes mighty works in Pennsylvania, and Mr Woodward embodies in a publication "surprising accounts" of revivals in Kentucky and Tennessee, while others write of the same in Georgia, North Carolina, and almost all sections of the country, about the same time. And so "the word of the Lord grew and multiplied."

Interruptions there were during the long period now under our notice; and at some seasons, (for example, 1814 and 1831), the spiritual harvest was more abundant than at others; but upon the field as a whole Christ was triumphing gloriously. As Dr Gardiner Spring, of New York, remarks, the period commencing with the year 1792 and terminating with 1842, was a memorable period in the history of the American church. Scarcely any portion of it but was graciously visited by copious effusions of the Holy Spirit. At this last mentioned date, (with the previous year), the city of Boston was wonderfully blessed, and *four thousand* converts were added to the evangelical churches.

It has been estimated that from 1815 to 1840, the Spirit was poured out upon from *four to five hundred churches and congregations*, on an average, annually; and that during some particular years "from forty to fifty thousand were added by profession in a single twelvemonth."

Thus, whatever view we take of the work, this was a most gracious period in the religious history of Christendom. Besides the rich harvests of priceless souls then gathered, these revivals stand directly connected, as we shall see in the next chapter, with all those aggressive movements which are turning the world's wildernesses into fruitful fields.

Fifth Revival Period: 1857–1860 – It is an interesting fact in revivals that they frequently succeed some great calamity – a prevailing epidemic, a general financial embarrassment, or the like.

It was so with the wonderful work of grace to which we now come. The churches in this country were, to an alarming extent, characterised by coldness and conformity to the world. The greed of gain amounted to a mania; and it filled not only the commercial centres, but the villages; in fact the whole land. Speculation was at fever-heat, and the wildest projects turned men's brains, and drove them recklessly on in the race for riches. As a natural result, frauds, defalcations and failures became common; until finally the crash came, and the castles in the air, as well as the solid accumulations, were seen everywhere toppling to the fall. As with the twinkling of an eye, golden dreams vanished and millionaires became bankrupts.

God meant it for good. He would drive out mammon that He Himself might reign. He made poor the merchant princes that they might be rich in heavenly gain.

And now that the wheels of industry stood still, and the counting-houses in the metropolis were deserted, and gloom and disappointment settled down like a pall, a voice was heard whispering to the men of weary brain, "Come ye yourselves apart, and rest awhile." "Is any man afflicted, let him pray." Subdued, broken, tender, they answered, "Yes, for he hath wounded, and he can heal."

A little room in the lower part of New York, and immediately in the drifts of trade, on the third floor of the "Consistory" of the old Reformed Dutch Church, Fulton Street, was thrown open for a weekly noon-day prayer-meeting. It was one of the earliest manifestations of a special religious interest.

At first the good down-town city missionary, Mr Lanphier, who made the appointment, met there three persons; then six, then twenty. Next week they assembled on the floor below, and the Business Men's Prayer-meeting began to attract attention. One man, (speaking for many), said: "Prayer never was so great a blessing to me as it is in this time; I should certainly either break down or turn rascal, except for it. If I could not get some half hours every day to pray myself into a right state of mind, I should certainly either be overburdened and disheartened, or do such things as no Christian man ought to do."

A call was now made for a *daily* meeting. It was received with enthusiasm, and the meeting-room overflowed, and filled a second, and eventually a third room, in the same building; making three crowded prayer-meetings, one above another, in animated progress at one and the same hour. The seats were all filled, and the passages and entrances began to be choked with numbers, rendering it scarcely possible to pass in or out. The hundreds who daily went away disappointed of admission, created a visible demand for more room; and the John Street Methodist Church and lecture-room were both opened for daily noon prayer-meetings, by a committee of the Young Men's Christian Association, and were crowded at once with attendants. Meetings were multiplied in other parts of the city; and the example spread to Philadelphia, to Boston, and to other cities, until there was scarcely a town of importance in the United States, (save a few in the South), in which the Business Men's Daily Prayer-meeting was not a flourishing institution, and a leading agency in awakening public interest to religion.

These *morning or noon-day prayer-meetings* were a marked feature of the revival. And it should be added, that they were union prayer-meetings, attended by all classes, without respect to denominational differences. The middle walls of partition were never before so broken down; and evangelical Christians of every name found they could come together and pray for the outpouring of the Spirit without any sacrifice of church order.

Requests for prayer were another marked feature. There was scarcely a meeting anywhere without such being sent forward; and often scores of them were presented. The following are samples:

> "Prayers are requested for a young man who has thus far resisted all persuasions to attend these meetings, and who is in these rooms today for the first time."
>
> "A sister, who has been praying daily three years for the conversion of an only brother, asks an interest in your prayers."
>
> "A brother requests the earnest prayers of this meeting on behalf of a loved but thoughtless sister."
>
> "Prayers are requested for a sister who is given to intemperance."
>
> "A few praying souls in Spring Street Presbyterian Church, deeply bewailing the spiritual desolation of that Zion, beseech you to unite with them in wrestling and importuning on her behalf. Brethren and sisters, pray for us, and if you can, come over and help us."

The aid of the newspapers was another feature of this great work. The secular papers all spoke of it; and some of them made it a point to report the meetings fully. A pastor wrote to one of the papers thus: "The glorious summary, with the editorial remarks on the 'Great Revivals,' in your paper of the 4th instant, stirred my soul so powerfully that I felt something more must be done in our village; and I have called on the other ministers, and we have started a meeting, and the dews are falling on us."

The *telegraph* was also called into requisition. The reader can imagine the effect of such dispatches as these:

> New York, March 12, 1858
> *To the Philadelphia Union Prayer-meeting in Jayne's Hall:*

> Christian Brethren – The New York John Street Union Meeting sends you greeting in brotherly love. "The inhabitants of one city shall go to another, saying, Let us go speedily to pray before the Lord, and to seek the Lord of Hosts – I will go also." "Praise the Lord – call upon His name – declare His doings among the people – make mention that His name is exalted."
> Benjamin F Manierre & Cephas Brainard (Leaders)

To this dispatch the following reply was received, and read to the meeting in John Street:

> Philadelphia, March 12, 1858
> Jayne's Hall Daily Prayer-Meeting is crowded; upwards of 3,000 present. With one mind and heart they glorify our Father in heaven for the mighty work He is doing in our city and country, in the building up of saints and the conversion of sinners. The Lord hath done great things for us, whence joy to us is brought. May He who holds the seven stars in His right hand, and who walks in the midst of the churches, be with you by His Spirit this day. Grace, mercy and peace be with you.
> George H Stuart (Chairman of Meeting)

The telegraph offices sent messages to all parts of the country, announcing conversions. Many of them were exceedingly tender and touching. These are samples: "Dear mother, the revival continues, and I, too, have been converted." "My dear parents, you will rejoice to hear that I have found peace with God." "Tell my sister that I have come to the cross of Christ." "At last I have obtained faith and peace."

The *lay element* was prominent in this revival. The workers, mostly, were laymen. From the beginning, ministers of the gospel cheerfully stood by and saw the principal share of labour in the hands of their lay brethren.

The *pervasiveness* of the work was striking. In manufactories, counting-rooms, jobbing-houses, and business firms of all kinds, prayer-meetings were established and souls converted. New churches were springing up, and old ones were strengthened. The substance of letters received from every State of the Union was revivals, *glorious and widespread revivals!* In some places day-schools were suspended, and teachers, scholars and parents occupied the school-houses daily for worship.

Again; great *sobriety* characterised the work. There were few wild and fanatical excitements to mar the beautiful and blessed work of the Spirit. "The majesty of a just God overshadowed the cross, and though the way to that cross was open and free, it was yet a solemn way for the guilty sinner to tread in."

Another characteristic of the work was – *that sinners seemed readily to find peace in Christ.* Those deep, long-continued, despairing convictions of sin which arise from a profound view of the holiness of God's law and the strictness of His claims upon us, were not prominent in this work. The love of Christ was the constraining power. Almost before they called He answered.

The *rapidity and power* of this revival formed another glorious feature. Certainly never before were our great cities such radiating centres of spiritual light and heat. God seemed everywhere to go *before* his people, and prepare the way; and hence revivals instantaneously sprang up in city, town and hamlet, throughout the land.

The *results*, of course, cannot be recorded; not even the number of conversions. In New York State 200 towns were reported as having revivals, with 6,000 conversions. In the city, all the churches were largely increased in membership, in some cases 50, 100, 200, 350, being received upon profession. Rev George Duffield, Junior, of Philadelphia, communicated some very interesting facts to the Fulton Street prayer-meeting. He had been employed, as one of a committee, to compile the facts of the revival as pertaining to that city. He found that 3,010 had been added by profession to one denomination, 1,800 to another, 1,500 to another, 1,200 to another, and so on, till the aggregate was above 9,000. He believed there had been in that city 10,000 conversions within that current year.

In New Jersey the work was very extensive. The writer of this volume had the joy of receiving into the church of his charge, (First Baptist), 236 souls upon profession. He wrote thus to the Newark *Daily Advertiser:* "As a matter of permanent record and grateful remembrance, I have thought it well to ascertain facts on this point as fully as possible. Inquiries have been addressed to thirty pastors and teachers in the city, as to the probable number of conversions, within the limits of their respective congregations. The figures show an aggregate of 2,685. Several ministers have not been reached; and it is fair to put the number unreported at 100; which would make an aggregate of some 2,800 hopeful conversions."

Rev Dr Scott, (First Reformed Church), stated that the conversion of persons of the strongest and maturest mind in the community was among the characteristics of the work in Newark. If he had attempted to select from his congregation forty-five of its strongest minds, he would have generally taken the forty-five who had united with his church by profession. Sixty towns in the State reported revivals, with 5,000 to 6,000 conversions.

Statistics from other States need not be given, as these are but examples. It is estimated that 100,000 conversions occurred in the short space of four months; and that during a year from the commencement of the work, not less than 400,000 souls were brought to Christ. Some writers have added one quarter to the above numbers. Thus much for the United States.

Abroad, the work was also extensive and powerful. Dr J W Alexander writes that he was in Great Britain before the work arose here; and that the increase of endeavours to carry the gospel to the poor, in their most abject retreats – the continual use of open-air preaching – the rise of several evangelical ministers upon whose words the multitude were disposed to hang – the services in Exeter Hall, and even the opening of Westminster Abbey, spoke of zeal on one hand, and roused attention on the other. He once saw an assembly of ten thousand souls giving rapt attention at the Surrey Gardens to the great truths of salvation.

Such paragraphs as these appeared in the English papers: "A meeting for prayer is now held daily at two o'clock, pm, in the County Rooms, Aberdeen, specially with a view to plead for the outpouring of the Holy Spirit; it is said that it is attended by above a thousand persons daily." "The year 1859 will be remembered as a year of a fruitful harvest of souls in many countries in Europe. In Wales, it is estimated that the number of converts in the various denominations of orthodox Christians was from 30,000 to 35,000, a large number out of a population of a little over a million. It is known that 25,000 were added to the Welsh Calvinistic church. The instances of backsliding, in both Wales and Ireland, have been very rare, though many of the converts were from the lowest orders of society. The good effects of the revival in Ireland, witnessed in the remarkable freedom from lawsuits and crime, are testified to by many public men connected with the courts, who attribute it to the moral and religious movements of last year. At the last assizes in the county Antrim, there was not a single prisoner for trial."

Rev Dr Baron Stow, of Boston, in 1860, wrote thus as to Ireland, which he had just the year before visited: "It has been estimated that in Belfast, a city of 130,000 souls, there are *ten thousand* converts. These are being received slowly and cautiously into the churches. God has distinguished this work in the North of Ireland by extraordinary manifestations of His own sovereign, mysterious agency. There were at many points the usual antecedents of faithful teaching and earnest prayer; but the blessing came in unexpected forms, lighted down in uninviting places, and produced unanticipated effects; and few, either of the ministry or the laity, were prepared to deal intelligently with the cases which were suddenly multiplied. In almost every place the work commenced among the less instructed and more degraded classes, and was characterised, in its incipient stage, by physical accompaniments that amazed the inexperienced, alarmed the timid, and impressed with an indefinable awe nearly the whole community. But the changes wrought in character, speech, and conduct, soon became too demonstrative to admit a doubt as to the Higher Agency that had produced them; and when God had made Himself known as the Author of the moral transformations, and had thoroughly awakened attention to His claims, He gradually withdrew the physical operations, and the work assumed a more purely spiritual type. His design evidently comprehended more than the religious improvement of a province, or the salvation of thousands of its people. He would make a demonstration of His supremacy and power that should affect Christendom, and bring glory, on a broad field, to the riches of His grace. Many hundreds, not only from the unblessed districts of Ireland, but also from England and Scotland, and even from the Continent, hastened to the scene of the Spirit's wonder-working; and, while many remained longer than they intended, co-operating with the over-tasked labourers, few returned without the conviction that Ulster was pervaded by the power of the Highest."

The bishop of Hereford, (Dr Hampden), the same year, in his triennial charge to his clergy, warns them against "the movement in the North of Ireland," and against "similar agitation in his own county and neighbourhood," adding that "he greatly distrusts the work, and he is strengthened in this feeling by the recollection of the scenes which took place during the agitation which was commenced and carried on by John Wesley." "Many instances of insincerity," the Bishop says, "were found among the followers of Wesley." And the *Saturday Review* ridiculed the work, (thus acknowledging its extent), in saying, "Undoubtedly the thing is catching. An enthusiast, we suppose, emits some subtle *aura* which falls upon the nerves, or the gastric *plexus*, or the hysteric organs, which are predisposed for receiving or imbibing the poison."

On the other hand, in Dr Gibson's *Year of Grace*, (a carefully prepared work), we have abundant evidence of the power and genuineness of these awakenings in Ireland and Scotland.

The following abstract shows the comparative number, both of congregations visited by the revival, and of individuals added to the Church in connection with them, in the several counties of Ulster:

County	Congregations	Additional Communicants
Antrim	81	4353
Down	68	2107
Derry	36	1258
Tyrone	42	1189
Armagh	27	625
Donegal	23	502
Monaghan	18	412
Cavan	10	169
Fermanagh	1	21
Totals	306	10,636

America, however, was most favoured in this gracious visitation, and many will recognise in the following pen-picture, taken from one of the religious journals of March 1858, an accurate portraiture of the well-remembered scenes of those days:

"Such a time as the present was never known since the days of the Apostles, for revivals. The prostration of business, the downfall of Mammon, the great god of worship to the multitudes in this land, both in and out of the church, the sinfulness and vanity of earthly treasures, as the supreme good, have come home to the hearts and consciences of the millions in our land with a power that seems irresistible. Revivals now cover our very land, sweeping all before them, as on the day of Pentecost, exciting the earnest and simultaneous cry from thousands, 'What shall we do to be saved?' They have taken hold of the community at large to such an extent that now they are the engrossing theme of conversation in all circles of society. Ministers seem baptised with the Holy Ghost and preach with new power and earnestness, bringing the truth home to the conscience and life as rarely before. Meetings are held for prayer, for exhortation, and for conversation, with the deepest interest, and the most astonishing results. Not only are they held in the church and from house to house, but in the great marts of trade and centres of business. Halls are selected, where men may leave their worldly cares for an hour, and by multitudes, without form or ceremony, drop in, fall on their knees and pray, with a few words of exhortation and entreaty, and then go about their usual business. In New York there is a most astonishing interest in all the churches, seeming as if that great and populous and depraved city was enveloped in one conflagration of divine influence. Union prayer-meetings are held in the principal centres, and here thousands on thousands gather daily. Prayer and conference meetings are held in retired rooms connected with large commercial houses, and with the best effects. The large cities and towns generally from Maine to California are sharing in this great and glorious work. There is hardly a village or town to be found where a special divine power does not appear to be displayed. It really seems as if the Millennium was upon us in its glory."

At one of the great meetings for prayer, held at midday in the city of New York, a gentleman from Philadelphia rose and read, with thrilling effect, the following hymn. It was but another indication of the times:

Where'er we meet, you always say
  What's the news? What's the news?
Pray what's the order of the day?
  What's the news? What's the news?
Oh! I have got good news to tell;
My Saviour hath done all things well,
And triumphed over death and hell.
  That's the news! That's the news!

The Lamb was slain on Calvary,
  That's the news! That's the news!
To set a world of sinners free.
  That's the news! That's the news!
'Twas there His precious blood was shed,
'Twas there He bowed His sacred head;
But now He's risen from the dead,
  That's the news! That's the news!

To heav'n above the Conqueror's gone,
  That's the news! That's the news!
He's passed triumphant to His throne.
  That's the news! That's the news!
And on that throne He will remain
Until, as Judge He comes again,
Attended by a dazzling train,
  That's the news! That's the news!

His work's reviving all around –
  That's the news! That's the news!
And many have redemption found –
  That's the news! That's the news!
And since their souls have caught the flame,
They shout Hosanna to His name;
And all around they spread His fame –
  That's the news! That's the news!

The Lord has pardoned all my sin
  That's the news! That's the news!
I feel the witness now within –
  That's the news! That's the news!
And since He took my sins away,
And taught me how to watch and pray,
I'm happy now from day to day,
  That's the news! That's the news!

And Christ the Lord can save you, too –
  That's the news! That's the news!
Your sinful heart He can renew –
  That's the news! That's the news!
This moment, if for sins you grieve,
This moment, if you do believe,
A full acquittal you'll receive –
  That's the news! That's the news!

And now, if anyone should say,
  What's the news? What's the news?
Oh, tell him you've begun to pray –
  That's the news! That's the news! –
That you have joined the conquering band,
And now with joy at God's command,
You're marching to the better land.
  That's the news! That's the news!

It would be pleasant to dwell still longer on God's wondrous works during this last revival period; but our limits forbid.

In the chapter that follows are crystallised some of the more marked results of the several seasons of grace which have now been brought under review.

"O Lord, Revive Thy Work!"

3

What We Owe to Revivals

NO one can study the history of revivals and not be impressed with their mighty influence upon the destiny of the race. Not to speak of those of primitive times, what would have been the condition of the world today but for the great Reformation, the *spirit* of which, as we have seen, was but a series of revivals of religion? And what had been the state of this country, and of other lands, had not the Holy Ghost been poured down in those gracious revival periods recorded in the previous chapter? Let us, under several particulars, see what we owe to these refreshings from the presence of the Lord.

1. *Society at large has been uplifted by revivals.* Godliness has the promise of this life, as well as of that to come. When the divine grace is abundantly downpoured it is felt at the very springs of society, and there cannot but be a corresponding elevation. Exalted to be the sons of God, and thrilled with new impulses, men burst asunder the chains of superstition, tyranny, and vice, and come into a higher and broader development. The fountains of life are purified, and a social and civil renovation is the result. It is impossible that the heart be turned from the love of sin to the love of holiness without an external reformation.

Hence the wonderful changes for good which are reported in pagan or papal lands, where the gospel takes effect. And hence the cases under our eyes where revivals have renovated, not only the moral but the physical aspect of a community; driven away vice, encouraged industry, promoted intelligence, and caused the social virtues to prevail where before were discord and unblushing crime.

We boast of the progress of this age; and nothing is more astonishing than the recent advancement in science, philosophy, invention, learning, philanthropy, and civil jurisprudence. But it would be an interesting line of thought to show how this is attributable, in great part, to the religious awakenings of the last three hundred years. Our limits forbid it here; but let it be noted that *aroused intellect* has been behind of all this: and that revivals of religion are favourable to intellectual action, not only as they bring the mind at the time into vigorous exercise, and into contact with the mighty truths of God's Word, but as they originate in the subjects of them moral feelings and habits which are peculiarly favourable to the acquisition of useful knowledge.

When Wycliffe and his successors reopened the Bible, the revival of letters took place. Twenty-four universities arose in less than a hundred years. In the midst of this movement, the discovery of the art of printing gave a new impetus to literature, and provided the swift and subtle agent by which the infant Reformation was to surprise and overpower its great adversary unawares. At the same juncture the Mohammedan power, overwhelming the Eastern metropolis, swept the remnant of Greek learning into Europe. Finally, about the last half of the same memorable century, Luther, Zwingli, Cranmer, Melanchthon, Knox, and Calvin, with other mighty champions of truth, stepped forward to blow the trumpet of salvation and summon to new action the world's thought.

In due time Owen, Bunyan, Baxter, Milton, Leighton, Flavel, and other luminaries of the seventeenth century, burning with the love of God, gave to the world for the first time an evangelical literature, and thereby a mighty acceleration to human progress. "We hazard little," remarks an authority, "in saying that for doctrinal, practical, and experimental religious instruction and authorship, it was the golden age in the fatherland." What other age has produced so many volumes full of the marrow of the gospel, and indicted as it were so close on the verge of heaven? What thousands have been guided in the Way of Life by Bunyan's *Pilgrim's Progress,* and his *Grace Abounding to the Chief of Sinners;* and what thousands more have had the fulness of Christ revealed to them in Flavel's *Fountain of Life* and *Method of Grace.*

What would our own land, as well as Great Britain, have been but for this revival period in the seventeenth century?

Then came that great uplifting of the English people by the revival under Whitefield and the Wesleys. John Wesley wrote theology, Charles Wesley put it into song, and Whitefield preached it to the masses. There was need enough of their best efforts; for the Establishment, with all its learning, opulence and dignity, was doing next to nothing for the elevation of the ignorant communities.

In Howitt's *Rural Life of England* is the following, with reference to the times under remark, which shows the elevating influence of revivals of religion:

"It is in the rural districts into which manufactories have spread – that are partly manufacturing and partly agricultural – that the population assumes its worst shape. And the Methodists have done much to check the progress of demoralisation in these districts. They have given vast numbers education; they have taken them away from the pot-house and the gambling-house; from low haunts and low pursuits. They have placed them in a certain circle, and invested them with a degree of moral and social importance. They have placed them where they have a character to sustain, and higher objects to strive after; where they have ceased to be operated upon by a perpetual series of evil influences, and have been brought under the regular operation of good ones. They have rescued them from brutality of mind and manners, and given them a more refined association on earth, and a warm hope of a still better existence hereafter. If they have not done all that could be desired, with such materials, they have done much, and the country owes them much."

This is a striking attestation to the beneficent influences of genuine revivals. And impartial history justifies the award. For the methods and means of education were improved, and the masses hungering for knowledge soon found their appetite gratified by public libraries, and the rapid issue of hymns and sermons, and treatises upon questions of current interest, and upon science and literature in a popularised form. In short, the trumpets of a grand moral, intellectual, and social resurrection were sounded throughout the realm by this spiritual awakening; and the people were elevated to higher aims and destinies.

It would be impossible to describe how much we in this country owe to the same revivals for our high position. The American Colonies felt the impulse of the intellectual advancement resulting from the awakenings in the old world, and were vastly indebted to them. Nor in the absence of such revivals could it have been said,

> "When, driven by oppression's rod
> Our fathers fled beyond the sea.
> Their care was first to honour God,
> And next to leave their children free.
> Above the forest's gloomy shade
> The *altar* and the *school* appeared:
> On that the gifts of faith were laid.
> On this their precious hopes were reared."

In fact, the Pilgrims and Puritans were *themselves the product* of those heavenly visitations. So that but for them we had not *had* such forefathers, of brain force, and conscience, and courage, and adamantine faith, and heroic virtue. And consequently we should not have had those institutions which have been bequeathed to us.

Not to insist on this, however, let it be remembered, that while the next subsequent great awakenings in the old and new world were progressing, the political agitations in this country were taking place. And who can doubt that they were coincident in purpose as well as in time? The first mentioned were designed, beyond question, to act upon the last mentioned, and both to coalesce in the elevation of man for the divine glory. And so while a popular government was to be planted, and the resources of the continent were making ready for development, constituting this the home of the nations, it was made sure that there should be special religious activities on the part of God's people. Thus were the moulding influences of Christianity operative in just that emergency – the formative state of society – blending its sanctified forces with the vigour of the youthful republic.

2. *Missionary movements came from revivals.* All those great benevolent enterprises which are the glory of this age originated thence.

Confining our view to the fourth revival period, 1790–1842, how apparent is the fact stated.

In 1784 at a Baptist Association held in Nottingham, England, it was determined "that one hour in the first Monday evening of every month should be devoted to solemn and special intercession for the Redeemer's Kingdom throughout the Earth." In the spring of 1791, at a meeting of ministers held at Clipston, in Northamptonshire, Messrs Sutcliff and Fuller delivered discourses adapted to fan into a flame the latent sparks of missionary zeal. At the annual association held that autumn at Nottingham, William Carey preached his famous sermon, "Enlarge the place of thy tent, ...," (*Isaiah 54*), urging that we were to "*Expect great things from God, and attempt great things for God.*"

On the 2nd of October, 1792, the ministers met at Kettering, and after the public services of the day, retired for prayer. Then they solemnly pledged themselves to God and to each other to make a trial for introducing the gospel among the heathen, subscribing as a fund for that purpose £13. 2s. 6d. A plan was adopted, and a society formed, designated "The Particular Baptist Society for Propagating the Gospel among the Heathen." The names of the twelve were John Ryland, Reynold Hogg, John Sutcliff, Andrew Fuller, Abraham Greenwood, Edward Sharman, Joshua Burton, Samuel Pearce, Thomas Blundel, William Heighton, John Eayres, Joseph Timms. William Carey immediately offered himself as a missionary. Mr John Thomas, who had already performed some Christian labour in Calcutta, while practising there as a surgeon, and was then in England, joined him. They sailed from England June 13, 1793. John Fountain followed them in 1796; and in 1799 Messrs Ward, Brundson, Grant, and Marshman, were added to the little band.

Thus was laid on a solid basis the first of the modern evangelical societies for the conversion of the pagans. Kindred societies, for home and foreign work, and for a variety of specific objects, (as we have seen in the previous chapter), were established in England about this time.

Still more visibly, if possible, were the great missionary movements of our own country connected with the revival period of which we now speak.

In the words of Dr Heman Humphrey, as to this era, when it dawned, there were no Missionary societies, foreign or domestic, no Bible societies, no Tract societies, no Education societies, no onward movements in the churches of any sort for the conversion of the world. At home it was deep spiritual apathy; abroad, over all the heathen lands, the calm of the Dead Sea – death, death, nothing but death.

All the first foreign missionaries, Hall, Newell, Mills, Judson, Nott, Rice, Bingham, King, Thruston, and others who entered the field a little later, were converted and received their missionary baptism in revivals. The American Board of Foreign Missions was formed in 1810, at the urging of the first band that went out from this country to India. But for their earnest solicitation to be sent forth with the glad tidings of the gospel upon their tongues, no such Board would have been formed, certainly not at that time; and if it had, it could not have done anything: there would have been no missionaries to send if God had not poured out His Spirit, and raised them up and prepared them to endure hardness as good soldiers of Jesus Christ. In these revivals the holy fire was kindled which waked up and warmed the churches to an onward aggressive movement such as had never been known in this country before. Other missionaries soon followed under the same Board. And about the same time the American Baptist Foreign Mission Board was organised, to sustain Judson and Rice who had changed their communion and commenced a mission in Burma.

From the same revival source, moreover, sprang home missions. It began to be felt that we have a wide and fast spreading population that must be cared for, and then domestic missionary societies were formed to meet the want. Nor was this enough. The churches having once waked up from their long slumbers, could not rest here. The destitute at home must have the Word of God put into their hands, and it must be sent abroad with the missionaries, and translated into the tongues wherein the heathen were born, that they might read the wonderful works of God and be turned from darkness to light, from the worship of dumb idols to the worship of Him who made the world. Hence sprang the American Bible Society, and in succession, its branches, and other kindred institutions.

Nor yet again could the yearnings of Christian benevolence, once excited, rest without still further expansion. A Christian literature, in a cheap and attractive form, must be created and diffused. Small religious tracts must be written, printed and scattered over the land. And to this end Tract and other Societies were organised.

If we would see more minutely the exact relation which revivals bore to these benevolent movements, we have but to consider such facts as these:

In the spring of 1806 Samuel John Mills joined Williams College, Massachusetts. Of him Dr Griffin says he "*had been prepared by the revival of Torringford,* Litchfield county, in 1798-9." Through Mr Mills, in great part, revival influences prevailed in the town and college, and among the converts was Gordon Hall. Says Dr Griffin, "Mills had devoted himself to the cause of missions from the commencement of his new existence, and by the influence of that revival he was enabled to diffuse his spirit through a choice circle who raised this college to the distinction of being the birthplace of American missions. In the spring of 1808 they formed a secret society, to extend their influences to other colleges, and to distinguished individuals in different parts of the country. One of them first roused the missionary energies of Pliny Fisk, who afterwards died in Palestine. In the autumn of that year, in a beautiful meadow on the banks of the Hoosack, these young Elijahs prayed into existence the embryo of American missions. In the fall of 1809, Mills, Richards and Robbins carried this society to Andover, where it roused the first missionary band that went out to India in 1812, and where it is still exerting a mighty influence on the interests of the world. In that band were Gordon Hall and Luther Rice, of this college, (and Adoniram Judson, converted at Andover). Richards soon followed and laid his bones in India. Mills and his co-adjutors were the means of forming the American Board of Commissioners for Foreign Missions, the American Bible Society, the United Foreign Missionary Society, and the African School under the care of the Synod of New York and New Jersey; besides all the impetus given to domestic missions, to the Colonisation Society, and to the general cause of benevolence in both hemispheres." Such were some of the fruits of the revivals of those times, regarded in the light of the benevolent enterprises to which they led.

In this survey we have not alluded to missionary movements among the Indians, resulting from the revivals in the time of the elder Edwards; nor to incipient organisations, (such as the Massachusetts Missionary Society, formed in Boston in 1799, and the Baptist Missionary Society of Massachusetts, formed in 1803), which were among the first fruits of the powerful awakenings about the beginning of the nineteenth century. But enough has been said to show the connection between missions and revivals.

It must be added, however, that the *funds* for the prosecution of these enterprises of benevolence would never have been forthcoming except for revivals. It is when God's people are vivified by the special power of the Spirit, that their hearts and their hands are open on behalf of those sitting in the region and shadow of death.

3. *An efficient ministry has come from revivals.* We hardly dare lift the curtain to see what the ministry was previous to some of the great historic revivals; as in the days of Wycliffe, Huss, and Luther; or when Whitefield began his career. The character of the English clergy of those times is but too well-known. Many of them could not even read the Bible. Of the clergy, even as late as 1781, Cowper could write without fear of contradiction:

> "Except a *few* with Eli's spirit blest,
> Hophni and Phineas may describe the rest."

It is also well-known that great numbers of the American Congregational clergy in the early part and about the middle of the eighteenth century, were not converted, nor even pretended to be. We are told that as many as *twenty ministers* were converted in and around Boston under Mr Whitefield's preaching, upon his third visit to America. Indeed, some men of eminence, (like Mr Stoddard at Northampton), maintained that "unconverted ministers have certain official duties which they may lawfully perform." Says Tracy, (in his *Great Awakening*): "A large majority in the Presbyterian Church, and many, if not most, in New England, held that the ministrations of unconverted men, if neither heretical in doctrine nor scandalous for immorality, were valid, and their labours useful. For years afterwards, this doctrine was publicly and furiously maintained."

The prodigious excitement created by Mr Tennent's famous Nottingham, (New Jersey), sermon, "On the danger of an unconverted ministry," is another indication of the times.

In the "improvement" part of the sermon he cries out, "What a scrole and scene of mourning, lamentation, and woe is opened, because of the swarms of locusts, the crowds of Pharisees, that have as covetously as cruelly crept into the ministry in this adulterous generation! who as nearly resemble the character given of the old Pharisees, in the doctrinal part of this discourse, as one crow's egg does another! It is true, some of the modern Pharisees have learned to prate a little more orthodoxly about the new birth, than their predecessor Nicodemus, who are, in the meantime, as great strangers to the feeling experience of it, as he. They are blind who see not this to be the case of the *body* of the clergy of this generation."

There was no doubt somewhat of exaggeration, as well as undue severity of expression, in this sermon; but it is certain that plain words were called for; and an unquestionable authority states that "to no other human agency as much as to this sermon is it owing that Presbyterian ministers at the present day are generally pious." Thus much as to the revivals of those times as related to a soundly converted ministry.

But there is a higher ministerial qualification than bare conversion: namely, the possession of a large measure of the Holy Spirit. And how many a minister has had his whole character and style of preaching remodelled by precious revival experiences. It has been remarked with truth that a minister can learn in a revival that which he can scarcely learn in any other circumstances. There he enjoys advantages which he can have nowhere else for becoming acquainted with the windings of the human heart; for ascertaining the influence of different truths upon different states of feeling; for learning how to detect false hopes and to ascertain and confirm good hopes; and for getting his own soul deeply imbued with the true spirit of his work. Hence ministers, after having passed through a revival, have preached, and prayed, and done their whole work with far more earnestness and effect than before; and they themselves have not infrequently acknowledged that what they had gained, during such a season, has been worth more to them than the study of years.

It must be remembered, too, that revivals mightily increase the number of ministers. It is when thousands of youth are gathered into the churches that our young men come forward, saying, "Here am I, send me." What an exhibit that would be if we were able to give the names of all the ministers of the last hundred years who were converted in revivals! We believe that *nine-tenths* of them were the children of revivals. Nor, if the repetition of such visitations were to cease, do we see any alternative except that the great work of the age must stand still for want of labourers, or be prosecuted by men lacking the most essential of all qualifications.

4. *Institutions of learning owe much to revivals.* Many of them originated directly in revivals. We have already seen that 24 universities sprang up within a century in the old world succeeding the labours

of Wycliffe. And the founding of Princeton College in this country is but one case of many where the beginnings were in revivals. It may also be mentioned that the same revival was the parent of Dartmouth College. Among the Mohegans converted in 1741, was Samson Occum, then seventeen years of age. In December 1743, Mr Wheelock, of Lebanon, received him as a pupil, and he pursued his studies in the family for several years. In 1748, Wheelock determined to commence a school for the education of Indian preachers, and a donation from Joshua Moor, a farmer in Mansfield, in 1754, gave it a permanent foundation. The influence of the revival on several Indian tribes helped to furnish him with pupils, and in 1762 he had more than twenty under his care. In 1766, Rev Nathaniel Whitaker, and Occum, who had become a preacher of some distinction, went to England to solicit funds for the institution. Occum attracted unusual attention, Whitefield aided them, and a large amount of funds was obtained. The school was afterwards removed to its present location, in New Hampshire, and Dartmouth College was added to it. And with the founding of the college there, a series of revivals commenced, extending through several years.

But, viewed in any aspect, what had been the fate of colleges without revivals? Take such facts as these as to the absence of revivals.

During the first seven years of the existence of Williams College – in which *ninety-three* graduated in six classes – there were but *five* professors of religion in the institution, exclusive of two who, seven months before the close of that period, were brought into the church by the revivals in Litchfield county. In three of those six classes there was not a single professor. From the commencement in 1798 till February, 1800, there was but *one* professor of religion in the college.

Dr Green, President of Princeton College, says that when in 1782 he entered the institution, there were but two professors of religion among the students, and not more than five or six who scrupled to use profane language in common conversation. The open and avowed infidelity of Paine, and other writers of the same character, produced incalculable injury to religion and morals throughout our whole country; and its effect on young men who valued themselves for genius, and were fond of novel speculations, was the greatest of all. And he says: "Dr Smith, then President of the college, told me that one man who sent his son, stated explicitly in a letter that *not a word was ever to be said to him on the subject of religion.*"

In some of the early years of Yale College there were not four in a year studying for the ministry. When Dr Dwight came to the Presidency, (in 1795), many of the leading students were tinctured with the French infidelity, and its bold champions.

Alas for college life if it had been thus barren of religious influence! But take such facts as the following. Speaking for Brown University, Providence, Rhode Island, President Manning, (also pastor of the Baptist Church there), wrote thus: "In the beginning of 1774 it pleased the Lord in a most remarkable manner to revive His work in the town of Providence, and more especially among the people of my charge. Such a time I never before saw. Our public assemblies by day and by night were crowded, and the auditors seemed to hear as for the life of their souls. It was frequently an hour before I could get from the pulpit to the door, on account of the numbers thronging to have an opportunity of stating the condition of their minds. And what added to my happiness, was, that the Lord visited the college as remarkably as the congregation. Frequently, when I went to the recitation room, I would find nearly all the students assembled, and joining in prayer and praise to God. Instead of my lectures on logic and philosophy, they would request me to speak to them of the things pertaining to the kingdom of God. In the space of six months I baptised more than a hundred persons."

In 1802 a revival in Yale shook the whole college, and "it seemed for the time that the whole mass of the students would press into the kingdom." And "nearly all the converts entered the ministry." No less than four revivals occurred under Dr Dwight's presidency, resulting in the conversion of two hundred and ten young men, who, in their turn, were the instruments of the salvation of thousands of souls.

In 1832, President Humphrey, of Amherst College writing as to revivals there up to his time says: "These times of refreshing have been of inestimable advantage to the college, by raising the standard of morals, and diffusing a strong religious influence throughout our whole youthful community. During the ten years that the institution has now existed, there has been a decided average majority of professed Christians in the four classes. In some years more than two-thirds have been professors. *Two hundred and seventy* have graduated

– more than two hundred of whom are hopefully pious; and about one-half of the number of students who have entered college without piety, since it was established, have, as we trust, found the pearl of great price before completing their academical course."

Says Dr Tyler, in his *Prayer for Colleges and Seminaries:* "In the space of ninety-six years, beginning with the great revival of 1741, and ending in 1837, there were twenty revivals in Yale College, in fourteen of which five hundred students were hopefully converted; and during the last twenty-five years of this same period, there were thirteen special revivals, or one every two years, besides several other seasons of more than usual religious interest."

Middlebury College has been blessed in forty years with ten revivals – some of them of great power. During the first twenty-five years of its history, every class but one was permitted to share in a religious awakening, and some classes received three or four such visits of mercy while in college. No class has ever yet left Amherst College without witnessing a powerful revival: and of the converts more than one hundred have been ministers, fifteen have been missionaries, twenty-eight officers of colleges and theological seminaries; and several were young men of genius and great promise, who died before entering upon a profession.

Nor must we forget to magnify the grace of God in the effusions of His Spirit upon our academies, high-schools, and other kindred educational seminaries, both male and female, where there have been hundreds upon hundreds of these revivals, making these schools emphatically nurseries of the churches.

In view of all this, who can calculate the influence of revivals upon our seats of learning? And from what source could faithful ministers have been obtained if these institutions had not thus been blessed?

5. Once more: *Strong churches have come from revivals.* The numerical aspect is one view of the case. It is of the very nature of revivals that multitudes flock into the kingdom. And what an accession to the praying and working force of the churches in the estimated 50,000 converts in this country during the awakening of 1730–1745; and the 40,000 to 50,000 *annually* for many years between 1790 and 1840; and the 400,000 additions in the revival of 1857-8. And what numbers of new churches during those seasons were organised.

It must also be taken into account, that in those earlier revivals great numbers of church-members were converted, and not put down among reported conversions. Says Tracy of the work at the time of Edwards, "The practice of admitting to the communion all persons neither heretical nor scandalous, was general in the Presbyterian church, and prevailed extensively among the Congregational churches. In consequence, a large proportion of the communicants in both were unconverted persons. Multitudes of these were converted. In some cases the revival seems to have been almost wholly within the church, and to have resulted in the conversion of nearly all the members." A large addition ought to be made, on this score, to the estimated number of conversions.

And of the work fifty years later an equally good authority says: "In New England, the old so-called Half Way Covenant system, by which many claimed for themselves and their children a visible relation to the church, while living in worldliness and neglecting the Lord's Table, was still widely prevalent, and though a large number of churches continued evangelical and spiritual, the great body had sunk into apathy and formality. As an illustration of the state of many churches, we have in mind one, now evangelical, in which, when a godly man was called to it, no prayer-meeting had been held for thirty years; family worship was maintained by very few; and the terms of admission to the church were little more than an assent to the truth of the Christian religion, and a wish to join."

Here was, then, a two-fold gain by the revivals – additions from *within* as well as from without. And this *re*-conversion of the churches was far more important than mere numerical accessions. Unconverted members are a dead weight, which no church can afford to carry: and the bodies were thus relieved from these encumbrances.

Again, a converted church membership was after this insisted upon; and had the opposite practice been continued, and become universal, it would have been more than a paralysis. The churches might have retained their names, but as true churches of Christ they would not have survived.

Another, and a most important advantage from the revivals was, that the preaching became more spiritual and discriminating, and the doctrines more evangelical. It was felt that every man is a "child of wrath" unless "born of the Spirit." Each individual saw that his most endeared friend, wife or husband, son or daughter, neighbour or acquaintance, was on the road to death unless created anew in Christ Jesus. Hence the latent Christian energies were called out.

Another result was the abolition of the union of church and state. The government of the founders of New England was a Theocracy, and it worked disastrously. In the words of the biographer of John Cotton, "it served both to embroil the state, and to *secularise* the church; and laid a foundation for that lamentable apostasy, in which not a few of the Pilgrim churches are sunk."

And yet the theory was clung to by very many. They shrank from the application of the principle of soul-liberty, now so common. Even to such men as Timothy Dwight and Lyman Beecher, it seemed dangerous to the interests of piety to disunite the churches from civil jurisdiction and support – the latter, as he said, being at first so unreconciled to it that he grieved and troubled himself over it day and night. Nor was it until a late day that the last link connecting church and state was broken by abolishing the assessments of church-rates. This was effected not alone by the great increase of the Baptists, who from the first heartily advocated it, but also by the increase of the *spiritual element* in all the religious bodies, which naturally found expression in this direction.

From these several points of observation, one cannot fail to be impressed with the conviction of an augmented church-power from revivals. Thence have come the vast majority of our Sunday School teachers and Christian workers, our most laborious and successful ministers and missionaries, and the most enterprising and influential churches.

In 1829 a letter was addressed to the Congregational ministers of Connecticut, proposing among other inquiries, the following – "1. What was the whole number of professors of religion in your church at the commencement of the year 1820? 2. What number were added to your church by profession during the years 1820,-1-2-3-4? 3. Of those who are now members of your church, what proportion may be considered as the fruit of a revival, and what is their comparative standing for piety and active benevolent enterprise?" And it appeared that a very large proportion of all who were members of the Congregational churches in that State, became such in consequence of revivals; that the relative proportion of such as revivals had been multiplying, had been continually increasing; that the most active and devoted Christians were among those who came into the church as fruits of revivals; that those churches in which revivals had been most frequent and powerful were the most numerous and flourishing, and that in all the churches thus visited with divine influence, there had been a great increase of Christian enterprise, and benevolent action.

Says Dr Joel Hawes, (in 1832), "It is now my sober judgment, that if there is among the people of my charge any cordial belief and love of the distinguishing doctrines of the gospel; any serious practical regard to the duties of the Christian life; any self-denial and bearing of the cross and following Christ according to his commands; any active benevolence and engaged-ness in doing good; in short, any pious efficient concern for the glory of God and the salvation of sinners, either at home or abroad, in Christian or in heathen lands – all this is to be traced, in no small part, to the influence of revivals of religion; and it is to be found, in an eminent degree, among those who have been added to the church as fruits of revivals."

The writer has been at considerable pains to verify this judgment of Dr Hawes as a general rule, by examining into the history of some of the strong churches of today. And the result is deeply interesting and instructive.

Beginning immediately under his personal observation, he finds that the First Presbyterian Church here, (Newark, New Jersey) – one of the oldest and strongest in the denomination, and from which have originated a goodly number of other bodies – is emphatically the offspring of revivals. Thus we read in a letter from Dr Griffin, that in 1806 "we were encouraged with symptoms of a revival in this village;" and that in 1807 "secret anxieties were preying upon a number of persons, and the desire for a revival was spreading rapidly through the church," and "the agonies of parents were such as to drive sleep from their eyes." Soon he tells of "the triumphs of the Prince of peace," and of "two hundred and thirty to two hundred and fifty" hopeful conversions. And Dr Stearns, (the present pastor), in his history of this body, narrates other mighty works of grace at various intervals. What would that congregation, (and the denomination in Newark), have been today but for those revivals? Almost all the strong men in these societies were the subjects of these revivals, twenty, thirty, forty, and some of them sixty years ago.

The history of the First Baptist church is much to the same effect. To the personal knowledge of the writer the main strength of this body is the direct fruit of revivals. Thus the 23 persons received in a gentle refreshing in 1810; the 28 in 1818; the 14 in 1833; the 23 in 1836; the 48 in 1840; the 30 in 1847 and 1850; and the *one thousand* souls added by profession since the last mentioned date, (230 in one revival) – these additions have been the very life-blood of the church. And other churches of this denomination, as well as of the Methodist, Congregational, and Reformed churches, have had a similar experience.

Passing to Elizabeth, (the same State), we find two old and very strong Presbyterian congregations. Trace their history back, and we meet such facts as these – In 1772, 1774, 1784, 1803, 1812, 1817, 1819, and 1825 there were revivals, when large numbers were added. "The young, and many of them children," added from 1817 to 1826, have been, chiefly, the strength of this denomination for many years. What a different aspect would those bodies wear today had there not been these great ingatherings.

Passing on to New Brunswick, (same State), we find there substantial Christian bodies – Reformed, Baptist, Presbyterian; and it is ascertained that *revivals* have chiefly made them what they are.

We visit Hartford, and New Haven, Connecticut; and turning to the narratives of wonderful works of grace in that State, we find that two hundred were added to the Congregational body in the former place in 1821: and, says the pastor in 1832, (Dr Hawes), "During the time I have been connected with the church, about five hundred and fifty have been added to its communion, not less than four-fifths of whom are to be regarded as the fruits of revivals."

In New Haven 300 were added to the Congregationalist church in 1820; and of 31 congregations in the county of New Haven, at least twenty-five were visited, during the winter and spring, with the special presence of the Lord; and it was estimated that within these limits between *fifteen hundred and two thousand* souls were called out of nature's darkness into light. Who fails to see that Congregationalism on those fields owes its strength today to those revivals?

In Boston and Providence, facts of the same nature might be abundantly gathered. Also in Pittsfield, Troy, Albany, and other cities.

Coming to New York, it is well-known that the "old Brick Church" has been for long years a tower of strength there. And now hear Dr Spring, for threescore years its pastor, tell how he felt in 1814 when it seemed that he "*must abandon*" his post through discouragement; until the time he had his first revival; and the ingathering, "though not great, was the finest of the wheat." And how in 1815, and five special seasons after that up to 1834, God graciously revived them – the converts added by profession being thirty, forty, or seventy, "*filling the broad aisle of the church* – a lovely spectacle to God, angels and men." What were that body today, and what had been its influence, but for such revivals?

Drs Dewitt and Mildoller tell us how the roots of the power of the Reformed churches struck deep in New York in such refreshings. And Dr Archibald Maclay narrates how the Baptists there had those growths which made them strong in after years, in blessed revival seasons.

Dr McIlvaine testifies, (in 1832, and also in 1858), to blessed works of grace "widely and wonderfully vouchsafed," which gave great strength to the Episcopal body. It would be easy to mention the names of some of the most influential Churchmen who were converted in a revival at West Point, when Dr McIlvaine was chaplain there.

This must suffice. And it but faintly shows what we owe to revivals. Revivals! what blessings have they brought to families, to neighbourhoods, and communities! What myriads of souls have they introduced into glory! What impulses have they given to Christian exertion, in home and foreign work! They have been the life of all the aggressive movements, evangelistic achievements, victories, conquests of the churches. They have made encroachments on the domains of darkness, turning the slaves of sin into soldiers of Jesus, and hastening the time of the millennium. They have made good citizens, good neighbours, faithful friends, useful labourers, wise parents, and dutiful children.

Blot out what God has done by revivals, and our sky would be shrouded in gloom; our sanctuaries would be vacant: our missionary agencies things unknown, and languor and death would be about us on every side.

"O Lord, Revive Thy Work!"

4

Divine Economy of Revivals

ARE revivals a part of God's plan? Are they ordained as one of the methods of the world's conversion? Do they enter into the economy of redemption?

For several reasons we believe this to be the case.

And first of all, because *from the beginning God has wrought prominently through revivals.* As we have seen in a previous chapter, the kingdom of Christ has thus far advanced chiefly by special seasons of gracious and rapid accomplishment of the work of conversion. And can any reason be found why God should work in that way in primeval and not in subsequent times? We question if the most ingenious opponent of these seasons, or if any Christian doubter, can invent any tolerably plausible reason for this – that God should work thus then, and not work thus now.

Again: many *scriptural utterances assume the existence of revivals, and anticipate them.* We refer to such as these: "Drop down, ye heavens, from above, and let the skies pour down righteousness." "I will pour water upon him that is thirsty, and floods upon the dry ground: I will pour my Spirit upon thy seed, and my blessing upon thine offspring: and they shall spring up as among the grass, as willows by the water-courses. One shall say, I am the Lord's; and another shall call himself by the name of Jacob; and another shall subscribe with his hand unto the Lord, and surname himself by the name of Israel." This prophecy is an exquisite representation of a revival, wherein newly converted souls are openly professing loyalty to their King. And these are but a few scriptures which encourage the expectation of revivals.

God's providences are adapted to move people in masses. Thus, often one member of a family falling in death is the means of the conversion of a household. So when pestilence spreads among a people, and thousands die; or famine is abroad on the earth, there is an appeal made to *communities;* and the thoughts of men, if any suitable impression were made, would be directed to God and to a better world. The times and seasons also preach to *communities*, as well as to men singly. There is neither a judgment of the Almighty, nor a blessing that comes from our great Father's hand, that is not fitted to impress *communities* with the importance of religion, and to lead alienated, social man, back to God. Thus threatening ruin roused Nineveh to repentance; and thus God visits the earth alike with judgment and mercy, to rouse the attention of whole communities, and direct their thoughts to eternity and to heaven.

Moreover, *the social character of man* must be taken into account. The world is not made up of independent individuals, but is bound together in tribes, communities, and families. There is a brotherhood of feeling and interest. If, then, religion is to exist in the world, we should expect to see it, at times, exerting a more widespread and potent influence over men's minds than at other times, and large masses of society moved as by a common influence. We think it would be rational beforehand to look for just such spiritual phenomena as every revival presents. We should expect that one mind, becoming strongly interested in the subject of salvation, would be the occasion of another mind being aroused to attend to the subject; and that this would lead to the same result in the case of another; and thus that the interest on this momentous subject, which perhaps began with an individual, would be, or easily might be, extended through a large community, until there should be but one paramount and absorbing object of pursuit throughout the whole body. And the denser the population in that community, and the more numerous the points of mutual contact among the members of that community, the more general and powerful, (should we expect), the revival would become. It would be strange if mankind, being placed together in organised society, and possessing such sameness of susceptibilities of being acted upon one by the other, should be serious and anxious about their salvation only one at a time, and each separately.

Again, how are *God's purposes of grace* to be fulfilled without this extensive moving of the masses? We do not see that the world can otherwise be converted. In the ordinary way of gaining converts to the Redeemer, without any such excitement of the public attention to the subject of religion as constitutes a revival, it would seem that the race could not be recovered from its ruined condition. The occurring of here and there a single solitary instance of conversion, will never bring about the conversion of the world. The common mass of the population, in any and every part of the world, must be moved. Thus, and thus only, can we reasonably expect that the inhabitants of this globe will be brought to give up their sins and lying vanities, and turn to the living God.

Again: by revivals *the atheistic spirit is rebuked.* Look at Christians. How apt are they to think that they can get along without God, even in the world's conversion. But leanness follows this self-consequence. And the churches finally come to see and feel that souls are not being saved; and they mourn over it, and in distress confess their pride and reliance on human agencies: upon which the Lord graciously appears to save. Thus are His creatures taught their dependence. When they are thrown upon the efficiency of their own efforts, they very soon find that their best strength and proudest doings avail nothing at all. In this way He glorifies His own great name. It is felt, and most heartily acknowledged, that the power is God's. Thus a discourse which a short time ago apparently accomplished no good, now goes with life and salvation to numerous hearts. Once no truth, no effort took effect. Now every word and work, in Christ's name, is charged with a benignly subduing efficacy. These very alternations produce more profoundly the conviction, and bring out more fully the declaration – it is the work of God – and more loudly the ascription – "to Him be all the glory."

Then look at Christ-less men. The best answer to their sneer, "Where is thy God?" is a glorious revival. The Most High takes this matter in hand. He comes in His great power. Seriousness settles on a community. Anxious inquiry and earnest prayer spread among the people with the rapidity of an electric shock. Every eye is open, every ear attentive, every conscience awake, every heart alive to the engrossing interest. Dissipation ceases; amusement is forgotten; the drinking saloons are less frequented; and where the wicked still congregate, perhaps to make sport of these sacred things, they yet see the handwriting on the wall, and their knees smite together like Belshazzar's; and perhaps next day they are found penitent and believing. The very atmosphere of the community seems charged with Divinity. Eternity is near. The world for the time is nothing. The soul is all. The invisible is seen. Spiritual things, before shadowy and distant, are real, and near, and urgent. It is as if the boundaries of earth and heaven were broken, and the veil of flesh removed – as if earth and seas had fled, and men were already standing before the throne of God.

These things are more potent than a thousand arguments to prove the divine existence. There is a God! There is no one but *knows* it, and *feels* it; and the whole ground of popular doubt is shaken, if not removed.

Thus does God by revivals rebuke atheism and infidelity. Scenes like these, scenes, we believe, yet to come with great and still greater power, are to be God's main argument upon an infidel age – ever growing more infidel and arrogant from the delay of His power – a mighty argument, an arresting, penetrating force, a fiery logic, writing in the inmost soul, the *demonstration* that a God and a gospel, and a heaven and a hell, are tremendous realities.

Particularly, is *Christ honoured* by revivals. Says Rev William Reid, "The quiet conversion of one sinner after another, under the ordinary ministry of the gospel, must always be regarded with feelings of satisfaction and gratitude by the ministers and disciples of Christ; but a periodical manifestation of the simultaneous conversion of thousands is also to be desired, because of its adaptation to afford a visible and impressive demonstration that God has made that same Jesus who was rejected and crucified, both Lord and Christ; and that, in virtue of His divine Mediatorship, He has assumed the royal sceptre of universal supremacy, and 'must reign till all his enemies be made His footstool.' It is therefore reasonable to expect that, from time to time, He will repeat that which on the day of Pentecost formed the conclusive and crowning evidence of His Messiahship and Sovereignty; and, by so doing, startle the slumbering souls of careless worldlings, gain the attentive ear of the unconverted, and, in a remarkable way, break in upon those brilliant dreams of earthly glory, grandeur, wealth, power, and happiness, which the rebellious and God-forgetting multitude so fondly cherish. Such an outpouring of the Holy Spirit, forms at once a demonstrative proof of the completeness and acceptance of His once offering of Himself as a sacrifice for sin, and a prophetic 'earnest' of the certainty that He 'shall appear the second time without sin unto salvation,' to judge the world in righteousness."

So is the *Spirit* honoured by revivals. One way this is done is by making effective in conversion the weakest instrumentalities. Said one as to the great revival in Dundee, Scotland: "The wonderful thing is, not only that people come – that labourers from a distance come night after night, but that the simplest statement of the truth in the simplest language seems to fall with power, and be listened to with the deepest interest." And ministers have often observed the same thing in revivals.

During the revival in Boston in 1842, it was often remarked how independent of ordinary agencies the Holy Spirit operated. A man in middle life, a Sabbath-breaker and a lover of pleasure, was awakened by shooting a pigeon on the wing. "There," said he to himself, "how quick that creature went out of existence! And I may go as suddenly and unexpectedly, and where would then my spirit be?"

One man was converted by observing that his dog after being fed seemed grateful. The thought came in his mind, "I am not so good as my dog; he is grateful to me for kindness, but God has always fed, clothed and taken care of me, and I have never been grateful at all." This discovered to him his heart, and brought him to repentance.

Thus by the use of insignificant means does the Holy Spirit manifest His being and power.

So does He do it by the quickness and the extent of the work. What weak men fail to do in years, the Spirit does instantly; and He does it on so grand a scale as to widely command attention. It was the greatness of the day, the prodigies of manifestation and power on the Pentecost, that brought the surrounding multitudes to a stand, rugged, resisting, defiant, as they were; and the Holy Ghost, through the truth, brought them down. The same holds all along in the history of the church. Some of the greatest prodigies of conviction and subjugation, the greater part of them – the all but miraculous making over of opposers and haters – have occurred in connection with special revival seasons.

These are some of the reasons why we may believe that revivals are a part of the divine economy. Dr Bushnell, (*Quarterly Christian*

Spectator for 1838), has very ably presented several points which we summarise in the following pages, leaving him, in the main, to speak in his own felicitous manner. Remarking upon an objection above referred to – the uneven character of the divine influence, he says it is instructing to advert to the various and periodical changes of temperament which affect men in other matters than religion. Sometimes one subject has a peculiar interest to the mind, sometimes another. Sometimes the feelings chime with music, which at others is not agreeable. Society of a given tone is shunned today, though eagerly sought yesterday. These fluctuations are epidemical, too, extending to whole communities, and infecting them with an ephemeral interest in various subjects, which afterwards they wonder at themselves, and can no way recall. No public speaker of observation ever failed to be convinced that man is a being, mentally, of moods and phases, which it were as vain to attempt the control of, as to push aside the stars.

These fluctuations, or mental tides, are due, perhaps, to physical changes, and perhaps not. They roll round the earth like invisible waves, and the chemist and physician tax their skill in vain to find the subtle powers that sway us. We only know that God is present in those fluctuations, whatever their real nature – and that they are all inhabited by the divine power. Is it incredible, then, that this same divine power should produce periodical influences in the matters of religion – times of peculiar, various, and periodical interest? For ourselves we are obliged to confess that we strongly suspect that sort of religion which boasts of no excitements, no temporary and changing states; for we observe, that it is only toward nothing, or about nothing, that we have always the same feeling.

Need we say, again, that progress, which is the law of all God's works and agencies, necessarily involves variety and change. Spring, for example, is the first stage of a progress. The newness thereof, the first beginnings of growth, must wax old and change their habit. So it is morally impossible that the first feelings of religious interest in the breast should remain. There is a degree of excitation in the strangeness of new feelings, and so likewise in the early scenes of a revival of religion, which belongs to their novelty, and which is by no means inconsiderable or improper. Such is human nature, that it could not be otherwise.

In fact, there is no reason to doubt that God, in framing the plan or system of his spiritual agencies, ordained fluctuations and changing types of spiritual exercise, that He might take advantage, at intervals, of novelty in arresting and swaying the minds of men.

These are the spring-times of His truth, otherwise in danger of uniform staleness. Thus He rouses the spiritual lethargy of men and communities, and sways their will to Himself by aid of scenes and manifestations not ordinary or familiar. Nor is it anything derogatory to the divine agency in the case that the spiritual spring cannot remain perpetual; for there is a progress in God's works, and He goes on through change and multiform culture to ripen His ends. Doubtless, too, there may be a degree of sound feeling, apart from all novelty in a revival of religion, which human nature is incompetent permanently to sustain; just as one may have a degree of intellectual excitement and intensity of operation, which he cannot sustain, but which is nevertheless a sound and healthy activity. In writing a sermon, for example, every minister draws on a fund of excitability which he knows cannot be kept up beyond a certain bound, and this without any derogation from his proper sanity.

Again: God has a given purpose to execute in those who have entered on the religious life, namely, to produce character in them. To this end He dwells in them, and this is the object of this spiritual culture, and here he meets, at the very beginning, this grand truth, that varieties of experience and exercise are necessary to the religious character. How then shall He adjust the scale of His action, if not to produce all such varieties as are necessary for his object? We have just remarked on the changes of temperament in men and communities, by which now one, now another, theme is brought to find a responsive note of interest. What is the end of this? Obviously it is, that we may be protected in all the many coloured varieties of feeling, and led over a wide empire of experience. Were it not for this – or if men were to live on, from childhood to the grave, in the same mood of feeling, and holding fast to the same unvarying topic of interest, they would grow to be little more than animals of one thought. To prevent which, and ripen what we call natural character to extension and maturity, God is ever leading us round and round invisibly, by new successions of providence and new affinities of feeling.

Precisely the same necessity requires that religious character be trained up under varieties of experience, and shaped on all sides by manifold workings of the Spirit. Now excitements must be applied; now checks to inspire caution or invigorate dependence. Now the intellect must be fed by a season of study and reflection; now the affections freshened by a season of social and glowing ardour. By one means bad habits are to be broken up, by another good habits consolidated. Love, it is true, must reign in the heart through all such varieties; but the principle of supreme love is one that can subsist in a thousand different connections of interest and temperaments of feeling. At one time it demands for its music a chorus of swelling voices, to bear aloft its exulting testimony of praise; at another, it may chime rather with the soft and melancholy wail just dying on its ear.

And so, in like manner, it needs a diversity of times, exercises, duties, and pleasures. It needs, and for that reason it has, not only revivals and times of tranquillity, but every sort of revival, every sort of tranquillity. Sometimes we are revived individually, sometimes as churches, sometimes as a whole people; and we have all degrees of excitation, all manner of incidents. Our more tranquil periods are sometimes specially occupied, or ought to be, in the correction of evil habits; or we are particularly interested in the study of religious doctrines necessary to the vigour of our growth and usefulness; or we are interested to acquire useful knowledge of a more general nature, in order to our public influence, and the efficient discharge of our offices. In revivals we generally prefer the more social spheres of religious exercise; afterwards the more private and solitary experiences may be cultivated. Such is the various travail which God has given to the sons of men to be exercised therewith.

Besides: through these changes the churches make a deeper impression on the minds of men. God is manifested in nature by the wheeling spheres, light, shade, tranquillity, storm – all the beauties and terrors of time. So the Spirit will reveal His divine presence through the churches by times of holy excitement, times of reflection, times of solitary communion, and times of patient hope. A church standing always in the same exact posture and mould of aspect, would be only a pillar of salt in the eyes of men; it would attract no attention, reveal no inhabitation of God's power. But suppose that now, in a period of no social excitement, it is seen to be growing in attachment to the Bible and the house of God, storing itself with divine or useful knowledge, manifesting a heavenly-minded habit in the midst of a general rage for gain, devising plans of charity to the poor and afflicted, reforming offensive habits, chastening bosom sins – suppose, in short, that principles adopted in a former revival are seen to hold fast as principles, to prove their reality and unfold their beauty, when there is no longer any excitement to sustain them – here the worth and reality of religious principles are established. And now let the Spirit move this solid enginery once more into glowing activity, let the church thus strengthened, be lifted into spiritual courage and exaltation, and its every look and act will seem to be inhabited by divine power – it will be as the chariot of God, and before it the enemies will tremble.

There is one more advantage in periodical or temporary dispensations; in the very fact that they are temporary. We often see that the certainty felt by those who are at any time enlightened and drawn by the Spirit that they will not long be dealt with as now – that by delay they may miss the grace of God and lose the favoured moment – is the strongest and most urgent of all motives to immediate repentance. This, in fact, is absolutely requisite to the stress and cogency of all means and agencies. Such is the procrastinating spirit of men; so fast bound are they in the love of sin, that however deeply they may feel their own guilt and lost estate, nothing but the fact that God is now giving them an opportunity and aid which are temporary, would ever foreclose them from delay. We need look no further to see the folly of supposing that God must not act periodically or variously, if He act at all, in renewing men. Why act uniformly when it would defeat all the ends of action?

We should be sorry if in what has been advanced a shadow of countenance has been given to the impression that the Christian is allowed, at some times, to be less religious than at others. He is under God's authority and bound by His law at all times. He must answer to God for each moment and thought of his life. His covenant oath consecrates all his life to God, and stipulates for no intermission of service. At no time can he shrink from religious obligation, without dishonour to his good faith, together with a loss of character and of God's favour. Furthermore still, it is his duty and privilege ever to be filled with the Spirit. The believer is one chosen for His indwelling.

He is consecrated to be the divine temple, and God will never leave His temple, except He is driven away by profanation – grieved away. "I have somewhat against thee," said the Saviour, "because thou hast left thy first love." He did not require, of course, that the novelty and first excitement of feeling should last; but that love, the real principle of love, should lose ground in them was criminal.

If it be asked, How can this be harmonised with the alternations of revivals? the answer is this – God favours and appoints different moods or kinds of religious interest, but not backslidings, or declensions of religious principle. There are diversities of gifts, but the same Spirit. There are diversities of operation, but it is the same God who worketh all and in all. There is a common mistake in supposing that the Spirit of God is present only in times of religious exaltation; or if it be true, that such need be the case. It is conceivable that He may be doing as glorious a work in the soul when there is but a very gentle, or almost no excitement of feeling. He may now be leading the mind after instruction, teaching the believer to collect himself and establish a regimen over his lawless will and passions, searching the motives, inducing a habit of reflection, teaching how to carry principles without excitement, drawing more into communion perhaps with God, and less for the time with men; and while He conducts the disciple through these rounds of heavenly discipline, we are by no means to think that he is, of course, less religious, or has less of supreme love to God than he had in the more fervid season of revival. A soldier is as much a soldier when he encamps as when he fights, when he stands with his loins girt about, and his feet shod with the preparation of the gospel as when he quenches the fiery darts. The Christian warfare is not all battle. There are times in it for polishing the armour, forming the tactics, and feeding the vigour of the host.

Hence we conclude that there is in what we call revivals of religion something of a divinely appointed periodical nature. But as far as they are what the name imports, revivals of *religion*, that is, of the principle of love and obedience, they are linked with dishonour; for they are made necessary by the instability and bad faith of Christ's disciples. But here it must be noted, that the dishonour does not belong to the revival, but to the decay of principles in the disciple which need reviving. There ought to be no declension of real principle; but if there is, no dishonour attaches to God in recovering his disciple from it, but the more illustrious honour is His due. Thus it is very often true, when a revival seems to have an extreme character, that the fact is due, not to the real state produced, but to the previous fall, the dearth and desolation with which it is contrasted. And generally, if the ridicule thrown upon a revival were thrown upon the worldliness, the dishonourable looseness of life and principle which preceded, it would not be misplaced.

We see then that revivals are in no degree desultory, except as they partake of human errors and infirmities. They lie embedded in that great system of universal being and event which the divine omnipresence fills, actuates and warms. As the gospel is enlarged in the world, and the Christian mind enlightened, they will gradually lose their extremes and dishonourable incidents, and will constitute an ebb and flow measured only by the pulses of the Spirit. The church will then make a glowing, various and happy impression. Her armour, though modified, will always shine, and will have a celestial temper in it. Changing her front, she will yet always present a host clad in the full panoply of God.

"O Lord, Revive Thy Work!"

5

Objections to Revivals

OBJECTIONS to revivals are no new thing, even from the friends of godliness. The primitive awakenings encountered them; and President Edwards complained of those in his day ready to say, "There is but little sober, solid religion in this work; it is little else but flash and noise." And he asks, "Is it not a shame to New England that such a work should be much doubted of here?" adding, "I suppose there is scarcely a minister in this land but from Sabbath to Sabbath used to *pray* that God would pour out his Spirit and work a reformation and a revival of religion in the country, and turn us from our intemperance, profaneness, uncleanness, worldliness and other sins. And we have kept, from year to year, days of public fasting and prayer to God, to acknowledge our backslidings and humble ourselves for our sins, and to seek of God forgiveness and reformation: and now when so great and extensive a reformation is so suddenly and wonderfully accomplished in those very things that we have sought to God for, shall we not acknowledge it?"

Whitefield preached to audiences in Boston, in 1740, that would be called great even at this day. At his farewell sermon on the 12th of October, on the Common, he had twenty thousand hearers; an assembly as large as two hundred thousand would now be, if regard be had to the population at the two dates. He had his enemies, however; and one writer gives it as his opinion that "every exhortation given here by Whitefield costs the people of Boston a thousand pounds!" The same writer described the preacher as a "vagrant enthusiast, with an ill-pointed zeal."

At a meeting of the General Association of the Colony of Connecticut, at Newington, June 18, 1745, the following action was had:

"*Voted*, Whereas there have of late years been many errors in doctrine and disorders in practice prevailing in the churches of this land, which seem to have a threatening aspect on these churches; and whereas Mr George Whitefield has been the promoter, or at least the faulty occasion of these errors and disorders; this Association thinks it needful to declare that if the said Mr Whitefield should make his progress through this government, it would by no means be advisable for any of our ministers to admit him into their pulpits, or for any people to attend on his preaching."

Although in our day the terms "religious excitement," "spasmodic effort," and the like are less frequently bandied than formerly, still there are many who gravely shake their heads when revivals are commended, and recoil at the mention of the very name, as if some evil inevitably lurked behind that designation.

Perhaps there is this poor apology for most of such persons, that they are constitutionally timid, or excessively conservative; or they may not have witnessed revivals, unless it be the most unfavourable specimens.

It is sad to be compelled to say that strong churches, (using a popular term), most often object to revivals; and that, too, when they owe their present strength to revivals. In conversation with Bishop Simpson, of the Methodist Episcopal Church, the writer was struck with the remark, that the wealthiest churches in that denomination, in New York and the other cities, were indebted to *revivals* for their independence; and that he extremely regretted the tendency often witnessed on the part of such churches, to think lightly of, and labour little for special outpourings of the Spirit.

In referring to the great benefits which the Presbyterian churches of Philadelphia have derived from *revivals* in the past, the *Presbyterian* of that city says: "But are any inclined to think that we have reached a stage to which such things are not adapted? – especially that revivals belong to the less cultivated, refined, wealthy, or fashionable congregations? Let it be remembered that the most intellectual ministers of our Church were converted through revival services; that in every revival period the ablest of judges, lawyers, and physicians in the neighbourhood, are numbered among the converts; that our continued salvation is worked out by awakenings in our colleges, in connection with which, through the labours of talented and refined Professors, the intellectual young men of the day are brought into the ministry of reconciliation. It is a great pity if any of our people who have risen in the scale of wealth, and desire to be considered especially respectable and fashionable, consider themselves above such precious influences, and unadvisedly imagine that these are only appropriate to the poorer and the less pretentious."

It may be asked at the outset, "*Do not revivals presuppose corresponding periods of declension?*" Suppose it be so; and that God foresaw these wicked backslidings of his people, and planned revivals to overbalance them. Is there any objection to this view? Another answer is this: It is not in contrast with religious *declension*, but *religious activity specially directed to other ends* – to the cultivation of Christian gifts and graces within the church itself – that we speak of this more direct and engrossing activity of the churches. Suppose we say, again, that God by thus doing adjusts Himself to the great law of change – the law and love of variety wrought, as it would seem, into the very substance and texture of the human mind. We see it to be the case that an equable perpetuity of interest is not according to man's nature. The mind freshens, then it flags; now moves more earnestly in this direction, now in that. It demands a certain sort of variety even in its religious interests and labours: now in the work of conversion; then in the work of edification, preparing Christians for the trials of their profession and the work of their calling. Suppose we say, too, that *business* has its revivals – *politics* its revivals – and *pleasure* its revivals. And cannot God rise higher than they, and put them down by giving better things the ascendancy?

We do not see why these considerations do not meet the difficulty.

The term *special effort* is odious to some. It is enough to disturb their nerves. Anything *new* is terrifying. With them the *extraordinary* is the *extravagant*. But we might show them how fertile in invention the men of the world are in carrying their points; quickly trying another measure where one does not succeed; and ask, Should not "the children of light" be equally wise? Such persons would do well to remember that without change there could be no progress. True conservatism is cautious, and not rash; but those who are ever bringing forward the past as a precedent for today, would do well to remember that the present itself was founded on the alteration of some past that went before it. Where had the churches been today had not Christian effort been breaking forth in new directions?

Excesses are pleaded as sufficient ground for being cautious as to revivals. We are sorry to admit that these have existed; and probably they will exist, to a greater or less extent, as long as men are what they are.

But is not a storm preferable to a parching drought? The economy of nature admits of the possibility of fearful torrents if it rain – brawling down the mountain sides, tearing up the meadows, and leaving sand instead of fertility on the plain. Why not, therefore, object to rain? Doubtless, on the whole, the atmospheric arrangement is a good one. Let us not, then, oppose revivals because occasionally the religious impulse rises above the usual level, and flows over the ordinary channels, and does some incidental mischief. Better have noisy animal excitement than that the sterile wastes of worldliness should not be transformed into fruitful gardens of the Lord. *The greatest possible evil is a deadly insensibility.* When the house is on fire and the family asleep, better that they be awakened by violence than consumed. Better rouse them even at the expense of insanity than let them perish in the flames.

We must also remember that the greatest and best actions have ever been performed in stages of excited feeling and high personal exaltation. And it is Dr Bushnell, we believe, who says, "If anyone expects to carry on the cause of salvation by a steady rolling on the same dead level, and fears continually lest the axles wax hot and kindle into a flame, he is too timorous to hold the reins in the Lord's chariot."

There is also this reply to be made to those who decry revivals because *they produce agitation*. They do not condemn excitement in other things. They will see as much enthusiasm in a political cabal, or in an election of civil officers, or in a commercial speculation, or even in the pursuits of science, as in a revival of religion, and not object to it. They will allow and demand excitement in the orator, the poet, the statesman, the warrior – a man may be ardent on any subject but religion, while on this subject they denounce fervour as fanaticism. Nobody complains of excitement when a ship is going down, or when half a city is on fire, or in political revolutions. And can any good reason be given, why, when the great majority of a congregation are slumbering on the brink of eternal ruin, they should not, if possible, be alarmed and excited "to flee from the wrath to come"? Mr Barnes once said, "From whence comes the objection that revivals are mere scenes of excitement? From that man *excited* throughout the whole week in pursuit of gain, feverish and restless, and unacquainted for one whole hour at a time with calm thought and repose; from that man whose life is spent in the whirlwind of political controversy or in the career of ambition; from that calm and interesting group preparing for the splendid party and the dance! O *there* all is calm and serene; but in religion all is excitement and commotion! Well may this objection be heard from the excited, agitated, tumultuous population of a city; a population more than any other on earth living in scenes of excitement; unhappy when they are not excited; fostering everywhere the means of excitement; and resisting all the means which the friends of religion can use to bring them to sober thought and calm reflection. What we aim at is that this excitement may be laid aside, and that the now busy multitude may be brought to *think soberly* about the immortal destiny beyond the tomb. We aim that they may lay down the exciting romance or novel, and take up the Bible – full of sober truth; that they may forsake the theatre – a place of mere excitement, and find happiness in the calmness of the closet, and the sober employments of the fireside; that they may turn away from the agitating scenes of political strife, and from the exciting of envy, and malice, and green-eyed jealousy, and ambition, and from the intoxicating bowl and the dance of pleasure, and devote themselves to the sober business of religion."

Further. Is the good to be denounced with the bad? Because there is undue enthusiasm, sometimes, in revivals, are we to be indifferent toward them? To borrow an illustration, if you should hear a lecture on science, or politics, or religion, in which you should discover a few mistakes, while nearly the whole of it was sound, and practical, and in a high degree instructive, would you condemn the whole for these trifling errors, and say it was all a mass of absurdity; or would you not rather treasure it up in your memory as in the main excellent, though you felt that, like everything human, it was marred by imperfection? And why should not the same principle be admitted in respect to revivals? Is it right, is it honest, because there may be in them a small admixture of enthusiasm, to treat them as if they were made up of enthusiasm and nothing else? Would it not be more equitable and more candid to separate the precious from the vile, rather than to lump together the devil's dross and the God-given ore? And we may say of the blessed works which we have traced in previous chapters, with Edwards, "If such things are enthusiasm, and the fruits of a distempered brain, let my brain be evermore possessed of that happy distemper! If this be distraction, I pray God that the world of mankind may be all seized with this benign, meek, beneficent, beatifical, glorious distraction!"

Spurious conversions, it is alleged, come of this excitement. But we may say "What is the chaff to the wheat?" Spurious conversions there no doubt are in revivals. So are there in seasons of coldness. And it is by no means clear that the proportion of false hopes cherished in revivals is greater than in other seasons.

Dr Humphrey tells of 85 converts added in one revival; and he is "able to say that now at the end of thirty-seven years from the time of their public espousals to Christ, there has not, so far as I can learn, been a single case of apostasy from the faith once delivered to the saints, nor of yielding to the mastery of any of those habits which disgrace the Christian name, and drown men in destruction and perdition."

Dr Nettleton said: "During the leisure occasioned by my late illness, I have been looking over the regions where God has revived His work for the two years past. The thousands who have professed Christ in this time, in general, appear to run well. Hitherto I think they have exhibited more of the Christian temper, and a better example than the same number who have professed religion when there was no revival. *If genuine religion is not found in revivals I have no evidence that it exists in our world.*" This is strong testimony; but no stronger than numerous pastors could present. And it confirms the view we would naturally receive of a powerful work of grace, namely, that just then we should have the best fruits – less of man's work, and more of God's; less of calculation, and more of conviction; less of head-work, and more of heart-work; less of theoretical persuasion, and more of direct, practical, moral earnestness – and so developing a purer, more vigorous, and more highly vitalised

Christian character than in times when there is less of "the demonstration of the Spirit and of power."

It is often objected to revivals that the *sympathies* are liable to be wrought upon. Now, as we have elsewhere insisted, it is of vast importance that in religious awakenings solid instruction be given, and the understanding be addressed. And if there be these clear and vivid exhibitions of divine truth, upon what ground is the excitement of the sympathies to be objected to? As God moves the mind according to its nature, why may He not employ the sympathetic principle to awaken, soften and prepare the way for conversion? "I have yet to learn," remarks Mr Barnes, "why religion is to be regarded as suspicious and tarnished because the pleadings of a father or mother, or the tears of a sister have been the *occasion*, though amidst deep excitement, of directing the thoughts to eternity. To me it seems there is a peculiar loveliness in the spread of religion in this way; and I love to contemplate Christianity calling to its aid whatever of tenderness, kindness and love there may be existing in the bosom of fallen and erring man. These sympathies are the precious remains of the joys of paradise lost; they may be made invaluable aids in the work of securing paradise again. They serve to distinguish man, though fallen, from the dis-social and un-sympathising apostasy of beings of pure malignancy in hell, and their existence in man *may* have been one of the reasons why he was selected for redemption, while fallen angels were passed by in their sins. On no subject have we so many common interests at stake as in religion. I look upon a family circle. What tender feelings! What mutual love! What common joys! What united sorrows! The blow that strikes one member, strikes all. The joy that lights up one countenance diffuses its smiles over all. Together they kneel by the side of the one that is sick; together they rejoice at his recovery; or they bow their heads and weep when he dies, and put on the same sad habiliments of grief and walk to his grave. Nor are these all their common joys and woes. They are plunged into the same guilt and danger. They are together under the fearful visitations of that curse which has travelled down from the first apostasy of man. They are going to a common abode beneath the ground. And that guilty and suffering circle, too, *may be* irradiated with the same beam of hope, and the same balm of Gilead, and the same great Physician may impart healing there. Now we ask why they may not become

Christians together? Sunk in the same woes, why may they not rise to the same immortal hope? When one member is awakened, why should not the same feeling run through the united group? When one is impressed with the great thoughts of immortality, why should not the same thoughts weigh on each spirit? And when the eyes of one kindle with the hope of eternal life, why should not every eye catch the immortal radiance, and every heart be filled with the hope of heaven? And why may we not appeal to them by all the hopes of sitting down together in a world of bliss, and by all the fears of being separated to different destinies in an eternal heaven or hell?"

In fact, it is one strong argument for revivals that this principle of sympathy is then brought into exercise. A parent, brother, sister, child, sees another member of the family weeping with a sense of sin, and asking prayers, or rejoicing in a new found hope, or separating, by profession, from the world and entering into the company of believers. The sight of the eye affects the heart, and the inquiry starts, "Am I to go to hell, while that dear one goes to heaven? Do not I need religion too?" And thus the current of thoughtlessness is interrupted, and the mind becomes impressible and attentive: and this gained, there is reason to hope that further progress will be made.

Thus viewed, an objection to revivals becomes an argument in their favour.

It is sometimes said that to expect revivals *prevents uniform effort.* We answer that it is only so with those who are not well-instructed. If the minister will keep prominent the duty of uniform effort, most of his people will respond to his views. And there is no question but that, as a rule, those ready to labour in revivals are just the persons engaged in steady work; while those who cry out "excitement" find it convenient, somehow, to be idlers in God's vineyard.

"But the excitement soon subsides, and then *there is a reaction.*" True, the special excitement is only temporary. In the nature of the case it could not be otherwise. And further, there may be reaction. Is there not in all special work, of every kind? But does the pastor, the politician, or the farmer decline special effort at special times from fear there will be reaction in the overworked brain, or body? What folly to plead the law of *rest against the law of special work!*

Let us add here the words of Rev T L Cuyler: "It is made an objection to revivals of religion that they are 'mere temporary excitements.' True enough. *Pentecost* lasted one day, but that one day changed the moral face of the globe. Luther's Reformation work was comprised within a few years; Europe and the world feel it to this hour. The memorable revival of 1857 began with a few praying hearts in New York – it culminated in a few weeks; its outward phenomena ceased after about a year. The influence spread across the seas, and around the globe. Did the results end with the end of the excitement? Have its converts all gone back to unbelief and ungodliness? No! That revival has its enduring monuments in nearly every church on this continent. Its history will blaze on one of the brightest pages of God's record-books which shall be opened on the Day of Judgment. Revivals *are* temporary in duration. This is partly to be accounted for through God's sovereignty, and partly through human imperfection. Revivals are commonly short-lived, and they often are attended with a few excesses and false conversions. But would any sane man object to copious rain because it did not continue to rain on for ever? Would he object to it, either, because it had swelled a few streams into a flood, and carried off a few mill-dams and bridges? Shall we do away with steam power simply because the boiler of the 'St John' exploded and blew a dozen human beings into eternity? Revivals are indeed attended with incidental dangers; but they are only such as belong to the constitution of imperfect human nature. They are in accordance with the divine plan. They are in harmony with church-agency in the best days of the church's history."

And it must further be said, that revivals are *not* followed by the same coldness and levity that preceded them. They leave an impression in the moral feelings of the community, which is not soon effaced. But, if it *were* true, as it regards the unconverted, it is what might be expected. It is only the relapse of minds ever averse to seriousness, and anxious for relief from the inquietudes of conscience, into their old and settled courses. Revivals do not *produce* the levity of worldly minds. They powerfully *interrupt* it. For the time being, and commonly long after, the ball-room and bar-room are deserted, comparatively if not entirely, and Sabbath-breakers find their way to the house of God. Is it any argument against revivals, that the depraved heart, though awed for the time by the manifest tokens of divine presence, can at last resist their influence and turn like the children of Israel before the mount of God, to idols of their own choosing?

But "*Is it not better to have conversions all the while?*" Certainly. Labour for them, and be not satisfied without them. And we admit that in an important sense that is a wrong state of things which needs a revival. Possibly the time will come when revivals will not be needed; when, as we might say, there will be a perpetual revival. But we are not to prescribe modes of operation to the Almighty. And if he choose to water his church by occasional showers, rather than with the perpetual dew of his grace; and this more at one period, and on one continent, than at other times and places, we should rejoice and be grateful for the rich effusions of His Spirit in any form and manner; and should endeavour to avail ourselves of these precious seasons, for the conversion of sinners. We know that many good men have supposed, and still suppose, that the best way to promote religion, is to go along *uniformly*, and gather in the ungodly gradually, and without excitement. But however sound such reasoning may appear in the abstract, *facts* demonstrate its futility. If churches were far enough advanced in knowledge, and had stability of principle enough to keep awake, such a course would do; but most Christians are so little enlightened, and there are so many counteracting causes, that they will not go steadily forward, and so must be impelled by special influences.

But, "*Is not a periodical and special divine influence on men for their conversion derogatory to God? Is He not always present and ready to bless?*" Yes; but our sins may separate between Him and us. And again, He may be as truly blessing the world in the edification of His people as by the direct conversion of sinners. But not to insist on this here, let it be observed that this objection is easily seen to be superficial. On this principle there ought to be no intervals of drought or rain – no revolving cycles of change, but either continuous drenching rains or ever-scorching suns. Instead of this, we see that while God is unchangeable in His purpose, He is various in His methods. Revivals are in accordance with the analogy of nature, which has its seasons of revivification and rapid growth, followed by seasons of ripening fruit and maturing strength. They are in harmony with the nature of man, who requires alternate seasons of activity and repose; of stirring labour and excitement on the one hand, and on the other of tranquil enjoyment and sober reflection; each in turn preparing the body and the mind for the other, and both in their due season imparting health and vigour to the system, and conspiring to produce the largest possible results. Revivals accord especially with the habits and spirit of the present age, which is an age of excitement, of division of labour, of associated feeling and action, of concentrated effort, and hurried enterprise and rapid locomotion.

"But why not be content with a *moderate growth* instead of *great and rapid ingatherings?*" Because it is not primitive; not after God's plan. In the early churches conversions were by the hundred and the thousand. The Word spread, not with that moderation insisted on by those who are always afraid of being charged with extravagance, but with the sweep and power of a divine movement. And the agents were borne onward as on the wings of the wind, willing to be a laughing-stock to men; willing to hear an outcry from the world which they were turning upside down.

But one sufficient answer is, that this "going on steadily," (which generally means *slowly*), leaves the great mass of men in their sins, and coolly consigns whole generations to hell! For *death* does not wait for our slow processes!

But "*Why do you have revivals at particular seasons*, as in the winter for example?" Suppose we ask in reply, "Why do you have your *Lecture seasons* in the winter, rather than summer? – and your social entertainments, and the like?" Is it unreasonable or arrogant to suppose that there are with God prudential considerations leading to this choice of times and seasons for His special and signal working, based upon this fact, that certain times are more favourable than others for His works?

We have thus alluded to some of the common objections to revivals. No doubt it is generally rather to some of their *incidental features* that objection is made than to revivals themselves. It is unfair and unreasonable, however, to hold revivals accountable for the evils that sometimes attach to them. When Whitefield was once preaching in Boston, a meeting-house was so packed that the gallery was supposed to be giving away, and there was a panic in which several persons were trampled to death. Did the blame attach to the revival? Persons sometimes take cold in a revival. Is that the fault of the revival?

This is a painful object to write upon. One might suppose that anything fraught with such blessings as are revivals would be welcomed universally; that churches long praying for such a time would gladly mark the first appearance of it, and that ministers long mourning their own and their people's deadness would rejoice in its approach. But alas! it is otherwise. "It is no new thing," says one, "for the world to spit upon Christ and revile Him – no new thing for unregenerate and foolish men to blaspheme the work of the Spirit; but sad indeed is it that any that are His should hide their faces from Him and from His work!"

Are none who ought to be leaders in the world's conquest, from this very cause failing of influence? Are no preachers open to the censure conveyed in the remark of a hearer, that his minister, apparently, would rather that souls should remain unconverted than be converted *in any way except his?*

Not far from the scene of a revival, one cold day, stood two men in conversation. They belonged to different churches, and the following was the substance of their discourse:

"What is the state of religion in your church?"

"Very cold, indeed, sir: it is as far below the freezing point as is the temperature of the atmosphere."

"And what is your minister preaching about?"

"He is labouring to show the danger of animal excitement in religion."

The conversation closed with the exclamation, "The danger of animal excitement! Why, surely the man's sermons would be better adapted to the state of his congregation if he were to preach on the danger of being spiritually frost-bitten!"

The pungent Mr Ryle, in one of his tracts, gives these utterances: "The plain truth is, that many believers in the present day seem so dreadfully afraid of doing harm that they hardly ever dare to do any good. There are many who are fruitful in objections, but barren in actions; rich in wet blankets, but poor in anything like Christian fire. They are like the Dutch deputies, who would never allow Marlborough to venture anything, and by their excessive caution, prevented many a victory from being won." It must be confessed that this representation is but too true.

A home missionary in the West wrote some time ago as follows: "If Christians were half as much excited about a *heavenly inheritance* as the people here are, and have been for a few months past, about

Government land, village lots, mill sites, cultivated farms, and so on, they would be branded at once with the wildest kind of fanaticism. How strange that professors of religion are fairly beside themselves in the anxiety to secure a little of this world's goods, and yet that some of them, if they chance to hear a poor sinner cry, 'God be merciful to me a sinner!' or witness deep anxiety for a lost world, are ready to cry, 'Excitement! Excitement! It is all excitement.' "

The very orthodoxy of some is made an occasion for inactivity. They cry out, "You are trying to get up a revival in your own strength: take care, you are interfering with the sovereignty of God: better keep along in the usual course, and let God give a revival when He thinks it is best: God is a sovereign, and it is very wrong for you to attempt to have a revival, just because *you think* a revival is needed!" Now no fact, (as we have elsewhere taken occasion to show), is more apparent in revivals than that of the divine sovereignty. But such talk as this is just what Satan likes, and men cannot do his work more effectually than by thus preaching up the sovereignty of God as a reason why we should not put forth revival efforts.

An actual *participation* and *personal experience* in precious revivals would dissipate many a man's objections. It makes a vast difference in one's estimate of a revival whether he enter into it or look at it. In the Memoirs of the late Mr William Dawson is the following anecdote:

Mr Dawson was one day accosted by an individual who said he had been present at a certain meeting; that he liked the preaching very well, but was much dissatisfied with the prayer-meeting; adding, that he usually lost all the good he had received during the sermon by remaining in these noisy meetings. Mr Dawson replied that he should have united with the people of God in the prayer-meeting, if he desired to profit by it. "Oh!" said the gentleman, "I went into the gallery, where I leaned over the front, and saw the whole. But I could get no good; I lost, indeed, all the benefit I had received during the sermon."

"It is easy to account for that," rejoined Mr Dawson.

"How so?" inquired the other.

"You mounted to the top of the house, and, on looking down your neighbour's chimney to see what kind of a fire he kept, you got your eyes filled with smoke. Had you entered by the door and gone into the room and mingled with the family around the household hearth, you would have enjoyed the benefit of the fire as well as they. Sir, you have got the smoke in your eyes!"

The writer would most earnestly entreat all opponents of revivals to look more thoroughly into the matter – to ascertain, as far as possible, in what a revival really consists – and to prove their own selves, lest it be found in the great day that they have been "fighting against God."

That man takes an awful responsibility who assumes to utter a word in disparagement of revivals of religion.

There are few names in our country's annals more conspicuous, for good or for evil, than that of Aaron Burr. Of his talents none can doubt. His defects were moral rather than intellectual, consisting in a total apostasy from the religion of his fathers, and in the lawlessness of one who had deliberately cast off fear and restrained prayer before God. His father was an earnest Christian minister; his mother one of the most devout women of her times, the daughter of Jonathan Edwards, and the off-shoot of a domestic circle which has been represented as more nearly resembling the life of heaven than any other on earth. Mr Parton, in his *Life of Aaron Burr*, perhaps without intending it, tells how this apostasy came about. During his last year in college, (at Princeton), there was a revival in the institution. "Burr confessed that he was moved by the revival. He respected the religion of his mother; he had taken for granted the creed in which he had been educated. Therefore, though he was repelled by the wild excitement which prevailed, and disgusted by the means employed to excite terror, his mind was not at ease. He consulted Dr Witherspoon in this perplexity. The clergymen of the time were divided in opinion upon the subject of revivals; those educated in the old country being generally opposed to them. President Witherspoon was of that number, and he accordingly told the anxious student that the raging excitement was fanatical, not truly religious, and Burr went away relieved." This is believed to be the key to Burr's apostate career.

Assuming that that opinion of the revival was the real cause of his going away "relieved," what terrible consequences followed that advice. For Burr proceeded to drink in with avidity the reasonings of the French and English infidels, which were much in vogue at the time. These prepared him for the profligate habits which distinguished him through life, which procured his arraignment at the bar of his country for high treason, which involved him in his fatal duel with Hamilton, and which made him ever after an outcast and a vagabond in the earth. It causes a shudder to think that possibly that depreciating remark as to the revival made him the libertine, the duellist, the plotter against his government, the heartless seducer, and the victim of a supreme selfishness that he was. And it is an illustration of the sad consequences that may follow the utterance of one word against revivals.

It will be remembered that our Saviour claimed for His miracles that they were wrought by the Spirit of God. The Pharisees attributed them to the agency of Satan. What that sin was the context tells us. "All manner of sin and blasphemy shall be forgiven unto men: but the blasphemy against the Holy Ghost shall not be forgiven unto men ... Whosoever speaketh a word against the Holy Ghost it shall not be forgiven him, neither in this world, neither in the world to come." *Revivals* also claim to be wrought by the Spirit of God. If *they are so*, what the sin of speaking against them is, it is not for us to say – further than that it is in *some* sense, at least, the sin of "speaking against the Holy Ghost." The degree of the guilt depends on the means of knowledge and the malignity of purpose. We would neither presume nor wish to say, that in any case it is unpardonable; but who would not shun the possibility of speaking contemptuously of the work of the Spirit? "Beware therefore," says an apostle, "lest that come upon you, which is spoken in the prophets; Behold, ye despisers, and wonder, and perish: for I work a work in your days, a work which ye shall in no wise believe, though a man declare it unto you." He that will speak lightly of revivals, should ponder these words deeply, and remember that he will be called upon in the great day to confront the fact that he took it upon himself to condemn those scenes of religious awakening which brought such gladness to such multitudes of souls.

Nor let it be forgotten, that one may be secretly doubtful and indifferent as to revivals; and so, though not openly opposing them, be practically against them. Such persons cannot be relieved of the responsibility of being opposed, in spirit and in practice, to revivals by their silent and negative course regarding them. To have no positive faith in revivals is to be averse and contrary to them. Revivals are so big with consequences, so instinct with life and power, that they cannot be objects of attention without moving the mind one way or another, without being hated where they are not loved, dreaded where they are not desired, though peculiar circumstances of expediency may repress positive expressions of aversion. Such persons will not only do nothing in favour of revivals, but amidst studied silence and reserve will do much against them. Can the preaching of ministers be otherwise than essentially hostile to revivals, who are not without doubts whether revivals are not the work of man, or perhaps of man and Satan united? The state of mind which dictates such a strain of preaching cannot but dictate a similar strain of conversation; and though direct unfriendliness may not be intended, yet it will be exerted, and exerted in the most decisive and effectual manner.

And this thought must be added; that ministers may believe in revivals, and still be practically opposed to them, because their one great, earnest aim is not to bring sinners to immediate repentance; which is the very spirit of revivals.

"O Lord, Revive Thy Work!"

6

Position of Evangelists

WE may define evangelists as preachers without pastoral charges. As thus defined, the apostles were evangelists – tellers of the good tidings to the people at large.

Paul was the prince of evangelists. In twenty-five years he travelled three times over a great part of Asia and Europe. Twice he spent two years as a prisoner, preaching to all who came to him, as well as to successive soldiers to whom he was chained. At one place he wintered, at another he spent a year and a half, at a third two whole years, so preaching "that all they that dwell in Asia heard the word of the Lord Jesus."

Our blessed Lord went from place to place preaching and performing His mighty works. In the three years of His public life He travelled three times over Galilee. Three times He visited Jerusalem. For weeks together He preached at Capernaum, a border town where many were coming and going. Six months He laboured beyond Jordan, and twice He sent out disciples to extend His work. He came not mainly to teach, and yet through His public life He laboured as an itinerant. It was thus that He spread His gospel among perhaps three million people.

Modern missionaries, in the main, are evangelists. So were many of the earnest preachers of early days. Whitefield spent most of his life as an evangelist. So did John Wesley, who rode on horseback 100,000 miles in his visits from place to place.

In this country from the earliest times, there have been men acting as evangelists. More than a hundred years ago the Philadelphia

Baptist Association appointed Rev Messrs Edwards and Gano to visit and preach as evangelists. Dr Nettleton, in the first half of the nineteenth century, was a famous evangelist. Inspired with the earnest wish to give himself to the foreign mission service, but prevented from so doing, he gave himself to the work of an evangelist; first among destitute churches, and then, upon the calls of his brethren, to the visitation of churches with pastors. And everywhere the Lord went with him and wonderfully blessed his labours. Eternity alone will tell the multitudes led to Christ in connection with his itinerant services. The names of others might be mentioned who were also much blessed in this work.

And yet such labours in our day are not looked upon with favour. A chief cause is found in the imprudence of some evangelists. Great scandal was brought upon this class of preachers by one James Davenport, more than a century ago. His excesses caused the ministry to look with suspicion upon this style of service, and to dread even the name evangelist. Rev Joseph Fish, of Stonington, Connecticut, in a sermon which he published in 1763, informs us of the visit of Mr Davenport to his church some twenty years previously. Speaking of the revivals of that day, he says, "In these strange operations, there was a marvellous mixture of almost everything *good and bad* – truth and error, chaff and wheat. For while the spirit of God wrought *powerfully*, Satan raged *maliciously*, and acted his old subtle part to deceive. This happened, or at least was carried to the highest pitch, under the preaching and ministrations of a wonderful, strange, good man, (the Rev James Davenport, of Long Island), who visited these parts in the time of our religious concern and awakening; a young man of undoubted real piety, fervent zeal for God, love to souls, and ardent desire to advance the Redeemer's kingdom. But, (thus it was permitted), a man, while with us, under the powerful influence of a *false spirit* in a great part of his conduct, as many then told him, and as he himself did afterwards acknowledge with deep abasement. Satan taking the advantage of his zeal in religion, transformed himself into an angel of light, and hurried him into extremes; yea, artfully carried him beside the truth and duty, and beyond the bounds of decency."

It is not difficult to trace the effects of the misguided zeal of this man in the existing coldness towards itinerating ministers.

And this has been enhanced by men since his time. Anyone familiar with the religious history of the churches for the last forty years, can recall the names of evangelists who have not commended themselves to the good judgment, (if indeed to the confidence), of their brethren generally. Dr Humphrey, in his *Revival Sketches*, says: "The great demand for preaching in western revivals, brought out a number of zealous young men with but little experience, who felt it their duty to enter into the work and help the pastors wherever their services were desired. They soon took the name of evangelists, or revivalists, as they were more commonly called. Some of them, in process of time, became zealous overmuch. They introduced measures which many pastors of riper judgment and more experience in revivals could not approve. And as their zeal increased, they wanted to go to places where they were not sent for. Nor would they be hindered for want of regular invitations. Influential members of the churches who sympathised with them were approached, and enlisted to overrule the judgment of their ministers, and wring from them a reluctant consent. If the ministers would not yield, they must be broken down, as the phrase was. This was often attempted, and sometimes succeeded. Nor would the evangelist long consent to labour under the advice and direction of the pastor. He must give up the reins, and stand aside and look on, or take a subordinate part in the revival. The consequence was, that divisions were created in the churches, part holding with the pastors and part with the evangelists; and though scores of converts might be announced, some churches were actually weakened, and to such a degree that if not quite broken up, in what has since been called the 'burnt district,' they have scarcely recovered to this day. Not only were good ministers driven from their congregations in this manner, but such prejudices against revivals were created by these extreme measures, that it has taken a whole generation to remove them."

But while eccentricities and rashness are justly chargeable to some who have acted as evangelists, it should not operate as an argument against this class of labourers. Richard Baxter remarks that though the Word of God is divine, our mode of dispensing it is human; and there is scarcely anything we have the handling of, but we leave on it the print of our fingers. Imperfection attaches to our best endeavours; and why should we be suspicious of a particular kind of labour because of the extravagance or unworthiness of some who have undertaken it? God knows more than we know; and it becomes us to be slow to denounce that upon which He bestows His blessing, even though it seem not to deserve our approval.

Much can be said in favour of this particular instrumentality. Undoubtedly it is of divine appointment, For "he gave some evangelists." And if it be insisted that their functions in primitive times were unlike those performed now, it devolves upon the objector to show the *essential* difference. True, they did not labour chiefly with churches, but outside of them; although this is not clear as to Apollos, at least, whose fame as an evangelist was in all the churches. But at first there were no churches with whom evangelists could labour. It was needful that they preach in new localities, like our modern missionaries. This carrying the gospel into "the regions beyond" engrossed all their time and attention; a prominent exception, however, being found in the apostle Paul, who, with other labours, visited and strengthened the churches – co-operating with the pastors. To reason from the early practice therefore, as against the present, seems scarcely allowable. We doubt whether an argument against modern evangelism can be drawn from New Testament order.

Again: experience attests to the great usefulness of this agency. We have spoken of Whitefield and Wesley. It is also well-known that Luther and his fellow-labourers carried forward the work more as *evangelists* than as pastors. Hosts of itinerant preachers and colporteurs went everywhere conveying the Word of life to the homes and hearts of the people.

The early revivals in this country were directly connected with the labours of Edwards, the Tennents, Wheelock, Pomroy, Pendleton, and many others, who either had no pastoral charges, or gave them up for the time, and went out as evangelists to places far and near, arousing the churches and warning men to repent. The same was true of the later revivals; as remarked above in regard to Nettleton and others.

It were not difficult to point to some men now who are honoured and beloved as the helpers of pastors in "bringing in sheaves," and the extent of whose usefulness it is impossible to overestimate. What multitudes of souls, both among those in glory and those toiling for

Christ, are witnesses to the good accomplished by the untiring energies of men whose names might be mentioned.

We are fully aware of the unfavourable opinion of many, as to some of the men and measures connected with evangelism during the last half century. Nor do we say there is no good ground for it. But it may well be asked, what had been the condition of the churches today without that class of labour to which exception is taken? Certainly the churches never made greater progress than within the period of modern evangelism. And who will undertake to say that it is not owing, largely, to the new impulses given through this particular branch of effort?

Further: we can easily see some peculiar advantages in evangelistic labour. For one thing, it stimulates expectation and hope, and impels to prayer and readiness for a blessing. Speaking of the great revivals at the beginning of this century, Baird says, "As one means of extending the work, ministers who had enjoyed the presence of God among their own people, were selected by some ecclesiastical body and sent forth, generally two together, on preaching tours among the neighbouring churches. The *expectation* of their coming drew large audiences wherever they preached."

"The churches which they visited being, in most cases, *prepared to receive them* by a previous season of fasting and prayer, and animated by their presence and labours to redoubled fervour of supplication, were, in many cases favoured with an immediate outpouring of the Holy Spirit. Under these and similar influences the work of God spread into more than one hundred towns in Massachusetts and Connecticut, and into a still greater number of places in the new settlements of Vermont, New Hampshire, Maine and New York, which had but recently formed a widespread field of missionary labour."

For the time being, as we see, these men were evangelists; and the facts alleged were what would have been expected. For, if a minister and church *know* of the speedy coming of an evangelist, the feeling is that they *must bestir themselves*. Sluggishness and procrastination are put away. The preaching is more earnest. Responsibility for the success of the proposed special effort is felt; prayers are more fervent and direct; and thus the way of the Lord is prepared.

Still further: expectation is awakened in the *community*, and the people are ready to come together, at least to hear the strangers, and to witness what occurs. And the first thing in saving men is to gain a hearing. A principal reason why the masses perish is because they *never* hear preaching.

Again: through the labours of evangelists the various gifts of the ministry are in a measure diffused. One man has specially the gift to *teach*, another to *incite*. Or, as we may say, the one *prepares* fuel, and the other *kindles* it. One preacher, too, may have no aptness in revival work, and another may excel in this, and in little else. Thus one class of talent is supplemented by the other.

Dr George B Ide, of Massachusetts, after a great revival among his people in connection with the labours of Mr Earle, said that his parish was like a garden in the spring with the beds all laid out, and the seeds all planted in them; and that it only needed the additional sunshine that came along with the evangelist to make the seeded rows shoot forth. So in multitudes of cases. One man plants, and another waters; while it is God that giveth the increase. One sows, (he is specially fitted for that), and another reaps, (he is specially fitted for that). And again one man excels in winning souls to Christ, and another in building them up in the faith. And why should not all the gifts of the ministry be brought into requisition, and diffused as far as possible among the churches for their edification?

How often, too, does a disheartened minister find cheer and strength in the coming of an evangelist. His work may drag heavily; and yet a *little* added power would accomplish wonders. Mr Earle once likened himself to the additional horse with whiffle-tree attached to hitch on and help pull the load up the hill. The disciples went forth two by two. But the pastor labours on alone; and like "the coming of Titus" of old, may be the visit of a brother minister. Iron sharpeneth iron; countenance cheers countenance; and so the feeble hands become strong, and the work goes bravely on. Often is a single visit of an evangelist the very thing that saves a church, and ensures a long and successful pastorate. But for this many a man had quitted his field, and let the interest die.

Hundreds upon hundreds of feeble churches, too, without settled pastors, have been saved from extinction by such visits of God's servants; and after that have been able to support a minister.

Further still: a pastor may be overworked; and a failure of health at the beginning of a revival among his people, may make the labours of an evangelist highly desirable for a few weeks or months. Anticipating this state of things, Dr Porter said: "Such help has often been furnished by the occasional labours of other pastors, who have had a short leave of absence from their own flocks. But perhaps the only adequate provision for such emergencies would be, that a few men, of rare endowments for this particular service – men of God, distinguished for judgment, fervour of piety and suavity of temper – should be held in reserve to labour where they are most needed, as assistants to stated pastors. These men, of course, should be ordained ministers, and hold themselves accountable to some regular ecclesiastical body."

Once more: there is no reason to doubt that it pleases God to bestow his converting grace in special measure in connection with the labours of some evangelists. It is undeniable that through them great numbers of souls are gathered into the Christian ranks; and there is no conceivable way of accounting for this acknowledged success but on the ground here indicated. It seems good to the Most High, in the sovereignty of his operations, to accompany with the extraordinary power of the Holy Ghost the preaching and the means, which are in themselves simple and in no wise remarkable, of men whom he has evidently raised up for this particular work. The names of Whitefield, Nettleton, the Tennents, Finney, Knapp, Inskip, Earle, Hammond, Dewitt, Graves, Caughey, and others, illustrate this remark. And we hold this to be a sufficient warrant for the employment of the agency in question.

Say what we will, God sets the seal of his approval on these labours; and what "he hath cleansed, that call thou not common or unclean."

Nor is it by any means certain that one reason for the infrequency of revivals is not to be found in the neglect of this instrumentality. And if churches generally, instead of viewing all evangelists with suspicion, and speaking evil of their work and their office, were to pray for more and better men of this class, it were a mighty gain to the cause of Christ. And when the harvest is so plenteous, and the labourers so few, it is little less than appalling to witness the frequent indiscriminate denunciation of a means which has been, and is, such a power for good.

In saying this, we are not depreciating the pastorate; far from it. Nor would we be understood to hold that the system of evangelism has not its drawbacks, and could not be improved. There is danger on the part of churches of a distrust of the established means of grace, and a morbid craving for extraordinary measures: and on the part of the evangelists, a longing for immediate rather than permanent results; an adoption of doubtful measures and management to hurry such results; and an unhealthy love of notoriety through the press, and the like. These, and perhaps other tendencies are to be guarded against. But such tendencies are not sound objections to the system itself; for there is nothing perfect beneath the sun. The field is wide for evangelistic labour, and in the time when many shall run to and fro and knowledge shall be increased, likely it will be more extensively called into requisition than now.

In just this connection some words of caution are appropriate. If reliance is placed upon foreign aid to such an extent as to diminish the sense of responsibility on the part of the church or the pastor, it is a serious evil. Sometimes the feeling is that without an evangelist nothing can be done; and so nothing is attempted. Sometimes the people *wait*, (in comparative indolence and hopelessness), *until* the promised visitation is realised. And sometimes the visit of the evangelist having come, it is felt that the work will go forward anyhow, as a necessary consequence.

All this is wrong. The pastor and his charge must feel that it devolves on *them*, not on him, to ensure success, in its human aspect. If the impression prevails that they are now relieved from obligation, and may be onlookers, no good can come. *The pressure must still lie upon their hearts.* No aid from abroad is useful which tends to release the church and the stated ministry from a full, undivided sense of responsibility for earnest, active, personal effort to carry on the revival.

Yet it should be added, that if a church and minister will not labour together without assistance, let them send for it. Better so than that the wise and foolish slumber on, and both perish together.

And the evangelist himself will need grace to act with discretion, in order to secure the greatest benefit. If wise, he will never use a style of preaching that is vulgar in diction or manner, or in any way offensive to good taste. He will be solemn and not trifling; always courteous, and never abrupt, rude, or coarse. He will everywhere be the Christian gentleman.

Moreover, he will be exceedingly careful in all his ways; and especially in his intercourse with the other sex will avoid even the very appearance of evil; for the eyes of gainsayers are upon him.

He will be patient, "not rendering railing for railing, but contrariwise, blessing." He will be much in prayer; will watch his own heart; will keep humble before God; will study to show himself approved of God, a workman that needeth not to be ashamed, rightly dividing the Word, and not handling the Word of God deceitfully. He will be thoroughly honest, not using anything of "pious fraud," or artifice of any kind to gain a present end, as is sometimes the case with revival labourers.

The good evangelist will also in every way help, and not harm the pastor. The pastor is the head of the flock, and cannot even temporarily abandon his post. He is responsible for results more than anyone else; and therefore his opinion and wishes are to be respected. Said Nettleton, "Settled pastors have, and ought to have, the entire management of their own congregations. Each one has a right to pursue his own measures, within his own limits; and no itinerant has any business to interfere or dictate. It will ever be regarded as intermeddling in other men's matters."

Good evangelists will not be ready to denounce those Christians and those ministers as enemies of revivals, who will not yield up to them the reins, nor sanction all their movements. There is danger of this from the nature of the case. *Their* minds are awake to the soul's salvation; and they are oppressed by its amazing importance. *They* feel that something efficient ought to be done – must be done to wake up a slumbering world; and they naturally desire that all Christians should go along with them in their efforts. In this state of mind they expect nothing but cordial co-operation; and where they do not find it, corrupt nature takes advantage of the excitement they have reached, and the disappointment they feel, (and perhaps withal of a naturally ardent temperament), to discharge itself not only in grievous complaints, but sometimes even bitter invective. All this should be guarded against with the greatest care.

It is a most delicate service for an itinerant preacher to go in and labour with a pastor of ordinary standing in a revival. And it requires great wisdom, prudence, and self-forgetfulness, lest the latter be thrown into the background, and his influence be unintentionally impaired. The biographer of Nettleton bestows high praise in saying, that an instance probably cannot be mentioned in which his influence led to the dismission of a pastor; but many instances might be mentioned in which he was instrumental in strengthening the hands of pastors. He would treat ministers with such kindness, and speak of them with such respect, as to make the impression on the minds of their people that they were worthy of their confidence; and thus not a few who had almost lost their influence, were firmly reinstated in the affections of their people.

Of course the true evangelist, as we have intimated, will *watch his own heart*, and be right before God. He will not act an assumed part; affecting a measure of sincerity and godliness that does not belong to him. How holy a man does it become him to be! How much on his knees! How intimate and uninterrupted his transactions with the Throne! If Luther trembled every time he entered the pulpit, well may an evangelist tremble as he sets foot on new ground, and puts himself into vital connection with a special work on behalf of God and men! His very zeal and success expose him to peril. Human passions, hateful pride, and uncharitable bitterness may be mixed with his zeal for the Lord; and when abundant blessings are showering down, the enemy of his soul is sure to attempt to puff him up with the idea that he has eminent gifts, and the highest tokens of God's favour, and so *he* may go forth and act among his fellow creatures as if peculiarly wise and strong and good.

President Edwards' words on this point are much in place; and no doubt they were called forth by some of the revival preachers of his time. He says: "There is also a great temptation to an assuming behaviour in some persons. When a minister is greatly succeeded from time to time, and so draws the eyes of the multitude upon him, and he sees himself flocked after and resorted to as an oracle, and people are ready to adore him and to offer sacrifice to him, as it was with Paul and Barnabas at Lystra, it is almost impossible for a man to avoid taking upon him the airs of a master. All young ministers in this day of bringing up the ark of God should take warning by the example of a young Levite in Israel, Uzzah, the son of Abinadab. He seemed to have a real concern for the ark of God, and to be zealous and engaged in his mind; but God smote him for his want of humility and taking too much upon himself."

Doubtless this is one reason why God subjects these his servants to so many humiliations, and defeats, and trials. In this way they are kept where He can consistently bestow upon their labours His blessing.

It must be added, that if the evangelist should respect the position of the pastor, so should the pastor respect the position of the evangelist. Obligations are not all on one side. It not infrequently happens that the evangelist is assailed, publicly or privately, and perhaps by those from whom better things should be expected. In such cases, the pastor, above all others, should "hold such in reputation." Sometimes it may be necessary, (not often), to resort to the public press to expose a base slander or a lurking insinuation. Possibly it may have to be done in the open assembly. Except in extreme cases, however, it is decidedly better that neither the assailed party nor the pastor take any notice of the matter. If the brethren of the church, including the minister, give to the evangelist their hearty and persevering support, all will be well. The "strife of tongues" will in this way be silenced; and God will take care of both the workman and the work.

But a pastor who is not ready to be the *true brother* to the evangelist, acts a very unworthy part in inviting him to come to his assistance.

In this connection we must record the belief, that the habit of some excellent brethren in the ministry of passing indiscriminate censure upon evangelists and their work, is a sin that ought to be repented of. Did not our Lord teach that speaking lightly of one of His servants was to "despise him that sent him?" If *ministers* denounce their brethren, (who at least have a *conscience* in pursuing their often thankless task), what must be expected of the world? We commend the thought to all preachers and theological teachers.

The following resolutions, adopted by an association in Maine, after a season of rich spiritual harvesting, embody sound views upon the topic under remark:

> "1. God honours the established ministry of the Christian religion by employing, in the conversion of sinners, usually, the truth as preached by his faithful ministers.
>
> "2. The establishment of such a ministry, however efficient and successful in any branch of the church, has by no means exhausted the instrumentalities of salvation; the prerogative being still the Lord's to project, even into the most cultivated portions of his vineyard, new and additional means.

"3. Masses of precious truth, imparted by many an able and faithful pulpit, sometimes lie inoperative, at least in that which is most essential, because un-quickened by the Spirit – by importunity of prayer – by devout ardour of sympathy – by fervour of appeal – and by variety of motive made intense and almost irresistible. To do this may demand, for a time, men and measures not usually employed.

"4. Evangelists are of divine appointment, and have their peculiar work. That work is never in derogation of, but always collateral and auxiliary to the established ministry; being designed merely to supplement its officers and labours, and thus be tributary to the conversion of souls, the spread of the Redeemer's kingdom, and the glory of his name."

"O Lord, Revive Thy Work!"

7
Child-Piety and Profession

CHILDREN have formed a substantial proportion of professed converts in the more recent revivals. Some look with favour upon this, and some with disfavour; but it certainly gives increased interest to the subject of child-piety and profession.

We take up the two points separately; and first ask as to the *possibility of child-piety*. Happily there is not ground for much discussion here. The very words of our Lord, "Suffer little children to come unto me, and forbid them not: for of such is the kingdom of God," make it sure that there is nothing on the part of God preventing the conversion of young children.

Is there anything on *their* part? We ask what is there in the gospel, and in the mind of the child, to prevent the apprehension of all saving truth? The gospel is comprehended in these two facts – *man a sinner, and Christ a Saviour*. Undoubtedly poor Jack, of whom we have read, had the whole of the gospel when he could repeat (and this was all he knew):

> "I'm a poor sinner and nothing at all,
> And Jesus Christ is my all and in all."

He who knows as much as that has the core of all Scripture. And cannot a child comprehend these two simple facts? When an infant, it understands what it is to disobey and displease a parent, and to feel sorry for it. Is it difficult to impart the idea that God may be disobeyed, and what it is to be penitent in view of it? A very young child may understand this.

And why not, also, *that Christ is a Saviour?* Children know much more than they are often supposed to know. Dr Archibald Alexander said that at *four years* of age he was interested to know the meaning of the words *anathema, maranatha*, as a minister was preaching on the text containing them; and that he watched for the explanation, and understood it, and never forgot it.

Besides the fact of the extreme simplicity of what is essentially the gospel, we add this thought; that Sunday School instruction, and Sunday School singing, and children's books and papers, have rendered intelligent the masses of children upon religious subjects to a very great extent; and that therefore they cannot be considered so ignorant of Scripture truth as to prevent their conversion. No: the blessed Spirit can find *truth* enough to work with in almost any child's mind. The prophecy is becoming fulfilled, that "There shall be no more an infant of days, (in respect to *knowledge*), for the child shall die an hundred years old."

Advancing a step, we remark that childhood is the most hopeful period of conversion. Consider this circumstance, which is a decided advantage on the part of the child over the adult; namely, that it has already many of the qualities that enter largely into the religious character and life. Our Lord meant at least this when he said, "Of such is the kingdom of heaven," for it is added, "Whosoever shall not receive the kingdom of God *as a little child*, shall not enter therein." And he once took to him a child to illustrate to his followers some of the qualities which they must possess.

These are readily seen. For instance, *love* is a marked feature in childhood; and so are *humility*, (or the want of ambition), and *teachability*, and *submission to authority*, and *hope*, and *faith*. And these are features of true piety. Now it is a gain to possess beforehand these features, though yet unsanctified. Other things being equal, a child will more readily believe than an adult; because, as we say, it is more natural to it.

A child will also be more ready to *submit to God's authority* because used to submit to parental authority; and the naturally loving and less selfish heart, will be more ready to *attach itself* to the dear Parent in heaven, than will be the heart of an adult. And so we might speak of other qualities. This being the case, if there is anything in being *fit subjects* for conversion, we should conclude that children are such.

And this is still more apparent if we remember the extreme susceptibility of childhood.

Human nature is then very plastic and ductile. It is yielding and shapeable. God may bless human efforts to the conversion of the most hardened: with Him nothing is impossible. But how much more reasonable to expect success in our trying to shape impressible childhood and youth into "vessels of honour," than in attempting it with those who have long been burnt and bronzed in the fires of passion and sin.

The difference between childhood and age, in regard to susceptibility, is like that between a page of type just set up, and a page that has been stereotyped. In the former case it is easy to make alterations; but how difficult in the latter. You may nearly as well break up the plate altogether as to attempt to alter it much. Or, the difference is like that between a young tree, and that same tree after many years' growth. The weight of a sparrow had bowed it when a sapling; now the strength of a Hercules cannot bend it. Or, the difference is like that between a wooden sailing craft and an iron-clad. The one is easily pierced, the other resists the heaviest shots.

Rev Dr Burchard, (whose letter is appended to this chapter), says on this matter of child-nature, "The skilful husbandman selects first a good farm, the freest from rocks and noxious roots, a deep, loamy soil, not overworked, susceptible, under proper culture, of the largest fruitage and abundance. Now our position is, that in all this wide extended and various field – '*the world*' – the best soil, the easiest cultivated, yielding the largest increase, is the *heart of childhood.* This is confirmed by the parable of the sower, in which some seed is represented as falling by the wayside, some upon stony places where there was not much earth, and some among thorns, and the result was there was no fruit. Whatever classes of persons may there be represented – the carefree, the frivolous, the hardened, the overburdened with care – surely this part of the parable is not intended to represent the *child's* character, or any obstacles therein to the growth of the spiritual seed. Who so free as children from temptation, from the cares of this world, the deceitfulness of riches, and all those hurtful influences which so effectually counteract the impressions of truth upon the mind? Their ardent sensibilities, their sensitive conscience unused to the process of moral hardening, render them pre-eminently the good ground of the parable; and here, if anywhere, may we look for the hundred-fold increase. Childhood is therefore peculiarly and emphatically the age designed by God in the constitution and condition of things, designated by the Scriptures, and demonstrated by experience, as the time for the successful application of the means of grace; the spring time, the time for sowing the good seed of the Word, the time which, above all others, invites effort, and gives promise of success."

We conclude, then, that little children *can* be converted, and that many circumstances strongly favour it. Scripture and analogy justify this belief. It requires no more intellect to love Christ, than to hate Him; to please than to displease Him, to serve than to disobey Him. As a little child can take its spoonful of milk, and be sustained by it as surely as the man is sustained by his strong meat, so the little child with its hand of faith can take as true a hold of Christ, and get life and salvation from Him as surely as an aged Christian. If old enough to sin, and be *punished* for it, why not old enough to *repent* and be saved? If old enough to hear the parental voice, why not *God's* voice?

We have seen little lambs in the fields run toward the keeper at his call; perhaps the quickest to catch his voice and be at his side. And

"When Israel's gentle Shepherd stands,
With all-engaging charms,
And sweetly calls the tender lambs
To fold them in His arms,"

shall we doubt whether they are old enough to know His voice? Shall we be suspicious of their coming? Shall we imitate those in Christ's day who forbade them to come? Let it not be. It is safe to follow in Christ's steps; and he said, "Suffer them to come, and forbid them not."

We come to another point – *the fact* of child-piety. Very little children *do* come to Christ. It is commonly held that Jeremiah and John the Baptist, who are spoken of in Scripture as sanctified from their birth, were early the children of grace: and also that King Josiah at the age of eight years, (when he began to reign), feared the Lord. There certainly were children among Christ's followers when on earth. Take this scene in His life: "When the chief priests and scribes saw the wonderful things that he did, and the children crying in the temple, and saying, Hosanna to the Son of David; they were sore displeased, and said unto him, Hearest thou what these say? And Jesus saith unto them, Yea; have ye never read, Out of the mouth of babes and sucklings thou hast perfected praise?" And then take this record concerning him: "In that hour Jesus rejoiced in spirit, and said, I thank thee, O Father, Lord of heaven and earth, that thou hast hid these things from the wise and prudent, and hast revealed them unto babes: even so, Father; for so it seemed good in thy sight." Were there not then some "babes," that is, very small children among those that received His gospel?

The early Christians embraced pious children. Thus Polycarp, martyred at the age of 95, declares he had served God 86 years; showing that he was converted at the age of nine years. And Justin Martyr testifies of many of both sexes "who had been made disciples to Christ from their infancy, and continued uncorrupted all their lives."

And coming to more modern times, it were easy to name many eminent servants of God who began to serve him in childhood: as Baxter for instance, who said he did not recollect the time when he did not love God and all that was good. Matthew Henry was converted before 11 years old, Mrs Isabel Graham at 10; President Edwards probably at 7, Dr Watts at 9, Bishop Hall and Robert Hall at 11 or 12.

Edwards, in his *Narrative* says, "It has heretofore been looked on as a strange thing, when any have seemed to be savingly wrought upon, and remarkably changed in their childhood; but now, I suppose, near thirty were to appearance so wrought upon between ten and fourteen years of age, and two between nine and ten, and one about *four* years of age; and because, I suppose, this last will be with most difficulty believed, I shall hereafter give a particular account of it. The influences of God's Spirit have also been very remarkable on children in some other places, particularly at Sunderland and South Hadley, and the west part of Suffield. There are several families in this town that are all hopefully pious; yea, there are several numerous families, in which, I think, we have reason to hope that all the children are truly godly, and that most of them have lately become so." He also remarks, "God in this work has shown a remarkable regard to little children; never was there such a glorious work amongst persons in their childhood, as has been of late in New England; He has been pleased in a wonderful manner to perfect praise out of the mouths of babes and sucklings; and many of them have more of that knowledge and wisdom that pleases Him, and renders their religious worship acceptable, than many of the great and learned men of the world."

To these utterances of Mr Edwards, we add other testimony as to child-piety and revivals.

Dr Griffin wrote the following as to a revival in Newark, New Jersey, under his ministry: "The appearance was as if a collection of waters long suspended over the town had fallen at once, and deluged the whole place. One Sabbath after the second service, when I had catechised and dismissed the little children, they gathered around me weeping and inquiring what they should do. I know not but a hundred were in tears at once. The scene was as affecting as it was unexpected."

Dr Archibald Maclay, of New York, thus speaks of the converts under his ministry: "Many of those who embraced the gospel at this period were young. One was only seven years old. She came to me in my study in great distress, asking if God could save her, for she had lived seven years without loving Him, and all the time sinning against Him. She united with the church, and has lived to train up a large family in the fear of God. Moreover, the great body of those who made a profession of religion have continued in the faith, rooted and grounded in love, and have not been moved away from the hope of the gospel."

One Mr Halley, in 1753, wrote thus of a work in Scotland: "Thirteen societies for prayer have been recently instituted, and a new one is about to be established. I cannot express how much I am charmed with the young people. Oh, to hear the young lambs crying after the great Shepherd – to hear them pouring out their souls with such fervour, with such beautiful expressions, with such copiousness and fulness, did not only strike me with admiration, but melted me into tears. I wished in my heart that all contradictors, gainsayers, and blasphemers of this work of God had been where I was that night."

The writer loves to recall the case of a little girl of nine years who had a very distinct perception of sin, and pleaded with God, in her room by herself, the promise, "Those that seek me early shall find me;" and then reassured her soul, saying "*Shall* find me! It does not say, (she said), *may* find me, but *shall* find me;" and finding the Saviour, truly, she became a bright ornament in the church. A child in Bridgeport, Connecticut, of some eight years, was asked why she thought she was a Christian; and she answered, "Because I believe all the words of the Lord Jesus." Could any person have given a better answer?

A sick girl of ten years of age was asked, "Is the matter settled between you and God?"

"Oh! Yes," was the calm reply.

"How did you get it settled?"

"Why, the *Lord Jesus Christ settled it for me!*"

"And when did He do that for you?"

"When He died on the cross for my sins!"

"How long is it since you knew this blessed and consoling fact?"

"About twelve months ago."

"How did you know that the work which Christ accomplished on the cross for sinners was done for *you?*"

She at once replied, "I read it in the *Bible, and believed that it was just so.*"

Who could ask for a better experience than this?

An eminent Scotch minister, (Dr W L Alexander), had doubted the genuineness of the great work going on near him among children, until he was once in a prayer-room where many little ones were praying; and he says of that scene: "I stood listening and the tears rushed down my cheeks as I listened. I could not help it, because I felt that I was reproved that I had doubted the work of God in that particular, and now he had brought me face to face with the work itself."

Would anyone want a better Christian experience than this from a little child in Boston: "I listened to the sermon and felt more sorry and more sorry for my sins; and a kind lady took me by the hand, and showed me the way to the blessed Saviour, and then, when I got home, I went straight to my bed-side, and prayed to God to give me a new heart and take Satan out of my heart, and to make me His child. And then I went and asked my mother's and father's forgiveness; and then I felt better. And then I prayed to God again, and then went to sleep. The next day I felt so happy that I felt like singing all the time. And now I feel as if I had given my heart to Christ."

If it be asked how early should we expect the conversion of our children? We answer, just as early as we begin to labour and pray in earnest for it. And should parents and Sunday School teachers do their full duty to children in this regard, adult conversion would become the rare exception, and early conversion the rule. There is a vast amount of scepticism on this subject among the churches, which must be removed before this world is given to Christ. As M'Cheyne has said, "Jesus has reason to complain of us that He can do no mighty works in our Sunday Schools because of our unbelief."

Approaching now the other part of our topic, child-*profession*, we are aware that it is more controversial ground. A hesitancy to receive quite young children to a public profession of religion is very general in all the churches.

In his *Letters to a Son in the Ministry*, Dr Heman Humphrey gives endorsement to this conservative view, as follows:

"You do not tell me whether the revival in L____ embraces children or not. This is not infrequently the case, and I have no doubt that many are renewed at a very tender age. But if there is any considerable number of the children of your congregation excited to make the great inquiry, 'What shall we do?' I am sure, that while you rejoice to see them flocking around for advice, it will occasion you a great deal of solicitude. You will find it extremely difficult to determine how much of the interest which they manifest arises from mere sympathy, and how much from the striving of the Spirit – how much they talk and exhort and pray from imitation, and how much from the impulse of religious feeling. You will often be astonished at the apparent maturity of their views and genuineness of their experience, and will probably look upon many more of them as truly converted than really are so. A few months will convince you that much of what appeared so promising was 'the morning cloud and the early dew.' Some however, will, it is to be hoped, give increasing evidence of a real change of heart, and the question of receiving them into the church will come up at no distant day. They may wish very much to be admitted, and their friends perhaps will urge it; but I hope you will take time and look at the question in all its bearings, before you give your consent. A great many young people in some parts of the land are now in the churches, who are quite sure they never had any religion, and who exceedingly regret that they were encouraged, or allowed to make a profession at so early an age. It appears to me the cases are very rare, in which children should be received under *fourteen;* and that it is not safe to admit many, till they are still older. The true way, I cannot help thinking is, to form them into a class of *catechumens*, under such a course of religious instruction, as is best calculated to imbue their minds with the essential doctrines of the gospel; to make them acquainted with the nature and evidences of true piety, and to prepare them for admission to the Lord's Table, after a suitable probation. Precisely how long they should be kept in the class of catechumens, I am not prepared to say. Doubtless some may be admitted into the church earlier than others; but I think there is more danger of moving too fast, than too slow."

We fail to see, however, why there is not here a false distinction between what is, after all, but a question of *evidence*. Why be so cautious as to the testimony of a *child?* Is it merely because the subject is a child? That were folly indeed. Since, then, it is a question of *validity* of evidence, why not frankly weigh the testimony and act accordingly? Why give credence to the experience of the adult and reject or refuse to accept, the experience of the child?

Certainly there is no foundation for this hesitancy in the Scriptures; and we cannot see why it is not unfairness to the child, and every way unwise. If a babe ever needs the mother's breast, it is just after it is born: and the same must be true of spiritual babes. And if one class more than another needs the church's embrace, it is those young in years. How un-philosophical, (as well as unfair), to keep the child outside the church till piety be *proved*, when this is not exacted of adults?

We are told that the church of which Dr Cox was pastor for a long time, in Brooklyn, once had a rule prohibiting children under fourteen years of age from becoming members of the church. At that time a very intelligent girl asked for admittance. The session did not wish to tell her that they could not receive her. They made excuses and put her off from time to time, until at last the pastor was obliged to tell her that she could not be received. She was familiarly acquainted with Dr Cox, and for a moment she laid her head upon his shoulder and wept. Then lifting her eyes pathetically to his, she said, "Dr Cox, Jesus Christ would not treat me so; he says, 'Suffer little children to come unto me.'" Upon which the pastor exclaimed, "Away with all church rules that conflict with Christ's word."

It is related that a certain deacon in Maine would not let his converted boy join the church because he was "too young." "Wait," said he, "till you *show* that you are pious." The minister, who did not share in his views, found the deacon one cold spring day toward night, getting the sheep and lambs into the barn. "Why do you do this?" he asked. "Because I fear these lambs will freeze to death if I leave them out over night," replied the deacon. "But," said the minister, "would it not be as well to leave them out till they *show* that they are going to live, and then get them in?" The deacon took the hint; and said, "I shan't prevent my boy's joining the church any longer!" It were well for all objectors to ponder and apply the narrative.

We talk to our children in the family and Sunday School about Jesus loving little children, and being ready to receive them. We urge them to begin now to love him, repeating, "I love them that love me; and those that seek me early shall find me." We tell them they may die early, and that that is a reason why they should repent now. And we pray for their immediate conversion, and teach them to sing of the loveliness of infant piety. But when they tell us they love Jesus, and would like to profess their love for Him, we hesitate, and advise caution and delay. Even where parents are compelled to acknowledge a great change in the child, and see better evidence of piety, (as they admit), in the child than in themselves, they oppose the idea of joining the church.

Alas, for such inconsistency. Do we not thus show that our prayers for their speedy conversion were faithless? Do we not depreciate and undo our own teaching? And do we not cast discredit upon the work of the Holy Spirit, and discourage all efforts on the part of the child to follow the divine requirements?

It is astonishing that the teaching and the practice of Christians here are so at variance. Why not cease this perpetual talk about child-piety, or else accept its consequences? If we *believe* what we preach, namely, that the children *ought* to love Christ, and should now, at once, give their little hearts to him, (the staple of Sunday School addresses), then why not acknowledge child-piety where it is apparent? Why try to lead the children to Christ, and then shut the door of Christ's church against them? Why in our homes and sanctuaries entreat them with tears and loving words to be Christians now, and then doubtfully shake the head when the question comes of their admission to the communion?

Many a parent perusing these lines may remember how a dear child spoke of having found Jesus. You heard the simple tale with tearful interest, and said, "I am glad of it, darling." You gave thanks for it in the closet; and felt unspeakable joy at seeing the new sweetness of temper in the child, the increased dutifulness, and lovingness, and prayerfulness.

Then the child said, "May I join the church?" You said, "Wait a little, my dear." The child submitted, (though with disappointment), to your superior judgment.

Months passed. Again the child said, "What do you think about my joining the church now? I would *like* to do it if you approve of it." You said, "You know you are very young; hadn't you better wait a little longer?" So it passed on.

At length, years after, (if God did not take the precious one to Himself), the minister, upon exhorting this youth to become pious, finds traces of existing godliness. "How long have you felt so?" "Why, for years." The pastor calls to see you as to the child's profession. You consent, and the child is taken into the church. But, what a loss has already been experienced! Darkness and doubt gathered upon the young mind, from the fact that you seemed to question the reality of the change. Perplexity arose on a thousand points. Coldness ensued, and wanderings in evil ways; until at last in another work of grace, that poor thing again through fearful struggles came into the light – to regret till a dying day that there had not been experienced during those years the warm sympathies of the church, instead of the chilling influences of the world.

This is by no means an overdrawn or unusual case. There are thousands of Christians who might have sat for the picture. And in this light, how much is the practice under remark to be deprecated.

A minister of much observation says: "I have not a doubt that thousands of child-converts have gone through life and never joined any church, but lingered long, full of doubts and fears and darkness, and in this way have spent their days, and gone to the grave without the comforts or the usefulness which they might have enjoyed, simply because the church, in her folly, suffered them to wait outside of her pale, to see whether they would grow and thrive without those ordinances which Jesus Christ established particularly for their benefit. Why thus turn them out alone upon the cold mountains, among the wild beasts, to starve or perish, to see whether they are alive or not? This whole system is as un-philosophical as it is unscriptural. It is almost as absurd as it would be to throw out a young child into the street, to see whether it will live – to say, 'If it lives and promises to be a healthy child, we will take care of it,' when that is the very time it wants nursing. Should the church throw her new-born children out to the winds, and say, if they live there, let them be raised; but if they die, they ought to die. We earnestly pray that the time may speedily come when such folly shall cease."

Abundant testimony could here be introduced as to the worthy lives of professors received into fellowship in childhood. An able minister once affirmed in public, that in his ministry he had admitted three or four hundred persons to the church. Of these, one hundred were children; and he believed that fewer mistakes had been made in admitting them than in the case of the adults.

Another experienced pastor says, "I may safely say that the most satisfactory cases have been those of children and quite young persons." "For myself," says another pastor, "I have reason to thank God for permitting me the joy of seeing scores of children coming to Christ. No more satisfactory cases of conversion have ever come under my observation than among children."

And another says, "I here record the gratifying fact, that under my pastorate I do not recall an instance where the church has been compelled to exclude a member received in early childhood; while among the most active and useful persons in my charge are many who came in as children." Mr Spurgeon, also, lately used almost these very words. These are but samples of many that might be given.

The writer recently addressed a communication to several distinguished ministers of different denominations, requesting their views upon three points: 1. The *fact* of child-piety as a thing to be *expected* and *laboured* for. 2. The wisdom of *early profession;* especially the *results* under their own observation. 3. Is the prevailing hesitancy as to receiving young but apparently pious children to a public profession, to be approved and encouraged, or otherwise?

The following responses will be read with interest:

From Rev Dr Goodwin, Chicago, Illinois:

My Dear Brother:

I am only too glad to note, in a most hasty way, such replies to the inquiries you raise as my experience and observation suggest.

1. I have no doubt whatsoever as to the possibility of early piety, and none as to the duty, and that a *most imperative one*, of labouring to secure such piety in the *very earliest years*.

And I believe further, that one of the grand mistakes made in many of our churches, and almost generally throughout the range of our Protestant faith, is that we forget that, "of such is the kingdom of heaven." We perpetually lay out all our strength, marshal all our arguments, and multiply all our agencies to reach adults, and bring them to a knowledge of the truth; while the real development and exquisite power of the gospel does not lie that way, but lies rather in the "nurture and admonition of the Lord."

2. I *believe fully in the wisdom of early professions* – such being always made upon evidence satisfactory to parents, (who believe of course, in the piety of children – as alas! how many do not). I would not encourage such professions, in any case, without someone – either a parent, or warm, earnest disciple in the household, or faithful teacher – to watch over the child, and lead it lovingly in the way. My experience is – and I have received a large number – that such young persons give as clear and satisfactory proof of the leadings of the Spirit, and just as truly and consistently honour their professions, as do older disciples. Indeed, as concerns pliability, readiness to receive and to put in practice Christian instruction, sincerity of motive, simplicity and conscientiousness of conduct – I have always found the youth, the children, far in advance of older people.

I think they ought not to be received, (as is so often done), and then all instruction or attempts to shape their character be dropped. There is clear need that catechetical classes, children's meetings or circles, or some method, by either the pastor or a competent Sabbath school superintendent – or better still, a wise and loving woman – shall help them to know Christ, and to *put Him on* in daily life, and *grow up* into Him in all things.

3. As I have intimated, I strongly *disapprove* the existing hesitancy on the part of many as to receiving children into the church. If the church is Christ's school, then why leave the children to pick up Christ's teaching by such chance-instruction as they may happen upon? If the church is God's family, and the children have any relation

to it, why keep them out when they need most nursing? Must they prove that they can go alone without help before we are ready to give them the atmosphere and encouragement of the household? I am glad you have taken so good a work in hand; it is greatly needed.

Very truly yours,

E P Goodwin.

From Dr Stephen H Tyng, New York,

Rev and Dear Brother:

My intense occupations have prevented a due notice of your communication and request. I have not time to go into any discussion or exposition of views upon the general subject of your note, in theory. It has been my constant practice to make no objection to age in a Christian profession, if I am satisfied on the two points of actual personal conversion and intelligence. When the Spirit of God anoints a soul to Christ, and gives His witness of personal ability to love and serve the Saviour, in reality and truth, who am I that my unbelieving fears should be interposed as an obstacle to His work and will? I have received a profession at eight years of age; I think no instance has occurred to me younger.

Yours fraternally,

Stephen H Tyng.

From Rev Dr Webb, Boston, Massachusetts

My Dear Brother:

You wish in reply to your questions, I suppose, not the most, but the least I can say. My belief is that piety in the children of Christian parents is to be expected.

My experience does not disappoint my theory. And children giving evidence of piety must be taken into the church.

But as to the evidence, I wait for it to be developed somewhat. The Christian family is a sort of room in the church, and the child is not going to lose his regeneration there. I make the time between the beginning of evidence, and the entrance into the church, longer in the case of children than of adults. I have weekly meetings, and all hopeful converts are formed into a kind of class; and I instruct them in our articles of faith – in experimental religion, etc. And from this class I select, from time to time, such as seem to me qualified to take upon them church responsibilities.

With all our machinery, the great want is, on the part of those who come into our churches, old and young, a better, deeper understanding of the truths and doctrines of religion, and a deeper, surer heart-acquaintance, or experience.

In the case of an adult, having been subjected to the influences and temptations of the world, he knows himself better; and uniting with the church is a change of relations, and an assumption of responsibilities, that he will ponder and feel.

A child in a Christian family, however, comes along without any such break or turn, and therefore is not likely to ponder the matter so sharply.

But children well instructed by the minister, encouraged to open all their mind to him, tell their temptations and purposes, and ask questions – children thus developed and matured under my eye – I receive joyfully. I hope this forthcoming book will be as good and timely as *Primitive Piety Revived.*

Yours cordially,

E B Webb.

From Rev Dr Richard Fuller, Baltimore, Maryland

Dear Brother:

I comply with your request the more readily, because I once thought I was doing God's service in opposing the reception of young children into the church, and was most thoroughly and touchingly corrected by my own first-born. At the age of ten she told me of her conversion, and desired baptism. "My darling child," I replied, "you are young and your gay relatives and companions may lead you into the world." "My father," she said, "am I too young to love *you* and my *mother?* And ought I not to love *Jesus* before all and above all?" – Since then I have rejoiced to welcome children to him who says, "Suffer little children to come unto me, and forbid them not," – thus rebuking in his apostles the very prejudice we now encounter. I may add, that the death-bed of this precious daughter, at the age of twenty-three, was so triumphant a termination to a life of purity and love, that Dr Wayland wrote to ask me if angels really appeared in her room. Never have I known or read of such bodily suffering, but of such exultation in Jesus. (*Forgive a father's feelings.*)

As to the questions you propose, I answer thus, after much experience and prayer: First. We believe in a change of heart by which "a child of wrath" becomes "a child of God." Let us hold fast to this, especially at this day. If there be conversion, the earlier the better. Paul speaks with a holy envy of those who "were in Christ before" him. To say nothing of the larger term for service, how many painful conflicts are we spared by conversion in our first years!

Second. For worlds we would do nothing which Jesus has not commanded; but for worlds we would not omit anything which he has commanded. And a convert ought to be *at once baptised* – it is the voluntary obedience of an intelligent believer.

But as to the reality of the change, the church must decide each case as it does in the examination of grown persons; with this difference, that the testimony of the parents ought to go very far in deciding the question, and the opinion of the Sabbath school teacher ought to be almost conclusive.

Sunday Schools have changed almost wholly the economy of churches belonging to a former age; but teachers have yet to feel that their one great business is the conversion of their scholars. When we consider this advantage in dealing with docile minds, and tender consciences, and susceptible hearts, it is a lamentation, and should be for a lamentation, that more children are not savingly united to Jesus.

Affectionately in the Redeemer,

R Fuller

From Rev Dr Burchard, New York.

My Dear Brother:

The early conversion of children is a subject of deep and growing interest. Doubt and indifference have lamentably characterised the past. Christians, from the early disciples downward, seem to have discouraged any attempt to bring young children to Christ. Even the most earnest of them have not laboured in faith for their conversion. While they have sowed the seed on the mellowest and best soil, they have felt that they must wait through many long years, before there could be any real germination, any positive fruit.

With this prevailing view, the conversion of children has been infrequent, and if occasionally *real*, regarded rather as a marvel than the natural effect of God's fidelity and gracious promise to His believing people; and if such converted children were finally received to the communion of the church, it was usually after the test and tutelage of years.

This, however, amid the culminating light of modern revivals, and a better interpretation of Scripture, has come to be regarded as a most dangerous heresy. The efforts and prayers of Christians are now turned to the young, as the most hopeful field, as furnishing the best soil for the seed which is to produce an hundred fold.

Some of the most active and spiritual members of our churches were regenerated in childhood. One of the most useful and prominent pastors in the city of New York, was received into full fellowship of the church at the early age of eight years, and was hopefully converted at a much earlier period. The intimation of Paul is that Timothy became the subject of grace, and a student of Scripture, when quite a youth.

During a ministry of more than thirty years, I have received a goodly number to the church between the ages of nine and twelve, and they "have run well," giving good evidence that the work was thorough, and that they were born of the Spirit.

Why should not such cases of conversion be more frequent, and more generally expected? Why should the sunniest portion of life be given to the service of Satan? Why should sin be suffered to propagate itself? Why should the seeds of the apostasy be permitted even to germinate, much less to produce a full harvest of vice and crime? Why should not the proclivities to evil in childhood be counteracted by those moral forces implied and involved in the gospel plan of mercy? In the atoning blood of Jesus there is the needed element for changing the original character of the soil, and making it good ground for the reception of the spiritual seed-grain. We have in the "exceedingly rich and precious promises," and in the influences of the divine Spirit, the glorious sunshine and showers, so essential to healthy germination, efflorescence and fruitage.

If, then, children may be converted, why should they not be received to the care and fellowship of the church? The church is God's seminary of instruction and preparation for the higher honours of heaven; and should she not take under her tutelage the younger disciples, the very "babes in Christ," who more than any other, need the "sincere milk of the word," as well as the tender care of our common mother, the church? They are members with us of the household of faith, and they should not be exiled from the family board or disinherited of their birthright. They are lambs of Christ's flock, and his charge to Peter is still imperative, "Feed my lambs." They, more than all others, need protection from the storms of this world, the pitfalls and perils of the wilderness, the fury of wild beasts; and to this end, they must be gathered into the fold, under the care of the good Shepherd. The idea of keeping them out of the church in their weakness and helplessness, when they most need shelter and protection, is simply absurd.

In my early Christian life, I witnessed a scene which opened a full fountain of sympathy for the young and tender lambs of the flock. Little Martha, the granddaughter of the officiating clergyman, appeared before the proper officers of the church to be examined for admission to its communion. She *was* examined thoroughly, and the examination showed satisfactorily that she had met with a change; and yet the officers, said, "Martha, you are very young, and had better wait till you are older before you make a public profession of religion." She did wait patiently for three months, and then appeared again, telling the same sweet story of Jesus and His love; and yet she was advised to wait. Again she appeared, hopeful now, but was again disappointed. And when a whole year had passed, and she was again advised to wait, her breaking heart sobbed out, "Oh! Grandpapa, how old must I be before I may love Jesus, and sit with Him at his table?" The old prejudice gave way. She was received, and became an ornament and a blessing to the church.

Whom Christ has received, however young, the church may not reject; and those who are fitted for his church above are surely fitted for its fellowship here.

Yours in the gospel,
S D Burchard

In view of the foregoing, let all join the more heartily in the prayer of Dr Bonar, of Scotland: "Lord, sharpen our sickles when we go to reap thy harvest among the young. For we have heard thee say, 'Have ye not read; Out of the mouths of babes and sucklings thou hast perfected praise?'"

"O Lord, Revive Thy Work!"

8

Indications of a Revival

BEFORE a copious rain we may expect the "little cloud like a man's hand." A *determination to have*, by God's help, a *better state of things*, must be set down as a first indication of a revival. We must *desire* a thing before having it. It is when we stir up ourselves to call on God, and to put forth effort, because we are tired of the present state of things and intent on improvement, that the blessing may be expected – not before. Said an eminent divine, "I never had a revival under my ministry without *labouring* for it, and *expecting* it."

Distress of soul over prevailing desolations must accompany this desire for improvement. "As soon as Zion travailed she brought forth children," said the Prophet Isaiah. Soul-savers are not ignorant of birth-pangs. This is imaged to us in our Master's character. He is the great Saviour of men; but before He could save others He learned in their flesh to sympathise with them. He wept over Jerusalem. He sweat great drops of blood in Gethsemane. He was, and is, a high priest who is touched with the feeling of our infirmities. As the Captain of our salvation, in bringing many sons unto glory, He was made perfect by sufferings. Even He went not forth to rescue the perishing until he had spent nights in intercessory prayer, and uttered strong crying and tears for their salvation.

We have heard Mr Earle urge God's people to go down into Gethsemane with Christ; and insist, most tenderly, that they *must* feel something of these agonies before souls would be brought in; and our own pastoral experience is in the same direction. We well remember the mountain weight more than once pressing down on the soul, so that the feet seemed to stagger on the pavements, and sleep departed from the eyes at night time.

The power in the hand of God for conversions is heart coming into contact with heart. This is God's battle-axe and weapon of war, in His crusade. He is pleased to use the yearnings, longings, and sympathies of Christian men, as the means of compelling the careless to think, constraining the hardened to feel, and driving the unbelieving to consider. "I have little confidence in elaborate speech and polished sentences," says Spurgeon, "as the means of reaching men's hearts; but I have great faith in that simple-minded Christian woman, who *must* have souls converted or she will weep her eyes out over them; and in that humble Christian who prays day and night in secret, and then avails himself of every opportunity to address a loving word to sinners. The emotion we feel, and the affection we bear, are the most powerful implements of soul-winning. God the Holy Ghost usually breaks hard hearts by tender hearts."

There is a deep philosophy in this soul-yearning before conversions. One reason for it, doubtless, is that the travail qualifies for the proper taking care of the offspring. God does not commit His new-born children to people who do not care to see conversions. If He ever allows them to fall into such hands, they suffer very serious loss thereby. Who is so fit to encourage a new-born believer as the man who first anguished before the Lord for that conversion? Those whom you have wept over, and prayed for, you will be sure to love and assist. The church that never travailed, should God send her converts, would be unfit to train them. She would not know what to do with them. Another reason is, that God's glory is thereby promoted. In our extremity we are ready to ascribe all to the sovereign Spirit; and not till then can God help us; for He will not give His glory to another.

Again: *the providence of God* sometimes indicates that a revival is at hand. There is a conspiring of events to open the way, a preparation of circumstances to favour a revival, so that those who are looking out can see that one is at hand almost as plainly as if it had been revealed from heaven. Cases have occurred in this country, says one of experience, where the providential manifestations were so plain that those who were careful observers felt no hesitation in saying that God was coming to pour out his Spirit.

The *praying meeting will improve* when a revival commences. The "two or three" are pressed in spirit, and speak often to one another about it. A passion to see the church revived rules them. By degrees, individuals are drawn together by sacred affinity, and the prayer-meetings become very different. The brother who talked twenty minutes in what *he* called prayer, gives up his oration, and falls to pleading with tears and broken sentences; while the friend who used to relate his experience, and go through the doctrines of grace, and call that a prayer, forgets that, and begins agonising before the throne. And not only this, but little knots here and there come together in their cottages, and in their quiet rooms cry mightily to God. The result will be that the minister, even if he does not know of this feeling in the hearts of his people, will grow fervent himself. He will preach more tenderly and earnestly.

A *thirst for the preached Word* and a *deep interest* in it, is a revival indication. In a declension there is nothing resembling an appetite, a thirst for the Word; there is no deep, soul-penetrating, soul-subduing interest felt in hearing it. The whole of this is reversed in a revived, living church. The souls of the people open at once to the Word of God, and melt and bend beneath the most simple truths presented in the simplest Scripture dress. In an account from the island of Arran, dated 1812, we read: "For some months after the commencement of the awakening, the subjects of it manifested an uncommon thirst after the means of grace. Both old and young flocked in multitudes to hear the Word of God. The house, and the place employed for private meetings, were frequently so crowded that the people, as it were, trod one upon another. To travel ten or fifteen miles to hear a sermon was considered as a very small matter." So, too, when the returning captives lingered about the ruins of Jerusalem and the temple, and the very stones of the fallen walls and buildings appeared to them as dear as jewels, and even the dust in the deserted streets seemed to them precious, the period of prophecy was almost determined; the time to rebuild Jerusalem and the temple was well-nigh come. Thus, while a decline of interest in even the external order of religion supposes commensurate spiritual declension, a quickened interest in that order argues spiritual revival.

Sorrow and shame for backsliding are a symptom of improvement. The Scriptures are clear and explicit on this point. "I will pour upon the house of David and upon the inhabitants of Jerusalem, the Spirit of grace and of supplication." And what shall be the fruit – what the result of this outpouring of the Holy Ghost? Is it joy simply? Is it change of conduct and life simply? Nay, joy were but delusion in this case apart from sorrow. Change of conduct were but hypocrisy without grief and shame for conduct past. "I will pour upon them the Spirit of grace – and they shall look upon me whom they have pierced, *and they shall mourn for him,*" – not believe on him simply, but *mourn* for him – mourn for *him* for dishonours done to *him* – for ignominy cast upon *him* – for their wicked unbelief, impenitence, and estrangement from God in time past.

With this there will be *mutual confessions*, and *restitutions*. The command to "confess your faults one to another," is not neglected; but where hardness and estrangement have existed, it is acknowledged, and the alienated ones beg pardon of each other, and the breaches are healed.

Especially will there be a readiness to make amends for injury or injustice. It is a rule in the isles of the Hebrides, that when a man meets a stray sheep on the moor, he is entitled to carry it home as his own, and obliged to make an equivalent offering in the collection for the poor on the Sabbath day. After the commencement of the revival in the Lewis, says a writer, "many came to confess to their minister the trouble of conscience they experienced by reason of having what they called a *black sheep in their flocks* – some having had them for several winters. The minister always directed them to make restitution now in the appointed way; and in one season, the sum of £16 was deposited in the plate. The number of sheep annually lost has wonderfully diminished since the commencement of the revival, leading to the conclusion that the loss imputed to accident arose from dishonesty."

Together with this will there be *hearty renunciation of sin, and a new dedication to God.* If the Lord is near, the "idols" are put away, and the appeal has not been without response, "Who will consecrate himself this day unto the Lord?"

Importunate prayer for a revival, and readiness to work in it, is evidence of its commencement. Sometimes Christians are not engaged in prayer *for a revival,* not even when they are engaged generally in prayer. Their minds are upon something else; they are praying for something else – the salvation of the heathen and the like – and not for a revival among themselves. But when they feel the want of a revival, they pray as if their hearts were set upon it, and as if they could not be denied. And they are willing to *sacrifice* for the success of the work.

Hence, an *immediate and earnest coming up to the help of the Lord against the mighty*, is evidence of the special presence of the Spirit. Mr Nettleton wrote in 1822, of his preaching in Somers, Connecticut, and seeing no such indications. He tells of the "*turning point*" thus: I said, "*When* will you take up the great subject of a revival in earnest? I alluded to what I had often been informed had been the state of things in this place for several years past. They had often imagined themselves on the very eve of a revival; appearances seemed to justify this expectation; but they have uniformly subsided, and no general revival had been witnessed; and at this moment I hear the sound of something. Is it the abundance of rain? I cannot tell; this awful suspense will not continue long." That afternoon the great question about a revival was graciously settled, for the people put away indifference and procrastination.

Another revival indication is *zeal for the conversion of others*. When the Christians of the Pentecostal church were scattered abroad in the persecution upon the death of Stephen, we are told that "they went everywhere preaching the word." Most of them, doubtless, were private Christians; yet, wherever they went, it seems they carried the news of Christ along with them. "The love of Christ constrained them." "They could not but speak the things which they had seen and heard." They could not but say to men – "Come with us, and we will do you good:" "We have found the Messiah:" "Come see a man that told me all that ever I did; is not this the Christ?" And so it will be with Christians now if the revival spirit has kindled upon them.

Finally: *Conviction of sinners in considerable numbers* indicates the beginning of a revival. Sometimes the change in this respect is very gradual; and for a considerable time nothing more can be said than that there is a more listening ear, and a more serious aspect than usual under the preaching of the Word; and this increased attention is gradually matured into deep solemnity and pungent conviction. In other cases, the reigning lethargy is suddenly broken up, as if there had come a thunderbolt from eternity; and multitudes are heard simultaneously inquiring what they shall do to be saved.

Some of the foregoing views are confirmed in a sentence from Dr Humphrey's Letters to his son which is here reproduced. "Favourable indications may pass away as the morning cloud and the early dew. I have myself experienced several such alternations of hope and discouragement before the revival actually came. There are, however, signs and evidences on which you may rely. If there are great searchings of heart in the church; if old hopes are shaken; if differences of long standing are healed by mutual confessions; if Christians are remarkably humble and prayerful; if they speak often one to another, and if their bowels yearn over the impenitent, then is a revival begun. There can be no doubt of it. And when in connection with such a state of things in the church, sinners in considerable numbers are awakened, when you find here and there cases of genuine conviction, and some individuals giving striking evidence that they have been born again, you need not doubt that a real work of grace has commenced in the congregation as well as in the church. But even then you should guard against expressing yourself too sanguinely, when you speak on the subject, and should exhort the church to '*rejoice with trembling.*' It is not certain that because God has begun to revive His work He will carry it on; that because a few have been converted many more will be. The Holy Spirit may be grieved and may depart ere you have sung out your first song."

"O Lord, Revive Thy Work!"

9

Revivals Hindered and Arrested

IF there be one momentous question, it is this; Why are not revivals more general, more permanent, more extensive?

And the answer must be, that there are hindrances to their commencement, and that they are often arrested after they have begun. We take the two points separately.

1. *There are hindrances preventing the existence of revivals.*

The great hindering cause is that *the churches are not living in keeping with their chief design.* They do not make the conversion of the ungodly their one grand aim. The very intention of the church of the Lord Jesus, as a *converting agency*, seems lost sight of.

The followers of Christ are chiefly engaged about other business than that which *ought* to absorb their attention. That business, unquestionably, is the salvation of men, the conversion of the world. This was the mission which brought Christ Himself into the world, and which, when He was about to leave the world, He committed to the hands of His disciples of all generations, as the high purpose of their existence. His first disciples, full of the Holy Ghost and of faith, entered on this work, and spent their lives and their all in performing it. They planted churches in almost every part of the civilised world. But nearly eighteen centuries have elapsed since they fell asleep, and there has scarcely been, until of late, any enlargement of Christianity beyond the bounds to which they carried it; while within these bounds it has been, for the most part, in a state of deplorable infirmity or monstrous perversion.

The reason was, that succeeding generations of Christians ceased from the work to which the first disciples devoted their lives. Christians have recently had a partial awakening from this mighty infatuation; but partial it truly is. Anyone who will lift up his eyes and look, in the spirit of Christ, over the length and breadth of the most evangelical countries, will see the vast multitude of professed Christians engaged about almost every thing rather than fulfilling the un-revoked command of their Lord, to teach all nations, and preach the gospel to every creature.

This, with the love of ease, money, pleasure, honour, among professors of religion, rather than an ardent and laborious desire for the conversion of perishing sinners, and a lack of holiness, humility, and dependence upon God on the part of preachers, most certainly is the greatest hindrance to revivals – the mighty mountain which stands in the way of the church's enlargement.

Distrust of revivals is another hindering cause. Sometimes this takes the shape of positive opposition; and the solemn words of Dr Porter deserve to be rung out in awful tones in the ears of opposers. Speaking of the revivals in the early part of this century, he says; "In a few instances the Holy Spirit was hindered among a people by decided opposition on the part of the pastor, or leading members of a church. As there is a sin which shall never have forgiveness, when committed by obdurate contemners of God and his grace – a sin that is unpardonable, not because it transcends the mercy of God or the merits of Christ, but because the sinner will be left to himself, and therefore will never repent – so a church whose minister or members revile the special work of the Holy Spirit, ascribing it to fanaticism, or satanic agency, are sometimes left to wither under a judicial dereliction, like the mountains of Gilboa on which there was neither rain nor dew. Some awful examples of this sort are upon record in the history of New England."

But there may be feelings of distrust when there is no open opposition. And where these feelings prevail, it cannot be a matter of surprise that no extended and powerful revivals should exist. For there the means ordinarily essential to their existence will not be used, but on the contrary will be carefully avoided. If at any time symptoms should be discovered of the public mind becoming more than usually interested in the subject of religion, efforts would then be made to guard against the incipient and dreaded evil. Who can reasonably wonder that under such circumstances there should be no revivals? Would it not rather be strange if the fact were otherwise? Is there evidence that God ever revives His work where it is not wished for? "If I knew," says one, "that anywhere revivals were not desired, but rather dreaded, I should want no other explanation of the fact that they are not enjoyed; this is reason enough."

We greatly fear that a distrust of revivals in the minds of some, even of pastors, and a doubt, on the whole, of their desirableness, has grieved the gracious Spirit, and hindered his visits to cheer and bless the churches of the land. Undoubtedly it is one of the most serious impediments to revivals. The obstructions with which they meet from open opposers are trifling compared with the cold indifference of those who ought to be their friends and helpers. The plants of a greenhouse can endure the storms without, but when masses of ice are in the enclosure, how can they grow?

Hence it is a solemn duty of each objector that he examine his own heart, and the grounds of his indifference or opposition to revivals. If they are the genuine work of God; if they accord with the statements of the Bible; if they are such results as he has a right to expect under the preaching of the gospel, he is bound, by all the love which he bears to his Saviour, and to the souls of men, to desire and pray for their increase and extension.

It is much, it is everything, when Christians intelligently, and on settled grounds, believe in the existence and value of revivals of religion; and we cannot hope for these descending influences until they shall think on this subject as the Saviour thought, and feel as He felt.

Mr Barnes once put to his congregation some questions which any pastor might press home upon all his hearers. They were like these: Are there none of you who start back at the word *revival*, and who feel an instinctive dislike to the name? Are there none in whose minds the word suggests the idea of mere excitement; of scenes of enthusiasm and disorder; of irregularity and wildfire? Are there none who, when they pray, and with very honest intentions in the main, for a revival, do it with many qualifications and mental reservations, and with an apprehension or fear that the prayer may be answered – who pray from the custom of using such language, rather than from any intelligent and sincere wish that such scenes may be witnessed?

When prayers are offered *for* revivals, are there, *practically*, no prayers against them? While the fervent petitions of a portion of an assembled church ascend to heaven for the descent of the Holy Spirit like floods and showers, are there no *counter*-petitions that cross and recross the prayers of those who love revivals, as they ascend up to God?

On this theme of such incalculable importance to the churches, we subjoin a passage from a discourse by Dr Skinner, which is worthy of prayerful consideration. "No man should allow himself any distrust or misgiving of religious revivals, such as have rendered our land almost peculiar in the eyes of the old world. If some of the evils of the day are to be referred to them as the occasion, what good or desirable thing is there among us which is not indebted to them, under God, as the chief support and encouragement, if not the origin? If we stand in doubt whether these remarkable effusions of the Spirit be desirable or not, should we not, in order to be consistent with ourselves, begin to question the ultimate success of Christianity? What manner of persons must they be, in heaviness and sorrow, or else in hardness of heart, who can allow themselves in distrustful thoughts concerning the desirableness of religious revivals? Evils, it is true, are incidental to revivals; but all is ultimately lost without them. And when one begins to object to good and necessary things because of the evils of which they may be the occasion, where will he find a stopping-place until he has objected to the incarnation of Christ, the preaching of the gospel, the government of God, his own existence, and even the creation of the world?"

To proceed: *a pastor may prevent the beginning of a revival.* History is instructive on this point. A writer upon the progress of the churches in New England some half century ago, states that there were congregations amid the surrounding showers of divine influence which were entirely passed by; and that "the pastor was the greatest obstacle to a revival among his people. And this was true, though he was not chargeable with any heresy, or immorality, or hostility to revivals." He specifies that brother A was of a sluggish temperament. Brother B was of a literary taste, an idolater of books, especially of popular literature, by which his spirituality was impaired. Brother C was fond of social and fashionable entertainments, and in the habit of jesting and story-telling, which destroyed the savour of godliness and unfitted him for revival work. Brother D hurt his usefulness by the multiplicity of worldly things that filled his hands, and he had not time or heart to help forward special services. Brother E was so ambitious of a classical style that he sacrificed pungency and power to rhetorical embellishment. And brother F was one of the "moral preachers," who condemned vices and extolled the virtues, but did not preach sin and redemption. "These ministers saw no revivals, and themselves were the principal cause of it."

Further: *want of action at the right time* may occasion the loss of a revival. Especially if God is pouring out His Spirit around us, it is the time for us to work. "If one sigh of a true Christian," says an old divine, "wafts the bark to the desired haven, or stirreth Zion's ship, how much more a gale of sighs breathed by hundreds of believers! If one trumpet sounds so loudly in the ears of God, how much more a concert of all the silver trumpets in Zion sounding together! Where so many hands are lifted up, how many blessings may they not pull down from heaven!"

"Often have I observed," says an experienced winner of souls, "a time when the heavens were big with rain," and yet the thirsty land remained un-watered because we were slothful to do God's work in His time.

We read in *2 Kings 13:18-19* that the dying Elisha commanded King Joash to take a bunch of arrows, and smite the ground with them. "And he smote thrice, and stayed." The dying prophet was deeply grieved in spirit, and said, "Thou shouldest have smitten five or six times; then thou hadst smitten Syria till thou hadst consumed it: whereas, now thou shalt smite Syria but thrice." He finally obtained only three victories over the enemies of Israel, when it would appear that God intended to have given him five or six signal victories – quite to the overthrow of Syria. Upon which it has been remarked that his three strokes indicated his tendency to slackness or indolence, and also were an intimation that a few victories over the enemies of his God would satisfy a soul fond of ease and quiet, and these were all the Lord gave him. This but illustrates how a church may, from irresolution and lack of promptness, lose a splendid victory.

In a time of general awakening, Dr Nettleton wrote in the following strain to one of his brethren in the ministry:

"It becomes every friend of Zion to prepare the way of the Lord through all the towns in this region. The fields are whitening all around us; and though God can create and gather the harvest without human instrumentality, yet we do not expect it. A revival *begun* is likely to subside without the constant pressure of gospel motives on the consciences of the awakened. It is obvious from experience, that God generally blesses far more extensively the means for extending His work, than He does for commencing it in the midst of surrounding darkness. As the conversion of one sinner is often the means of awakening every member of the family, and the impulse is again felt through every kindred branch, and through the village and town; so one town may be the means of revival in another, and that in another. Though some ministers feel the truth of this remark, yet few, if any, realise it in its full force. There is as really a season of harvest in the moral as in the natural world. Now every hand that can hold a sickle needs all its strength. The harvest *fully ripe*, neglected a few days, is forever lost. Other fields may whiten, and the same field a second time, but the former neglected harvest is lost forever. There is a crisis in the feelings of a people, which, if not improved, the souls of that generation will not be gathered. In the season of a revival more *may* be done – more *is* often done to secure the salvation of souls, in a few days, or weeks, than in years spent in preaching at other times. One sermon, in a revival, often does more execution than a hundred equally good out of it. And I verily believe that more good may be *lost* for the want of that *one*, than can be done with it, and with a thousand like it, when the crisis is past."

Again: *inactivity in the church* may prevent a revival. Mr Edwards, in the great revival under his eye, complained of those, "standing at a distance, and keeping silence;" and he declared that such exposed themselves to the curse of Meroz, for not "coming up to the help of the Lord against the mighty." Commenting upon this curse of old, Mr Spurgeon forcibly says that some such curse will assuredly come upon every professing Christian who is backward in helping the church in the day of her soul's travail. "And we shall be hindering the travail of the church if we do not share in it. Many church-members think that if they do nothing wrong, and make no trouble, then they are all right. Not at all, sir; not at all. Here is a chariot, and we are all engaged to drag it. Some of you do not put out your hands to pull; well then, the rest of us have to labour so much the more; and the worst of it is, we have to draw you also. While you do not add to the strength which draws, you increase the weight that is to be drawn. It is all very well for you to say, 'But I do not hinder;' you do hinder, you cannot help hindering. If a man's leg does not help him in walking, it certainly hinders him. Oh, I cannot bear to think of it. That I should be a hindrance to my own soul's growth is bad indeed; but that I should stand in the way of the people of God and cool their courage, and damp their ardour – my Master, let it never be! Sooner let me sleep among the clods of the valley than be a hindrance to the meanest work that is done for Thy name."

Many an earnest minister, with a soul panting for conversions, has lamented this lack of co-operation on the part of his brethren, and been nearly killed by it. An inert, inefficient church, or one self-willed and sluggish church-member, will often defeat the best-directed efforts of the wisest and best minister.

2. But *revivals may be arrested.* Let us turn to this thought. There is a sense in which, after they have been in progress for a season, they may be expected to decline, and probably will decline – perhaps *must* decline. They will decline in respect to the degree of vividness and force with which truth will blaze upon the mind, and get hold of the feelings of the heart. As man is now constituted, and amid the objects by which he is now surrounded, perhaps it is not possible that the mind should have, for any great length of time together, those vivid and impressive views of spiritual objects which for a season it may have, and which in a revival of religion it often does have. We are inclined to think that the laws of mind, as man is in the present world, forbid it. In this sense, then, it may be expected that revivals will, (perhaps in some degree *must*), decline. They may be expected to decline, also, in regard to the number of minds simultaneously affected by them. There will be a season during which the number of the anxious and the rejoicing will increase; and after a while that number will reach its highest point and begin to decline, and then the revival *in this respect* will be at stand, or begin to decline. And this, we think, is a result which no human power or skill in the use of means can prevent.

Conversions ought to be expected to continue. In fact, we have no right to be satisfied unless they are perpetually occurring. Moreover, the quickened graces of the children of God are to be kept alive, and more and more operative. So that, in a sense, the work goes on, though less as a specialty, and more in another channel or direction.

It is only in a narrow sense then that we can justify any decline in a revival. And yet the fact in question is not to be overlooked.

Dr Lyman Beecher's remarks are judicious. He says of the *special sense* of rapid soul-saving, and of highly excited Christian feeling in that one direction, "It is never worthwhile to chase a revival after it is gone by. The laws of mind and of divine sovereignty are in unison, and after the greater stimulus has been applied and failed, it will do no good to apply the less. After one battle and victory, it remains to clear the decks and prepare for another. We often see an opposite policy followed. A pastor deplores that many in whom he is deeply interested are not converted; Christians mourn that the large results which seemed within reach are not attained; and they combine in the use of convulsive efforts to protract the interest and to awaken and convert the unsaved. The consequences are almost uniformly the same; the renewed efforts fail, and pastor and people, instead of rejoicing over the harvest gathered, are filled with despondency."

When we speak of a revival being arrested, then, we refer to its being stopped in its inception; or where it ought to go on to the gathering of many more souls. This frequently occurs; and it is a result to be most anxiously guarded against. We specify some of the causes.

Discouragement at the outset is a frequent cause. This may come from not seeing the whole church alive; perhaps but a very small part of the church. But as a rule the *whole* body is never awake – not even in the most extensive revivals. We are not to wait for this unanimous or general movement.

The writer once said to some brethren who were half-hearted from the inactivity of the body, "I never expect to see this whole church waked up till startled by the trump of the Archangel; let us do our duty, and not wait for others." And he here puts it upon record that in all the blessed revivals he has passed through he has never seen the whole of the church once thoroughly aroused. And this is a common experience with pastors.

Let not Christians spend their time, and divert their attention, by complaining to one another of those who stand back. It is not their business to censure them; neither to *wait* for them; but to *go forward* in the strength of the Lord. If but *two* of them become truly revived themselves, and agree together, and offer up the prayer of faith for a revival of religion, they may expect that the blessing will be granted.

Other causes may conspire to produce discouragement; such as the state of the weather; thinness of audiences; disability of working members, and the like. Hence it is peculiarly requisite in God's people to exercise great patience in *waiting on God under special difficulties and disadvantages.*

In fact, it often occurs that in this way or some other, the pastor, or the evangelist, is awfully tried and humbled at the beginning of a revival; thus being prepared for a rich blessing.

An experience of Dr Edward Payson, which he gives in his journal under date of February 21, 1815, is in place here. He says, of some revival efforts, "I expected severe trials, but had few fears of the event. The trials came, but they did not come in the way that I expected, and therefore I was surprised and overcome by them. The day of the fast was the most dreadful day of my life – the day in which I had most dreadful proofs of more than diabolical depravity of heart. The meeting-house was full, but things did not go on in the manner I had hoped and expected. I thought all was lost; and I now wonder that I lived through it – that a broken heart, (as Mr Newton says disappointed pride and madness are called), was not the consequence. For some days I saw and heard nothing encouraging, and my distress was unabated; but at the next inquiry meeting I found more than sixty inquirers." From that time the work went on.

Unbelief is a chief cause of the cessation of revivals. No sin is more dishonouring to God. It is discrediting the Word of the Almighty. We have the most awful warnings in his Word against indulging it. We read of one place where Jesus did not many mighty works because of the unbelief of the people. If He did not work miracles on account of their unbelief, will He revive His work and convert souls while His people are filled with unbelief? It has been found by universal experience that just in proportion as this prevails, the sinews of moral effort are severed. Let doubt and unbelief take the place of faith, and the Spirit is gone, courage is gone; men beat the air, or sit down in indifference, and the work wanes.

Cessation of a felt dependence on God will arrest a revival. We have a most striking illustration of the importance of this reliance on God in the experience of Dr Griffin; which we give in his own words:

"I preached my first sermon at New Hartford on October 26, 1794. In the fall of 1795 a revival commenced which in the course of the winter apparently brought about fifty to the knowledge of the truth. The neighbouring towns were not then visited: but in October 1798 a great revival began at West Simsbury on the east, and soon extended to Torringford on the west, and we were left like a parched island in the midst of surrounding floods. The agonies of that hour can never be told. First one, and then two, and afterwards more, met me in my study for prayer, and the wrestlings were such as I had never witnessed in a meeting before. On the 4th of November I went to the house of God, saying as I went, 'My soul, wait thou only, *only*, ONLY upon God, for my expectation is from him.' During the morning service I scarcely looked at the audience, and cared not whether they were asleep or awake, feeling that the question of a revival did not lie between me and them, but was to be settled in heaven. In the afternoon, in alluding to the fact that Jesus of Nazareth was passing by and we were left, and could hardly hope for another visit soon, and to the awful prospects of sinners in the middle of life if another revival should not come in twelve or fifteen years, I seemed to take an eternal leave of heads of families out of Christ. I came near falling. I thought I should be obliged to stop, but was carried through. The next day it was apparent that a revival had commenced. A dozen heads of families of the most respectable class were under conviction; and in the course of the winter and the following year a hundred were hopefully added to the Lord. The last time I heard that 4th of November referred to at New Hartford, I was told that between forty and fifty of those converted dated their convictions to that day."

One who does not know something of this experience has not been much in revivals. While this sense of *utter dependence* exists God can consistently bless. When it ceases, the work ceases. Let the example never be forgotten.

Hence, *resting on men or measures* will stop a revival. When an evangelist comes, or the pastor is specially engaged, or special meetings are commenced, the extreme danger is that *private duties* will be neglected – such as heart-searching humiliation, and communion with God. The unconscious feeling is, that *we can do without these now;* and so we part company with God our strength. Just here ministers and workers commit a serious evil. Engaged from day to day, and from evening to evening, in exhorting sinners to repent, and in praying for and comforting the penitent, they are very liable to excuse themselves from the duties of self-examination, and family and private prayer. They thus lose their *spirituality*, and consequently their energy and efficiency. Having put the car in motion, they leap on, and it ceases to move. We may backslide during the progress of a revival! Let it never be forgotten, that *a time of great blessing is a time of great peril!*

This resting on particular measures has another evil worthy of distinct mention. We often see revivals decline as soon as the special means are withdrawn; indicating that the *instrumentality* was made too prominent, and too much trusted in, to the exclusion of the Spirit and power of God and the simple exhibition of divine truth. God, having been overlooked, overlooks us. In the effort to bless ourselves we have lost the blessing of heaven.

Decline of prayerfulness will arrest a revival. Of the "taking hold on God" in times of a revival, Dr Lyman Beecher says that no one who ever felt it can fail to recognise it, as kindred cords are made to vibrate by each other's motion. It is a deep, constant, unutterable desire that God may be glorified in the salvation of souls – it is love to God – it is compassion for man – it is gratitude – it is broken-hearted, child-like desire, flowing from a full fountain, day and night, in ejaculations and protracted wrestlings at the throne of grace. And he says, "I bear testimony to the glory of God and the truth of His promises, that I have never known Him to say to a church in which such a spirit of prayer prevailed, 'Seek ye me in vain.' But without this spirit of prayer a *revival cannot be sustained;* and when it declines, the glorious work must stop. Whenever the humble boldness, the brokenness of heart, the prostration of spirit in the dust, are gone; the tender inimitable pathos of the soul evaporated; and the still small voice of simple unaffected importunity is exchanged for earnest, loud, confident, unhumbled supplication, we will soon witness the gradual suspension of divine influence."

Undue and premature rejoicing may hinder the progress of a revival. "Let not him that girdeth on his harness boast himself as he that putteth it off." A great general cried, "No shouting!" as some new recruits gained a slight victory. The writer has often said in the beginning of a revival, "Let it be headed in," – referring to cutting in trees to compel them to get roots. A revival must have bottom; and exulting belongs to the flowers and the leaves, not the roots.

No doubt incipient revivals are often checked by the confident and even boastful way in which they are regarded and spoken of. Wise leaders will watch this. The biographer of Mr Nettleton tells us that when things began to assume a favourable appearance, he did not like to see professors of religion elated, and disposed to talk about it with an air of exultation. He knew that flattering appearances often suddenly vanish, and he had learned that it is apt to be so when Christians begin to rejoice prematurely. He frowned upon everything like ostentation, and discouraged the disposition which too often prevails, to proclaim a revival upon the first indication of unusual seriousness.

And it must be added, that some, while publishing things to the praise and glory of God, have published things that savoured so strongly of a disposition to exalt themselves, and to make their own agency stand out conspicuously, as to create unhappy impressions and injure the work.

Satisfaction with present results may be in the way of progress. If it be felt that the harvest in the sheaf is all that can be gathered, Christians will be less on their knees with their faces in the dust, and less consecrated to the service of soul-saving.

A pastor of considerable experience in revivals, states that he thinks this a common cause of the cessation of the work. The impression is something like this: The blessing has already been larger than we could have hoped for, considering our infinite unworthiness, and we regard it as a rich earnest of what God will do for us when He shall be pleased to come and revive us again; but we must wait God's time for the conversion of the many who are left. In this way Satan gains an advantage over us.

Diversion of the public mind by any counter-excitement is hurtful to a revival. It is something to keep up the train of sacred associations; and whatever comes in to distract attention is to be avoided.

Hence *sectarian discussions* are hurtful. When these arise, especially if there be unhappy wranglings, the Spirit is grieved, and the revival may be considered at an end.

Indiscretions, wild excitement, and excesses of any kind harm and hinder a work. President Edwards says, "It has been a common device of the devil to overset a revival of religion, when he finds he can keep men quiet and secure no longer, by driving them to excesses and extravagances. He holds them back as long as he can, but when he can do it no longer, then he will push them on, and if possible run them upon their heads. And it has been by this means chiefly that he has been successful, in several instances, to overthrow most promising works."

In summary, *whatever grieves the Spirit* must tend to arrest a work of grace. And if it seems to come to a stand, it ought to alarm Christians, and prompt them to detect and correct the hindering cause.

Happy is that people with whom is found no hindrance to the commencement of a revival! And happy is that people, who, when it has begun, opposes no barrier to its progress!

"O Lord, Revive Thy Work!"

10

Revival Means and Methods

DIVINE sovereignty is nowhere more conspicuous than in revivals of religion. In very many respects, such as their origin, progress, instrumentalities, time, locality, continuance, occurrence here and not there, and the like, all we can say is, "Even so, Father, for so it seemeth good in thy sight."

And hence to many persons there is something offensive in the language commonly used respecting revivals. When they hear or read of directions "how to promote a revival," and "how to conduct a revival," they are apt to feel as if there was of necessity something profane, if not positively impious, in such language. It seems as if man were presuming to attempt, by his own devices and arrangements, to originate and guide the operations of the Holy Spirit. Yet there is no real ground for such an idea. All will admit that even in the economy of grace, the law of cause and effect prevails, though not always discoverable.

And God, in accomplishing His purposes, not only makes use of means, but adapts means to ends. He raises up instruments, and fits them for the work which they are destined to perform. Although no labour of the husbandman will insure to him a harvest, yet he has no reason to expect a harvest without labour: nor has he a right to conclude that it is a matter of indifference what kind of labour he employs. He knows it to be important to till his ground, and to sow in it good seed. So in the moral world must means be adapted to the end. Although Paul plant and Apollos water, while God alone gives the increase, yet we are not to suppose that it is of no consequence what seed is planted, or how it is planted and watered. It is true God might bring to pass different results when the same means are used, yet ordinarily when the results are different there is some difference in the means or the manner of employing them.

With reference to the revival in his day, Mr Edwards affirms that it is the work of God, and not of man. "Its beginning has not been of man's power or device, and its being carried on depends not on our strength or wisdom." But he adds: "God yet expects of all that they use their utmost endeavours to promote it, and that the hearts of all should be greatly engaged in it, and that we should improve our utmost strength in it, however vain human strength is without the power of God."

This is the true view in respect to all revivals. Here, as everywhere, there are to be specific adaptations of means to ends. And we are to *labour* as though the work were entirely our own, and *feel* as if it were God's work alone.

As another general remark, it may be observed that particular revival means and measures greatly change in effectiveness, and often cease to be operative. What was once useful seems worn out, and has to be laid aside. And this is so ordered, probably, that reliance should not be placed on the instrumentality rather than on God.

It is unsafe therefore to predict how revivals will be best carried on in the after time; though of their existence and great extension there cannot be a doubt. Agencies are at God's disposal; and He will shift them as often as He sees fit. We speak here, of course, of *special* agencies; for to the end of the world the ordinary means of grace, properly so-called, will remain the same.

The question may here arise whether we are justified in going about to *produce* a revival spirit – whether, in the absence of any signs of a revival, *special means* may be entered upon to secure a better state of things. Shall we wait for indications of a revival before any particular means are used; or shall we rather use special means to bring into existence those indications?

Different views would be taken of this question. Generally there would be a hesitancy as to employing specific agencies to *produce* a revival spirit. Some would be ready to attach to this the odious term of "getting up" a revival. And yet much can be said in favour of the opposite view. Who would object, for instance, to *praying* more when the state of religion is low? Who would object to *preaching* with more pungency, and perhaps more frequency? Who would object to the 'two or three' getting together more often for crying out with one heart and voice, "Spare, Lord, and give not thine heritage to reproach!" But in such a case special means and measures are *already being employed* to produce a better state of things. We see, then, that it is a matter of *methods*, rather than the thing itself, about which there would be hesitancy.

How, then, are revivals to be promoted? We know not where to find a more comprehensive answer than in the words of a missionary in the West, who wrote thus respecting his people: "We are obediently waiting, anxiously looking, fervently praying, confidently hoping, and every day living, for a revival of the work of God in our charge."

Dr Francis Wayland, in 1832, says of the revival about that period, "The *means* most successfully used for the obtaining of this blessing are these:

1. On the part of the church, putting away all known sin. The enforcement of strict discipline, the universal engagement in behalf of temperance, the renewal of covenants with God, more universal separation from the world, have all been frequently followed by seasons of revival.

2. Setting apart seasons of fasting, and prayer, and humiliation, both individually and collectively, has very commonly been attended with a blessing. Those seasons which have been followed by most powerful revivals have been marked by unusual confession of sin, deep humility, earnest longing for the salvation of others, specially of parents for children and of relatives for relatives. In innumerable cases, such prayers have been in a remarkable manner answered.

3. The more frequent and more faithful preaching of the gospel has been generally followed by an increase of religious attention in a congregation. Meetings for conference, or for exhortation and prayer, by lay brethren, have been very common, and have been very useful."

As an instance of getting ready, or preparing the way for a revival, when as yet there were no indications of one, we mention the great work in Salem, New Jersey, a few years ago; the particulars of which are given by Rev Dr Murphy, then the pastor. He says, "Early in last summer the church resolved to hold a series of meetings, to commence in autumn. From that time many in the church were constantly looking forward to the anticipated meetings, and earnestly praying that God would open the way and prepare His people for the work. The city and vicinity was divided into convenient districts for tract distribution, and personal visiting and conversation on the subject of religion. The sermons and lectures of the pastor, for months, were prepared in view of this special work, and often the burden of prayer in our social meetings had reference to the same end. The condition of the church at that time did not promise any great results. While there were no great difficulties in the way, yet there was a very general apathy and coldness. The pastor canvassed the families connected with the church, taking down the names of the unconverted, and reported to the church that there were more than two hundred of this class. We tried to hold these facts before us. We talked them over in our personal and social intercourse. We laid them before God as we knelt in private and social prayer. Special meetings were appointed to pray for the outpouring of the Holy Spirit. These grew in interest and attendance. As our hearts grew warm under these influences, words of confession and of renewed consecration to God were frequently heard. Just before our special meetings commenced, we had a notice of the meetings printed on the back of one page tracts, cordially inviting all to attend; requesting the sympathies and prayers of Christians in our efforts, and kindly urging the unconverted to prepare to meet God. One of these, with a suitable four page tract, was enclosed in an envelope, bearing the printed inscription: 'Please take this home; read the enclosed carefully; think about the subject earnestly; act honestly and promptly. Time is short.' Packages of these were placed in the hands of distributors, with instructions how to distribute them. Hundreds of them were distributed in the city and surrounding country. Frequently a written note was added, and the whole enclosed in another envelope, directed to some friend, and sent through the post-office, or by the hand of a messenger. Thus we sought to *prepare the way* of the Lord. Special meetings commenced on Sabbath, November 8th, and continued on till Sabbath, March 20th. During this entire time, of 134 days, there were meetings every evening except six. There were also frequent afternoon meetings for prayer and conference, or to meet inquirers, or hear the experience of candidates for baptism. From the very first there was a good attendance, and soon there were anxious inquirers. Rev H G DeWitt, evangelist, of Canandaigua, New York, had been engaged to assist us. He came on the second week of our meetings, and remained nearly four weeks, preaching every evening. His labours were greatly blessed to both the church and community."

Two hundred and fifty were added to the church upon profession in connection with this revival. All would be ready to say, if this be in any sense a going to work to "get up a revival," more of it would be desirable.

The following excellent suggestions were compiled and printed in view of special meetings, by Rev Dr S H Hall; and were a means of good to his people, among whom they were freely distributed.

1. If these meetings are not blessed, not only are the fairest opportunities and the most promising means for the conversion of sinners lost, but the hearts of sinners are rendered more callous to the truth. Therefore *resolve*, before God, to avoid every sin by which the usefulness of these meetings may be prevented, and perform every duty devolving on you to render them successful.

2. Some meetings are not blessed for the want of earnest, importunate, believing prayer. Therefore *resolve* to "pray without ceasing," and to present your prayers in humility and faith.

3. Some meetings are not blessed because men rely too much upon an arm of flesh. Therefore *resolve* to cherish constantly the conviction that without the Holy Spirit no good effects can be expected.

4. These meetings are sometimes unsuccessful because the people of God make such a reliance on divine sovereignty that they neglect to pray or labour with earnestness and fervour, forgetting the uniform and necessary connection between the means and the end. Therefore *resolve* faithfully to use those means which God has promised to bless, namely, Christian example, direct personal conversation, believing prayer.

5. Sometimes these meetings fail of the greatest usefulness because the lay members of the church depend too much upon the minister, or upon each other. Therefore *resolve* to cherish a sense of your personal responsibility; and remember that to labour for the salvation of souls is a common Christian duty.

6. Sometimes these meetings are not blessed because they are not well attended. Therefore *resolve* to attend as much as practicable

yourself; to arrange your domestic concerns so as to permit your family to attend, and to endeavour to persuade your friends and neighbours to attend.

7. Sometimes the cause of sinners remaining unconverted is, that nothing is said to them but from the pulpit. Therefore *resolve* to embrace every proper opportunity to converse with them on the subject of their souls' salvation.

8. Prayers and exhortations that are too long, or on subjects too various, prevent the impression of divine truth, or tend to dissipate impressions when made. Therefore *resolve* that when called upon to pray or speak, you will have your prayers or exhortation *short* and *bearing upon the express object* of the meeting.

9. The harbouring of unkind feelings, the want of charity and forbearance, ill will, the indulgence of former prejudices or animosities, may prevent the outpouring of God's Spirit. Therefore *resolve* that no such unholy feeling shall find a place in your bosom for a moment. Seek reconciliation where you have given or taken offence, and endeavour to cherish toward all your brethren a spirit of Christian fellowship and kindness, and toward every enemy a spirit of forgiveness and affection.

10. Though "hand join in hand," the united efforts of thousands of impenitent sinners cannot prevent a blessing; yet one lukewarm, sinful child of God may do it. Therefore *resolve* to be free from this sin. Renew your covenant engagement. Return to your first love. Come up with greater zeal to "the help of the Lord," that the blood of souls may not be found in your skirts. Remember Achan, (*1 Chronicles 2:7*).

This was a wise method of preparing the way of the Lord; and may well be followed.

There is a large amount of practical common sense in an article which appeared some years ago in a religious weekly, from a pastor whose name was not given. He says, as to preparing for a revival, "I would endeavour to gain clear views of the soul's immense value, by contemplating its nature, its capabilities, what it cost to procure redemption for it, what God is doing to try to save it, what evil angels are doing to try to ruin it, and where it will be ten thousand years hence if saved, or if lost. Remember that each man, and woman, and child in your congregation is the owner of such a soul, and is to have the disposing of it for a long eternity. Ask yourself, can nothing more be done to arouse these immortal beings from their death slumbers? Have I preached to them faithfully, affectionately, plainly? Have I brought the truth on their consciences in private conversation as well as in public? Can I honestly and truthfully say, I am free from all their blood? If you see shortcomings – and doubtless you will see many of them – humble yourself at the foot of the cross, and obtain a fresh baptism of the Holy Ghost. If God has restored to you the joy of His salvation, and imparted a fresh unction from on high, go to the best brother you have in your church, take him alone, and lay open your whole heart to him. Tell him the anxiety you feel for souls, and the desire you have for their salvation. Cordially counsel together, and unite in prayer. If this brother sympathises with you in your views and feelings, invite one or two others to join you, and let them into your secret feelings and purposes. Should you and they think it advisable to have a protracted meeting, then consult whether you will be likely to need any ministerial aid.

"As many people within the bounds of your parish live at a distance from church, special pains should be taken to inform them of the contemplated meeting, and to invite them to attend. That this business may be done thoroughly, it may be well to hold meetings in the different out-neighbourhoods a few days before the services in the church are to commence. Each family in the respective neighbourhoods should be visited by the minister and one of the brethren, or by two brethren in company, and invited to the meeting that evening in their school-house, and also to the contemplated protracted meeting. The evening meeting should be as interesting and solemn as you can possibly make it. Testify to the hearers like one pressed in spirit. Tell them that now is the accepted time, and the day of salvation. Tell them that the opportunity about to be afforded them is like the harvest time to the farmer, and that those who let the opportunity pass without improving it, will be likely to take up the bitter lamentation hereafter: 'The harvest is past; the summer is ended; and we are not saved.' Urge them to come up to the Lord's house during the special effort, and to come regularly.

"On the Sabbath on which, or before which, the protracted meeting is to commence, you should be sure to go into the pulpit full of faith and of the Holy Ghost, and preach as though you never expected to preach again – preach as Paul and Barnabas did in Iconium, where they so spake that a multitude believed. And let your prayers show that you have just come down from the mount. Let the love of souls fill your heart, and fire your tongue. Let your eyes run down with weeping – let your cheeks be wet with tears. Endeavour to lead the church to feel that *fearful responsibility* rests upon them in the coming struggle. Tell them about Meroz, which received a curse instead of a blessing, because she came not up to the help of the Lord against the mighty. In giving the invitation to the unconverted, affectionately urge them to attend the meetings as much as possible, and tell them it may be their last opportunity. Tell them it is a time of merciful visitation, and exhort them not to be like the Jews over whom the Saviour wept because they knew not the time of their visitation, till the things which belonged to their peace were hid from their eyes.

"Having thus prepared the way for commencing a protracted meeting, you need not fear to begin it. I have been in some sixty protracted meetings, and not one of this number which was commenced under anything like the above favourable circumstances, has failed of resulting in a good number of conversions."

Coming to particulars, the first thing as to revival means and methods is, to have our own heart right. Says Mr Earle, whose extensive experience enables him to speak intelligently here, "A revival of religion, like a fire, must begin somewhere 'Behold, how great a matter a little fire kindleth!' A fire often begins with a little match, and works its way through the combustible material about it until it has swept over an extensive region. So a work of grace often commences with a single Christian – never with the whole church. As soon as that one Christian is filled with the Holy Spirit, he goes after others, to lead them to the Saviour, or to induce believers to join him in efforts for a revival. Jesus fulfils his promise, 'Lo, I am with you;' and others are soon moved and melted, and the work begins to widen. So that whoever would promote a revival of religion should begin *with his own heart*, and pray, and confess, and believe, until he feels his heart all subdued and melted by the Holy Spirit – until his love to Christ is glowing, fervid, burning – until he finds himself groaning over the lost condition of men, and, like Jesus, being in an agony, prays more earnestly."

Especially should the *minister first be right.* The reservoir will not rise higher than the fountain. A cold heart will never make other hearts hot. Nor will any *feigned* heat suffice. It must be the fire of the Holy Ghost. Says Edwards, "Especially we that are *ministers* not only have need of some true experience of the saving influence of the Spirit of God upon our heart, but we need a *double portion* of the Spirit of God at such a time as this. We have need to be as full of light as a glass held out in the sun; and with respect to love and zeal, to be like the angels that are a flame of fire. The state of the times requires a *fulness of the divine Spirit in ministers*, and we ought to give ourselves no rest until we have obtained it."

It is a grave mistake that many a minister makes just at this point. If, instead of trying to "marshal a movement," he were reviewing his own deficiencies of heart and duty, charging himself anew with his responsibilities, and devoting himself more faithfully to his people and to God's whole truth, it were far better. A secret work thus begun, is enough to move, in due time, a whole community; and it is the more powerful, because it moves in the legitimate order of action. It begins, bowing to duty first and chief, and leaves results for the most part to come in their natural shape. It works in the hand of God, trustfully, humbly, pertinaciously, and following whithersoever He leads. And when *God* leads His servant into a crisis of great moment, He is in it *naturally*, He moulds it to Himself as if constituted for the time to be its presiding power.

Family work is next to be done. This is the divine order; first the individual, then the household.

Next, *the church is to be right.* Perhaps discipline will need to be resorted to before a revival can be expected. Dr Porter, in his *Lectures*, states that with churches in New England where discipline was neglected, and immorality countenanced, refreshings were not enjoyed. We are to "take up the stumbling-blocks out of the way." Where great obstacles exist, they must be removed. This is the first step.

Fasting and prayer have always been resorted to in order that the church might be in a right state. Dr Payson says: "We have found no means so much blessed to keep religion alive in the church as fasting and prayer. Ever since my settlement, the church has set apart one day quarterly for this purpose." Plainly, such setting apart of whole days for prayer and humiliation before God must be of great advantage. As one result, it tends most forcibly to arrest incipient declension in the church when such declension has begun, and to bring them up anew to the work; and it is like barbed arrows in the hearts of the impenitent sinners. Cases have been known in which they have been awakened while merely passing the place where such meetings were held.

Let Christians also abound in *moral practices*, such as acts of righteousness, truth, meekness, forgiveness, and love towards our neighbour; which are of much greater importance in the sight of God than all the externals of His worship. Let them also be *filled with contrition*. The command of God is to "break up the fallow ground." – *to break up our hearts* – to prepare our minds to bring forth fruit unto God.

In these ways, and others, should the church strive after nearness to God, and fitness to carry on His work.

An excellent deacon once said to his pastor, after a powerful revival, "I wondered, before the work commenced, why you preached so long and pointedly to the church. I knew we were in a cold state, and needed to be woken up; but at the time it seemed almost cruel in you to lay the blame of our never having had a general revival so heavily upon the church. I now see that we needed it, and bless God that he moved you to deal so faithfully with us, both in the pulpit and out of it." If we had all the facts, it would no doubt be found that nearly all of the most powerful revivals have been immediately preceded by a loud and earnest sounding of alarm in the ears of the churches. What a record is this: "When Jesus returned, the people gladly received him; *for they were all waiting for him*."

We cannot but give here some weighty words of Mr Earle: "It is not enough for those of us who preach, that our sermons be able, sound, and well delivered, or that we preach what are sometimes called revival sermons, and that we also visit and converse with men about their souls' interest. It is not enough that the church be aroused and go to work actively for a revival: all this can be done, and but few souls be saved. Nothing can be a substitute for real '*power from on high*.' No amount of study or talent, no effort, however untiring, can take the place of the fulness of Christ's love; 'Not by might nor by power [human], but by my Spirit, saith the Lord.' I have known ministers to preach, and their churches to unite with them, day after day, for weeks together, for a revival, and yet very little to be accomplished. The failure was not because the Spirit was unwilling to work with them and bless their efforts, nor because a continued meeting is not of divine appointment, but because they had not the needed power with God. I am often invited to assist pastors and churches in a series of meetings, with a view of gathering in the multitudes, who are unreached by the ordinary means of grace. Important as it is to reach this class, I have never found any way of doing so, or of reaching the unconverted in the regular congregations, until Christians were filled with the Spirit, and humbled in the dust in agonising prayer."

"Let me say, then, to pastors and to the churches: If you believe the glory of God demands a revival in your midst, and you desire to be instrumental in advancing the work and bringing sinners to the Saviour, first see that your own hearts are thoroughly melted and subdued under a deep sense of the condition of lost men, and that you are filled with the Spirit. Spend days and nights, if necessary, in humiliation, fasting, and prayer, until the Spirit comes down upon you, and you feel that you have power with God; then you will have power with men."

We add a few other particulars:

Contact with revivals is a means of spreading the heavenly flame. Edwards says of the work in Northampton: "There is no one thing that I know of, that God has made such a means of promoting His work among us as *the news of others' conversion*, in the awakening of sinners, and engaging them earnestly to seek the same blessing, and in the quickening of saints."

Pastors, therefore, will do well to *read* of revivals and *visit* revival scenes, and talk of them; and to get their brethren and sisters to do the same.

Suitable *tracts and books* are useful in promoting a revival. The writer well remembers how a youth under his charge, (now a distinguished professor in one of our colleges), was finally brought to repentance through the *Great Inquiry*, which he gave to him, accompanying it with an affectionate letter and many prayers. And in all the revivals among his people, he has freely used such tracts as *Don't put it off; What is it to believe on Christ? Come to Jesus*, (by Newman Hall), and his own *Two Questions:* ["Is your soul safe?"

and "How can I be saved?"] He can safely say that he has known of hundreds of conversions as the consequence.

Personal visitation and conversation should not be neglected. It should be entered upon systematically by the pastor and members, and kept up as far as possible.

Protracted meetings are prominent among revival means and methods. Daily meetings were held in apostolic times. The primitive churches considered this example of Christ and the apostles as authority for them; and they continued, down into the fourth century, to make *daily, direct and earnest efforts* for the conversion of men. Dr Lardner, in his *Ecclesiastical History*, says: "At first the churches assembled every day; and traces of this are found in later times." Bingham, in his *Antiquities of the Church*, says: "The most noted and usual times of meeting, besides the Lord's Day, were the morning and evening of every day, which in times of peace were *constantly and regularly observed*."

In 1866, a paper upon *special revival efforts* was issued in Boston over the signatures of some sixty well-known ministers, of the different evangelical denominations, which deserves to be incorporated in this volume. They say that it is abundantly evident that the conversion of the world was advancing far more rapidly during the first three centuries, and was prospectively much nearer its final completion fifteen hundred years ago than it is today. Why this difference in the success of the primitive and the modern churches? Our answer is, *few modern churches make all the effort that primitive churches made; and that but occasionally*. Look at the reformation in the sixteenth century. That glorious revival of religion, which spread over Western Europe, was begun and carried on by labours not unlike those of the apostolic and primitive churches. It was not by Sabbath service merely. It was by *daily, direct and earnest efforts for that special purpose*, that that great work was promoted. Moreover, the great and powerful revivals for which our own country has been distinguished, in former years, were the results of special efforts. In the revival of 1735, which extended through Western Massachusetts, and parts of Connecticut and New Jersey, bringing many thousands into the church, President Edwards, Mr Enfield, Wheelock, Pomroy and others, left their own pulpits for months together, and laboured as evangelists in distant places, *preaching several times a week*, or *daily*.

Their preaching was direct and pungent, and aimed at the immediate conversion of sinners; and was attended with great success. In 1740, Mr, Whitefield, Pendleton, the Tennents and others, went on preaching tours through the country, from Maine to Philadelphia, arousing the churches and sinners to repentance; and the result was, that in eighteen months, probably not less than forty thousand souls were added to the Lord, or about one-sixth part of the whole population in this section of the country.

The great revival of 1797, which lasted five or six years, was promoted by preaching tours, ministers being sent out by the associations, two and two, for six months at a time, performing the work of evangelists. The churches prepared for their coming by fasting and prayer, renewal of covenant, and so on, and a revival almost always followed. The powerful work which extended from Ohio, through Kentucky, to the Carolinas and Georgia, in 1802-3, was promoted by similar efforts of the different denominations united. Next comes a period of continuous revivals for twenty-five years, beginning about 1807, which spread over the whole country. Here we need not detail facts which are familiar to all. It is well-known that the labours of such men as Messrs Nettleton, Finney, Smith, Parmerlee, Foot, Saxton, McAuley, Kirk and many others, were intimately connected with these extensive triumphs of the gospel.

Again; the importance of supplementing the labours of the Sabbath with direct and earnest efforts during the week was also clearly seen in the great revival of 1857-8. Dr Prime, in his "authentic account" of the rise and progress of that work, says, that "in New York and Brooklyn there were not less than one hundred and fifty daily prayer-meetings established, many extra places being fitted up for that purpose." He also says, that "a thoroughly organised plan of systematic visitation, adopted and carried out by these two cities, *had much to do* with the beginning, spread and continuance of this revival." A convention on revivals was held at Pittsburgh, in the autumn of 1857. This convention continued in session three days, for the purpose of considering the necessity of *a general revival* in all the churches. A plan of personal visitation was adopted, by which every family should be visited by the pastor and some experienced member, and on the first Sabbath in January, multitudes of ministers delivered discourses on the necessity and practicability of revivals; and the following Thursday was observed as a day of humiliation, fasting and prayer. All these arrangements powerfully affected the country. Immediately after this convention at Pittsburgh, another was called at Cincinnati, having the same object in view. It was largely attended, and followed by similar results. Thus the public mind was thoroughly aroused. And it is to be noticed, that churches which made no special effort at that time added comparatively few to their numbers by profession; as may be seen by referring to the *Congregational Quarterly*, January numbers, for the years 1858 and 1859.

Again; during the last four or five years, churches that have connected "special efforts" with the ordinary means, though only for short periods, have added converts by scores and hundreds; while those churches that have not made such efforts have not averaged two conversions a year. Statistics show that the Orthodox churches in the United States have not made an average net gain of one and one half members a year for the last eight years; and probably not for the last twenty-five years. Aside from the results of "special revival efforts" made by a few churches, the body of Orthodox churches have not made a net gain of one member each, for the last eight years; and probably not for the last thirty years. So far as can be ascertained from their statistical reports, the churches of the other evangelical denominations have not averaged a greater number of additions by profession during this period. Whoever will examine the reports of additions by profession to those churches that make no "special revival efforts," and compare them with those churches known to make such efforts, will be satisfied as to the comparative value of the two systems of means for the conversion of men.

Again; an examination of these statistical reports will show, that the great mass of churches that rely on the ordinary means alone, barely hold their own from year to year. Dr E Porter, in his *Letters on Revivals*, says: "With no greater degree of sanctifying influence than has been enjoyed for the last half century, (ending 1832), which has been a comparatively favoured period, the church could scarcely hold her own." How much less, then, in ordinary times. These statistics further show that many churches, in cities especially, lose more by death from year to year, than they add by profession; and are sustained chiefly by additions by letter. They are among those churches which make no special effort for the conversion of men. Sixty-one churches in the nine principal cities of New England, in 1864, lost by death more than they gained upon profession. The body of Orthodox churches of Connecticut, lost in five years, ending 1864, 480 by death more than they gained by profession.

The General Conference of Maine in 1864, reported two hundred and thirty-seven churches, with a gain of only one hundred and sixty-two members over losses, or less than one to a church; while the other ten churches, by *extra efforts* for a few weeks, added two hundred and seventy-two by profession, or twenty-seven to a church.

The General Association of New Hampshire in 1864, reported one hundred and eighty churches, with a gain of only twenty-three over losses, or one to every seven churches; while the other three churches, by *extra efforts*, gained by profession one hundred and forty-three over losses, which is more than three hundred per cent, in favour of "extra efforts."

The General Convention of Vermont, in 1864, reported one hundred and ninety-two churches, with a gain of only nineteen over losses, or one to every ten churches.

The General Association of Massachusetts in 1864, reported four hundred and seventy-four churches, with a *loss* of eighty-four by death more than they gained by profession, while fifteen churches, that made *extra efforts*, added, by profession, three hundred and seventy-seven over losses.

The General Association of Connecticut, in 1864, reported a loss in five years, ending 1864, of four hundred and eighty more than they gained by profession, there having been little or no "*extra efforts.*"

According to statistics given in the tract of Dr A Wilbur, of Boston, a quarter of a century ago, and subsequently published in the appendix of Rev Jacob Knapp's *Autobiography*, five Baptist churches in Boston, which employed the labours of an evangelist, and held special meetings at that time, gained, during four years, fifty-one per cent, on their membership; and excluded fifteen per cent. All the rest of the churches of the city gained thirteen and a half per cent, and excluded nineteen per cent. Statistics of the whole State of Massachusetts, covering a period of eight years, showed a gain of membership in eleven Baptist churches employing an evangelist, of thirty-one, and an exclusion of twenty-three per cent; the rest of the churches of the State gaining a trifle over one per cent, and excluding twenty-eight and one-third per cent.[1]

From this brief survey, it is sufficiently evident that Sabbath services, in connection with frequent and protracted "special efforts," is the true gospel system of means for the conversion of men; and, that all theories and opinions to the contrary, and all objections to such efforts, are set aside by the authority of Christ and the apostles, and by the example of the primitive churches for three hundred years, and by the simple evidence of facts occurring among us at the present day. If these things are so, is it not the duty of the churches to address themselves to more continuous endeavours for the conversion of perishing mankind?

Having said thus much, some *cautions* are in place as to all protracted effort. The immediate aim should not be an excitement. Sad results have followed upon the track of preachers who have felt bound to get up a sensation, by foul means if they could not do it by fair. Oddity, noise, denunciation, attacks on private character, and everything to kindle the passions and set tongues in motion, are sometimes resorted to, to accomplish their object. The most deplorable effects have followed from such a policy.

Dr Porter makes some good points. "Let protracted meetings never supersede the stated, ordinary means of grace. Let them not disturb the customary worship of the Sabbath, nor impede the regular action of a local ministry. Let churches beware that they do not contract a false taste for preaching from love of novelty and excitement; and after having heard a few extra sermons, complain of ordinary discourses, such as their own pastors can prepare amid the pressing engagements of a revival. And let them beware, too, that their religion does not degenerate into mere alternations of zeal and apathy."

Very sensible and weighty is a caution from Dr Griffin as to neglect of *prayer*. He says: "God forbid that I should speak against protracted meetings; but I will speak against their abuse. In this imperfect world, it is almost impossible that such a stimulating institution should not be abused. It is so much easier to enter into the excitements of a protracted meeting than to 'tug at the oar of

---

1. The above is taken, mainly, from the paper of 1866, which we referred to. See also chapter 18 – *Revivals the Hope of the World.*

prayer' in secret, or even to exercise a holy heart – so much easier to move the people by these impassioned forms than to bring down the Holy Ghost by the struggles of faith – that there is the utmost danger that these meetings will be put in the room of secret prayer, and of the Holy Ghost, and even of personal religion. When I see them relied on to produce revivals without previous prayer, and a boast made that Christians were stupid when they began; when I see a revival of ten days produce its hundred converts, and the people who were stupid before relapse into the same stupidity at the end of the protracted meeting, I cannot but say, 'How different are these from the revivals of the last forty years, which were preceded by long agonies of desire and prayer, and which transmitted their spirit to many succeeding months.'"

Many questions may arise as to conducting *revival meetings*, which cannot in this place be noticed. [2] *Scripture truth* should be very largely, and every way, inculcated. The more interest, the more instruction, should be the rule. When Bible truth is shunned or rejected, then, neither noise nor excitement, the thronged assembly nor the crowded anxious seat, can be relied upon as an evidence of a work of grace.

Much more depends upon *little things* in revivals than is commonly supposed. As an illustration: Mr Nettleton, used to advise the people at the close of his meetings to go home as still as possible – to say nothing to each other on the way about the sermon, or anything else, but to "commune with their own hearts and be still."

Requests for prayer should always be encouraged. As we have seen elsewhere, in great revivals, such requests have been a prominent feature.

Prayer-meetings should hold a foremost place in all revival movements. It may be said that the revival of 1857–8 was mainly carried on by means of them. And the good sense exhibited in their management is worthy of imitation.

The *converts* may be helpful in carrying on a revival. On suitable occasions, let them relate briefly their religious exercises, exhort their impenitent companions, and lead in prayer in social meetings. This should, indeed, be managed with caution and skill; but when it is properly conducted, it is a powerful auxiliary in extending a work of grace.

2. See chapter 16 – *Treatment of Inquirers.*

Concluding this chapter, we say of those called to lead in revivals, let them enter into their work pouring out their hearts to God for a blessing. And whenever they see the want of any special means and methods to bring the truth more powerfully before the minds of the people, let them adopt them and not be afraid; and God will not withhold His blessing. Many a man has formed his plans in anticipation of a wished-for revival, but when it came, these were all swept away, and he felt he was just forced to do the Lord's work in the Lord's way. Christ will plead His own cause, and "Wisdom is justified of her children." There is no end to the objections of an ungodly world, and of carnal worldly professors. And one of the greatest errors to be dreaded, and watched and prayed against, is that of an excessive caution under the guise of prudence.

Obviously, we are justified in being intent "by all means" on "saving some, pulling them out of the fire." The great thing is to *work while God works*. The sunshine, while it lasts, must be fervidly improved. The tide must be waited on, and all hands must be at work. The Philippian jailor was converted at midnight; and Paul, once at least, continued his speech until the same hour. So even by *extraordinary measures* we must be anxious that men be saved from "the wrath to come."

"O Lord, Revive Thy Work!"

11

Preaching and Revivals

FOREMOST among the instrumentalities for saving men is the pulpit. "It pleased God by the foolishness of preaching to save them that believe."

But preaching is not alike effective. When God called Aaron to be high-priest, he said, as a reason, "I know that he can speak well." Of Paul and Barnabas it is written that "they so spake that a great multitude believed." Though a sovereign, yet the divine Being is not an arbitrary sovereign; and it cannot be denied that there is some connection between the means and the end in powerful preaching. What would affect a man *without* the Spirit, we might expect to be employed by the Spirit to carry conviction to the heart. Otherwise the kind of preaching were a matter of entire indifference.

Of Luther it was said each word was a thunderbolt. We are told that when Venn preached, men fell before the word like slaked lime. Baxter affirmed that he had reason to believe he never preached one sermon in vain.

A prevailing defect in preaching is, that it is not aimed at the conversion of men. Doubtless there are other legitimate ends; but this is not sufficiently a *chief end*. The thought may seem surprising, but there are multitudes of ministers, and deeply pious ones too, who never once in all their lives distinctly concentrated their purposes to the single point of converting men. It is related of two preachers that one had great success in bringing men to Christ; the other converting none. The latter inquired of the former what was the reason of this difference. "Why," replied the other, "the reason is that I *aim at a different end* from you in preaching. My object is to convert sinners, but you aim at no such thing; and then you lay it to sovereignty in God that you do not produce the same effect. Take one of my sermons, and preach it to your people, and see what the effect will be." The man did so, and preached the sermon, and it did produce effect; and he was almost frightened when sinners became concerned.

If one would be successful in soul-saving, there must be that home-dealing which means conversion. The people must be plied from day to day with plain, faithful, scriptural preaching to them, and not merely *before them*. The conviction must be wrought on the mind that the preacher is in earnest; that he means and feels what he says; that, in the words of Baxter, he "*never expects to meet one of them in heaven unless they be truly converted.*"

The aim at bringing men to repentance, therefore, would greatly intensify the power of our pulpits. It is more needed than anything else. The defensive outworks of Christianity are strong enough, and the thing to do is to assume the offensive, and advance on the enemy, and "shell" him out of his entrenchments. Edwards said in his day: "Men may abound in light and have no heat. How much has there been of this sort in the Christian world in this age! Was there ever an age wherein strength and penetration of reason, extent of learning, exactness of distinction, correctness of style, and clarity of expression did so abound? And yet was there ever an age wherein there has been so little sense of the evil of sin, so little love to God? Our people do not so much need to have their heads stored, as to have their hearts touched."

More sermons are needed which are made and meant to *do execution* – sermons which grasp and make bare and wield some mighty idea, holding it up, and turning it around, and repeating it, if need be, as does Demosthenes the one main point in his oration on the Crown, until it becomes a palpable thing, and the audience *feel* its form and pressure – sermons having the "agonistical," the wrestling element in them, as Aristotle calls it – sermons put together on the principle that "force in writing consists in the maximum of sense with the minimum of words," whose sentences are pounded together until they crack; and where figure, trope, allegory, metaphor, antithesis, interrogation, anecdote – anything that can awaken interest and deepen impression is resorted to – sermons supported and sinewed with the, "Thus saith the Lord," and then charged with living truth and aimed *directly at the conscience and the heart*, singling out each hearer, and saying, "*Thou art the man*," and "*I have a message from God unto thee;*" and then making pursuit after that man, in clear, rapid, concentrated utterances, and pressing upon him, and narrowing his way, and hemming him in, and smiting him down with terrible volleys, until, quivering and breathless, he crouches between the law that condemns and the cross that saves.

Before the world is converted to Christ there will be much more of this sort of preaching.

It is highly instructive, in this connection, to study the preachers and preaching most blessed in revivals. These salient points are everywhere seen – *scripturalness in matter, and plainness, earnestness, directness and fervency in application and appeal.*

The Reformers found the world in ignorance of Scripture doctrine – especially of free salvation through Christ. Their power was in wielding the cross. Luther, in Germany, preached justification by faith. Calvin taught it in Switzerland, and parts of France and Italy. Knox in this way extended the Reformation in Scotland. And wherever a spiritual change was wrought in England, it was effected through grace by the doctrine of "Christ and him crucified." Whatever external form of organisation "the church" received, whether walking with the Establishment, or choosing to fall into the ranks of Dissent, its spiritual renovation occurred under the same truths. These were the truths which the English reformers and their successors, for more than a hundred years inculcated on their hearers, and by them spiritual religion made conquests, and converts were multiplied.

Whitefield and the Wesleys, at a later day, in the rise of "Methodism" magnified these same doctrines, and by them wrought their glorious victories for Christ.

The American preachers, in the early revivals, found the cardinal facts of regeneration by the Holy Ghost, and the necessity of a converted church-membership, fallen into comparative neglect or contempt; and their power was in giving them prominence. This was the mighty upheaving force in those great revivals. Edwards, with the clarity of a sunbeam, insisted much on justification by faith alone. And he says, "The beginning of the late work of God in this place was so circumstanced, that I could not but look upon it as a remarkable testimony of God's approbation of the doctrine of justification by faith alone, here asserted and vindicated. *At that time*, while I was greatly reproached for defending this doctrine in the pulpit, and just upon my suffering a very open abuse for it, God's work wonderfully broke forth amongst us, and souls began to flock to Christ as the Saviour in whose righteousness alone they hoped to be justified."

Seizing upon a resultant fact of this doctrine of justification by faith, Mr Edwards wrote that terrible sermon, *Sinners in the hands of an angry God*. He went down to Enfield and preached it there on July 8th, 1741. While the people of the neighbouring towns, says Trumbull, were in great distress about their souls, the inhabitants of Enfield were very secure, loose and vain. A lecture had been appointed there, and the neighbouring people were so affected at the thoughtlessness of the inhabitants, and had so much fear that God would, in His righteous judgment, pass them by, that many of them were prostrate before him a considerable part of the previous evening, supplicating the mercy of heaven on their behalf. And when the time appointed for the lecture came, a number of the surrounding ministers were present, as well as some from a distance – a proof of the prayerful interest felt on behalf of the town. Mr Edwards chose for his text, the words, 'Their foot shall slide in due time,' (*Deuteronomy 32:35*). When they went into the meeting-house, the appearance of the assembly was thoughtless and vain; the people scarcely conducted themselves with common decency. But as the sermon proceeded, the audience became so overwhelmed with distress and weeping, that the preacher was obliged to speak to the people and desire silence, that he might be heard. The excitement soon became intense; and it is said that a minister who sat in the pulpit with Mr Edwards, in the agitation of his feelings, caught the preacher by the skirt of his dress, and said, 'Mr Edwards! Mr Edwards! is not God a God of mercy?' Many of the hearers were seen unconsciously clinging by their hands to the posts, and the sides of the pews, as though they already felt themselves sliding into the pit. This fact has often been mentioned as a proof of the strong and scriptural character of Edwards' peculiar eloquence – the eloquence of truth attended by the influence from heaven – for his sermons were read without gestures." [1]

Davies, of Virginia, saw more conversions under his ministry than did Edwards. He preached the same truths, however, and with the same intense earnestness and unflinching fidelity. No one can read his published sermons without having his spirit stirred as with the sound of a trumpet. And under such breathing thoughts and burning words, multitudes bowed as before the majesty of God.

It has been remarked upon as an interesting fact, that three such men as Jonathan Edwards, George Whitefield, and Samuel Davies should have been contemporary. They differed widely in their characteristics; but they were all "sons of thunder." Davies was less logical than Edwards, and had less extemporaneous fluency than Whitefield; but he exceeded them both in true eloquence. Edwards acted upon men through their understanding; Whitefield through their imagination and passions; Davies through all the soul's avenues. He had such command of every faculty and affection, that he swept the whole field of intellect and feeling. By fact, by argument, by description, by appeal, by entreaty, by expostulation, he addressed man's entire spiritual nature, and roused it from its lowest depths. Edwards caused men to think deeply, and Whitefield made them feel strongly. But Davies accomplished both – awakening at once thought and emotion.

The successful preachers in later revivals, pressed the consciences of men with the same truths and terrible earnestness as did their predecessors. Dr Lyman Beecher, speaking of his preaching before a work of grace, says, "My object was to cut and thrust, hip and thigh, and not to ease off. I had been working a good part of a year with my heart burning, and my people feeling nothing. Now I took hold without mittens."

Says one, speaking from experience concerning the preaching of that day, "Oh how we smarted under it. I remember it well in my own case. We complained of some of Paul's hard sayings, and wondered why our ministers dwelt so much upon them. We wanted to get to heaven in some easier way. But instead of abating one jot or tittle to relieve us, they pressed harder and harder, driving us from one

1. See the sermon, and criticisms, in *History and Repository of Pulpit Eloquence*, Volume 2, page 395.

refuge to another, till there was no hiding-place left. The law, which we had broken times without number, we were made to feel was just; its fiery penalty hung over our heads, and we must submit or die."

Dr Griffin's statement on this point is worthy of careful study – the more so as he was a prince in pulpit oratory, and greatly blessed in revivals. He says: "Sinners have been constantly urged to immediate repentance, and every excuse has been taken away. At the same time we have not denied or concealed their dependence for the sake of convincing them of their obligations. On the contrary, we have esteemed it vital to urge their dependence in order to drive them from all reliance on their own strength, and to make them *die* to every hope from themselves. All that you can possibly gain by flattering their independence, is to extort a confession of their *obligations;* for as to matter of fact, they *will not* submit until they are made willing in the day of God's power. And if you can fasten upon them their obligations without that falsehood which robs God of His glory, pray let it be done. This we have found it possible to do. We have shown them that their obligations rest on their faculties, and are as reasonable and as complete as though the thing required was merely to walk across the floor; that their faculties constitute a natural ability, that is, a *full power to love and serve God, if their hearts were well disposed*, leaving nothing in the way but a bad heart, for which they are wholly to blame if there is any blame in the universe; that sin can rest nowhere but in the heart, and that if you drive it beyond the heart, you drive it out of existence; that *they alone* create the necessity for God to conquer them, and to decide whether He will conquer them or not; that it is an everlasting blot on creation that God has to speak a second time to induce creatures to love Him, much more that He has to constrain them by His conquering power; and yet after all His provisions and invitations – after He has sent His Son and His Spirit to save them – after He has opened the door wide and stands with open arms to receive them – they will still break their way to perdition if His almighty power do not prevent; that by their own fatal obstinacy they are cast entirely upon His will; that they are wholly in His hands – that if He frown they die, if He smile they live for ever. This is the grandest of all means to press them out of themselves, to cast them dead and helpless upon God, to make them *die* that they may be made alive."

At a later day came Nettleton, so highly honoured of God in soul-saving. In 1825 Rev Mr Cobb, (of Taunton, Massachusetts), who heard him preach sixty times, gave a description of the man and his preaching to this effect: "His sermons were clear, sound, able, full of thought, direct and simple, with unity of design. He seemed to be destined to be understood. As the revival progressed, he preached more and more closely and doctrinally. The great truths of the gospel were the weapons of his warfare, and were wielded with a spirit and an energy which the people were unable to gainsay or resist. He was remarkably clear and forcible in his illustrations of the sinner's total depravity, and his utter inability to procure salvation by unregenerate works, or any desperate efforts. He showed the sinner that his unregenerate prayers for a new heart, his impenitent seeking, striving and knocking would be of no avail; and that absolute, unconditional submission to a sovereign God was the first thing to be done."

In another description we are told that he was solemn, affectionate, and remarkably plain. His style was simple, perspicuous and energetic. His illustrations were familiar and striking; such as rendered his discourses intelligible to persons of the weakest capacity, and at the same time interesting to persons of the most cultivated intellect. He always commanded the attention of the audience. There was an earnestness in his manner which carried conviction to the minds of his hearers that he *believed* what he spoke, and that he believed it to be truth of *everlasting moment*, and there was also a directness in his preaching, which made the hearers feel that *they* were the persons addressed.

While on a visit to Scotland, Dr Nettleton preached in Edinburgh; and during the sermon, while pressing home the high claims of the Almighty, a woman who sat in a remote part of the house was so affected that, leaving her seat, and walking up in front of the pulpit, she spoke aloud, "Dear sir, don't forget, that 'God so loved the world that he gave his only begotten son, that whosoever believeth on him might not perish, but have everlasting life.' "

Among living preachers who are successful in leading souls to Christ, few are more blessed of God than Rev A B Earle. It has been the writer's privilege to be with him in a series of meetings, and to know him intimately as a brother beloved. He has travelled in almost all parts of the country, and preached *seventeen thousand* sermons. On the matter of "Preaching and Revivals," such an example is deserving of study. It is often asked, "Where is his power?" We answer, obviously *from God.* Like all good ministers of Jesus Christ, he lives in communion with the skies, and is invested with an energy more than human. As has been remarked of him, one can hardly be with him long without a persuasion that he loves God, and loves the gospel, and loves the souls of men – without a persuasion that with him, "religion is the chief concern," and that it possesses his mind and heart and life.

But he is also skilled in the work of an evangelist; and his preaching, while apparently deficient in some elements of power, is eminently powerful. "It would be difficult," writes Rev Dr Yerkes, of New Jersey, with whom he has laboured successfully, "to analyse his preaching; yet considering its power, I esteem it worthy of study. Doubtless it is largely adapted to revival work; yet there is an element in it that would give power to all preaching. Where is that power? We do not find it if we judge the preacher according to the schools; and yet there are, I presume, men who have been trained in our schools, and possessed of scholastic attainments of the highest order, who confess his power as a preacher of the gospel. He would not, perhaps, be regarded as a logical preacher, and yet no arrangement of logic could be better adapted to secure the results contemplated. The right thing is said in the right place and at the right time. His discourses are rarely marked by that thoroughness of treatment which presents a complete picture, but they do impress the hearer with the greatness of the truth preached, in a way that makes them thoroughly effective. Nor would Mr Earle be considered an eloquent preacher; yet he moves men as they are not often moved by public discourse. If we are not charmed by eloquence of speech, we must confess the effects of true eloquence. Pascal says that eloquence makes the hearer feel the theme as the orator himself feels it. Mr Earle's preaching does produce that feeling. It is not an excitement, but deep feeling upon the most important subject which can engage the attention of mortals. Without the coherency of logic, his sermons are forceful. Without the appearance of thoroughness, they are complete when considered in their adaptation to the end of preaching – which is not merely to mouth truth, but to impress it upon the heart."

An eminent Methodist clergyman, (Rev Dr Steele, of Massachusetts), writes, "Having recently heard him preach thirty sermons in two weeks, and closely watched in order that I might find the secret of his power, I deem it due to the cause of Christ, especially to his ministry, to report my observations. The hidings of his strength lie in his faith and philosophy. He has faith in God, simple, child-like, mighty trust. He is always praying. Previous to every sermon he would call me into his room to kneel down by his side at Jesus' feet and seek power from on high. Often in the public assembly he would call on all the people to bow down in prayer for himself, that the Spirit would attend the Word. He has faith in the truth, reading and expounding some portion of the Scriptures at every meeting. He reads the Bible as if he believed every syllable and comma to be inspired of God. He dwells much upon the historical parts of the Old Testament and extracts the marrow of the gospel from what many modern preachers regard as dry bones. His simple aim is to set the unadorned truth before the mind utterly regardless of elegance of style. Though naturally witty, he conscientiously suppresses everything which would divert from the clearest and most impressive exhibition of divine truth. His illustrations are almost always drawn from the incidents of his own long experience as an evangelist. He dwells upon the terrors of the Lord, and never speaks of hell as 'the great elsewhere.' Yet he holds up the sterner truths of the gospel no more frequently than did his Great Exemplar. In listening to him, one is strikingly convinced that the modern evangelical pulpit has, within a generation, largely dropped out the law and its penalties, under the influence of an excessive sentimentalism which is leaking insensibly into the minds of Christians from the subtle scepticism which pervades the atmosphere. His fearless proclamation of the painful, and hence neglected truths of the Gospel, in contrast with that insensible softening down of these truths prevalent in the modern pulpit, is no small element of brother Earle's power."

Rev Dr Richard Fuller, in the *Religious Herald*, Richmond, Virginia, in 1870, gave the following vivid description of Mr Earle and his preaching: "We have heard Mr Earle three times, and do not hesitate to pronounce him one of the ablest men we ever listened to. Some say, 'The secret of his power is in prayer.' Certainly, and the secret of all spiritual power with men, is power with God. This was true not only of Paul, but of Jesus, the only perfect preacher. To the prayer of faith we apply what the apostle says of charity, 'Though I speak with the tongues of men or angels, and though I have all knowledge that I can explain all mysteries and do not pray with faith,' it is all sounding brass and a tinkling cymbal. 'He leads a holy life.' Yes, but the success of one's ministry is no proof of holiness; it may be a fatal snare to the soul, as it was to those who said, 'Have we not prophesied,' etc. A blind man may hold up a torch for others to walk by.

"If these things are said as meaning that power in prayer and holiness are less than eloquence, they are even more wicked than foolish. If they are intended as deductions from Mr Earle's character as a sacred orator, they betray a sad misconception, we humbly conceive, as to the real elements of power in a preacher. His very appearance draws reverent attention. There is not a particle of that self-consciousness which sometimes shows itself in an affected simplicity and naturalness, in the awkward attempt to be easy, to put out the hand gracefully, to modulate the voice artistically. He plainly forgets himself; and before he has uttered twenty words, the people forget the man as completely as Peter was forgotten on the day of Pentecost; they are engrossed with the truths he is proclaiming.

"Brother Earle's intellectual endowments are remarkable; and would at once be felt were he at the bar or in Congress. The closest reasoning, the most natural wit and humour; a lively imagination, a correct taste; an intuitive insight into human nature; resources of strong native Saxon, of warm, gushing emotions, of incident and narrative and illustration drawn from every quarter – these attributes and advantages he possesses and uses without any effort, and with the entire self-possession which ever accompanies the sense of power. And even all this is comparatively little. The one grand peculiarity in all truly great men is thorough earnestness. On some summer's afternoon we have sat admiring the beautiful sheets of lightning which, now with one broad rosy suffusion, and then with white and yellow corruscations, illumined the sombre clouds piled up along the horizon. Afterwards the heavens have gathered blackness, and the living thunder has leapt from crag to crag, and the flowing bolt has shivered the solid oak in its resistless course. The difference between the electric fluid in its cold, ineffectual splendours, and that same element in its concentrated energy, is not too strong an illustration of the force of real earnestness in a preacher, compared with those graces and accomplishments which are often called sacred eloquence.

"Of M'Cheyne, a Scotch woman said, 'He preaches as if he is a dyin' a'most to have ye converted.' Mr Earle preaches just in that way. A man who believes what he says must be powerful. Our brother believes what he says. Do ministers read the Bible much? We fear not. Mr Earle *studies* the Bible, and really *believes* God's testimony. Hence he is full of 'divine simplicity.' Hence too his soul is ever at a white heat, and yet perfectly calm. And all this earnestness is inwrought in his heart and diffused through his pulses to his finger-tips, by a faith which never falters, by a love, a sympathy which often melts him into an agony of tears, and by the power of the Holy Spirit, who never disappoints the soul which hangs in utter dependence on Him."

From the foregoing, we have already an idea of the preaching which is adapted to awaken and save souls. For this reason the above examples are given. We may crystallise the essential elements of effective revival preaching into a few points.

God is honoured in all powerful preaching. "He makes God look big;" was the remark of a plain parishioner of one of the old-style New England divines. Evidently, God will honour that which honours Him. "I have found," says Edwards, "that no discourses have been more remarkably blessed than those in which the doctrine of God's absolute sovereignty with regard to the salvation of sinners, and His just liberty with regard to answering the prayers or succeeding the pains of mere natural men, continuing such, have been insisted on."

The *truth is honoured* in effective preaching. We find an illustration of this in the labours of Rev E P Hammond, evangelist. It is a marked feature in his meetings that he reads and comments upon the Scriptures, the Old and New Testaments; often giving a wonderful freshness and vividness to scenes and incidents and utterances there recorded. In his sermons, too, he deals largely in the true sayings of God. Rev Jacob Knapp's heavy blows are often simply solid Scripture utterances. The same is true of Rev J S Inskip, the Methodist evangelist.

We have already seen the same thing in the preachers of other days. Strong preachers have ever been Bible-preachers. The sermons of Bunyan, and Baxter, and Flavel, and men of their stamp, were full of God – instinct with living doctrines. Their very garb was after the Scripture pattern. Of Chalmers it has been said that, his sermons "held the Bible in solution." A peculiar energy attends the divine Word. It is the "Sword of the Spirit;" the "fire and the hammer that breaketh the rock in pieces." It is "quick and powerful, and sharper than any two-edged sword." It is "perfect, converting the soul," and "making wise the simple." "I will hazard the assertion," says Fisher Ames, "that no man ever did, or ever will become truly eloquent without being a constant reader of the Bible, and an admirer of the purity and sublimity of its language."

The Bible is the battery through which the Holy Spirit illuminates and saves. If one would have a felt power, let him keep these thunders rolling through the souls of the auditory.

Timeliness and adaptation are necessary to effectiveness in preaching. It needs special preaching to secure special ends. At the beginning of a revival, the preaching especially should be to Christians, urging upon them their obligations. Suppose a minister at such a time to bring before his people that fundamental truth in all religion – the existence of God, and to attempt, by a process of reasoning, to vindicate it against the objections of atheism; or suppose he were to discuss, in an elaborate manner, the historical evidence of Christianity – this, in certain circumstances, would be very proper; but it would be ill-adapted to awaken saints and guide souls to Christ: and so out of place now.

All successful revival preachers are thorough with the church in what may be called preparatory work. And as a rule, revivals are deep and thorough in proportion to the thoroughness of the preaching at the outset.

While, however, there should be great plainness in preaching to Christians, there should be great *kindness* and *tenderness* in doing it. President Edwards deplored a style of preaching which censured professed Christians as unconverted because they did not come up to the work. He terms it "the worst disease" that attended the revival, and altogether contrary to the spirit of the gospel. Mr Earle tells of a most interesting experience which he once had on this point. In beginning a series of union meetings, he thought himself fully prepared, and expected immediate results. "My first aim," he says, "was to preach so as to lead the churches nearer to Christ. Accordingly, I prepared five sermons for Christians, as clear and pointed as I knew how to make them. The first four had no apparent effect. I wondered at it. The fifth was prepared with a scorpion in the lash. It was a severe one, and the last harsh sermon I have preached, and the last I ever expect to preach: but this, too, was powerless. I then went to my closet, and there on my knees asked Jesus what could be the difficulty with those Christians. It did not enter my mind that the trouble could be anywhere else than among them. I had preached with tears in my eyes, and been anxious to see a revival, and had no thought but that the preacher was in a right state. But there in my closet, God revealed to me my own heart, showing me that the difficulty was with *myself*, and not with the church; I found myself as cold as those I was trying to benefit. My tears, even in the pulpit, had been like water running from the top of a cake of ice when the warm rays of the sun are falling upon its surface, but which becomes hard and cold again as soon as the sun goes down. I told the pastor of what I had discovered, and asked him the condition of his own heart. He frankly confessed that he was in the same state as myself.

"We prayed together several times. I felt that I could not live in that state and accomplish much. Accordingly, I went home and shut myself in my room, resolved to spend the night in prayer, if necessary. Oh, the struggle of that night! Hour after hour I wrestled alone with God. My heart had been full of coldness, and I not aware of it. No wonder the churches had not come up to the work! I renewedly and repeatedly gave myself to the Saviour, determined not to let the angel depart until my heart was filled and melted with the love of Jesus. Towards morning the victory came. The ice was all broken, melted, and carried away; the warmth and glow of my 'first love' filled my heart; the current of feeling was changed and deepened; the joy of salvation was restored. In the morning I went out, took the unconverted by the hand, and said the same things as on days previous; but now they were melted to tears over their sin and danger. I prepared and preached another sermon to the churches – no lash, nothing harsh about it. They broke down, confessed their own need of a special preparation of heart, and gave themselves anew to the work, which, from that hour, went forward rapidly and successfully."

Wisdom and skill are elements of effective preaching. "He that winneth souls is wise." For example, it is important to see when a point is made, and to *follow up* an impression – blow upon blow. It was said of a great commander, "he knew how to take advantage of a victory." A successful leader in revivals will both know how to make opportunities, (under God), and to take advantage of them. He will both make the iron hot by striking, and strike while it is hot.

Moreover, in his sermons and in the general management of the work, while he does not wait for happy junctures, he will yet be quick to *improve* them when they occur.

On one occasion as Mr Whitefield was preaching in Boston, a violent storm of thunder and lightning came on. In the midst of the sermon, it attained so alarming a height that the congregation sat in almost breathless awe. The preacher closed his note-book, and stepping into one of the wings of the desk, fell on his knees, and with much feeling and fine taste repeated:

> "Hark, the ETERNAL rends the sky!
> A mighty voice before Him goes –
> A voice of music to His friends,
> But threatening thunder to His foes.
>
> Come, children, to your Father's arms;
> Hide in the chambers of His grace,
> Till the fierce storm be overblown.
> And the avenging fury cease!"

Then he said, "Let us devoutly sing to the praise and glory of God this hymn, to Old Hundred." The whole congregation instantly rose, and poured forth the sacred song, in which they were accompanied by the organ, in a style of simple grandeur and heartfelt devotion that was probably never surpassed. By the time the hymn was finished the storm was hushed. The remainder of the services were well adapted to sustain the elevated feeling which had been produced; and the benediction with which the good man dismissed the flock was universally received with streaming eyes, and hearts overflowing with tenderness and love.

Rev James Caughey, a noted Methodist evangelist, relates a case where he was preaching day after day, with no distinct results, until one night, just as the audience were about to retire, a terrific thunderstorm burst upon the place. The windows of the church were unusually large, and they appeared all in a blaze, from the effect of the lightning. The storm raged in fury; and one of the preachers began to exhort, and wielded with power that passage in *Psalm 11*, – "*Upon the wicked he shall rain snares, fire and brimstone, and an horrible tempest; this shall be the portion of their cup.*" Thus, while God thundered and lightened outside, his minister did the same within. It was a scene of terror and awful grandeur, and sinners began to tremble and weep and pray. Still the storm continued, with peals of loudest thunder, which were re-echoed by successive appeals to the consciences of men. Nothing was heard but –

> "See the storm of vengeance gathering
> O'er the path you dare to tread;
> Hear the awful thunder rolling.
> Loud and louder, o'er your head!"

And this was attended by the deep and subdued groans of sinners, slain by the sword of the Spirit. It was a help in time of need; and victory from the Lord of hosts began with that hour.

It has been said of Dr Nettleton that he was pre-eminently a wise man; able to see the relations and tendencies of things, and to adapt means to ends, so as seldom to fail of an object desired. A distinguished clergyman who had been intimately acquainted with his history for several years, and who had noticed with admiration the skill with which he formed and executed his plans for doing good, exclaimed, "He is the wisest man I ever knew."

Intense yearning for souls is a condition of powerful preaching. Whitefield was remarkable for this. It spoke in his manner, his looks, his words. "I love those that thunder out the Word," he said; "the Christian world is in a deep sleep, and nothing but a loud voice can awaken them out of it." A certain baronet said to a friend, "Mr B, this Whitefield is truly a great man – he is the founder of a new religion."

"A new religion, sir!" exclaimed Mr B.

"Yes," said the baronet, "what do you call it?"

"Nothing," rejoined the other, "but the old religion revived with energy, and heated as if the minister really meant what he said."

It is said that Whitefield would sometimes rise in the pulpit, and for a minute or two, looking in silence around his vast audience, as if salvation or perdition teemed in every cast of his eye, would burst into tears; while the swift contagion reached every heart that could feel, and dimmed every eye that could weep. There was pleading for souls in his very looks. And it was the gushing of a full heart.

Of Rowland Hill it is related that while once preaching, he was carried away by the impetuous rush of his feelings, and raising himself to his full stature, he exclaimed, "Beware! I am in earnest! Men call me an enthusiast; but I am not; mine are words of truth and soberness. When I first came into this part of the country, I was walking on yonder hill. I saw a gravel pit fall in and bury three human beings alive. I lifted up my voice for help, so loud that I was heard in the town below, a distance of a mile. Help came and rescued two of the poor sufferers. No one called me an enthusiast then. And when I see eternal destruction ready to fall upon poor sinners, and about to entomb them irrecoverably in an eternal mass of woe, and call on them to escape, shall I be called an enthusiast?"

In Vincent's little book *God's Terrible Voice in the City*, is a description of the preaching of the few faithful ministers who stayed at their posts during the great plague and fire in London. These men lifted up their voices like a trumpet, and spared not. Every sermon might be their last. Graves were lying open around them; life seemed now not merely a handbreadth, but a hairbreadth; death was nearer now than ever; eternity stood out in all its vast reality; souls were felt to be precious; opportunities were no longer to be trifled away; every hour possessed a value beyond the wealth of kingdoms; the world was now a passing, vanishing shadow; and Man's days on earth had been cut down from threescore years and ten into the twinkling of an eye. "Oh, how they preached! No polished periods, no learned arguments, no laboured paragraphs chilled their appeals, or rendered their discourses unintelligible. No fear of man, no love of popular applause, no over-scrupulous dread of strong expressions, no fear of *excitement* or enthusiasm, prevented them from pouring out the whole fervour of their hearts, that yearned with tenderness unutterable over dying souls. Old Time, seemed to stand at the head of the pulpit, with his great scythe, saying, with a hoarse voice, 'Work while it is called today: at night I will mow thee down!' Grim Death seemed to stand at the side of the pulpit with his sharp arrow, saying, 'Do thou shoot God's arrows, or I will shoot mine!' The Grave seemed to lie open at the foot of the pulpit, saying –

"'Here thou must lie –
  Mouth stopped,
  Breath gone,
And silent in the dust.'"

Truly were ministers in earnest then – no coldness, no languor, no studied oratory. They preached as *dying men to dying men*, in very deed. And what an added power there would be in our pulpits if all ministers preached like this!

If a minister, then, through the blessing of God, would be powerful in converting men, let him eschew the idea of preaching for the mere purpose of preaching. Let him prepare and preach his discourses with a *straight aim!* Prettiness is *not* in place in the pulpit; certainly not in a revival. It is *not* the highest ideal of a sermon that it is precise and dignified, and offends nobody's taste! Foster complained of Blair that he kept his thoughts so long standing to be dressed, that they were chilled through before leaving his hands. Sermons may be elaborated till they are spoiled. They may be so "perfect" as to be perfectly worthless! They may be

"– correctly cold, and correctly dull.
Faultily faultless, icily regular, splendidly null."

Tholuck would call these literary properties "dried sweetmeats in a glass jar." Such sermons are good enough to lay away as embalmed beauties, but they are totally unfit to be preached to a living congregation. Souls never cry out under them. When ministers are full of the Holy Ghost they do not preach thus. They cannot do it. The moment they are in earnest, they preach in any way rather than this. And many a revival has been checked, and prematurely brought to a close, by not preaching plain, and homely, and solemn truths in a weighty and downright earnest manner.

Especially will one skilled in soul-saving *press the consciences* of his hearers. Rather than

"Smooth down the stubborn text to ears polite,
And snugly keep damnation out of sight,"

he will rally all his strength and lay siege to the sinner, and thunder at the door of the heart. When Popilius, by order of the Roman senate, required Antiochus to withdraw his army from the King of Egypt, and he desired time to deliberate, the haughty Roman drew a circle about him with his wand, and said, "*In hoc stans delibera,*" – "In this standing-place deliberate!" that is, *Answer before you move!* Thus must men be pressed to an immediate surrender to the demands of Almighty God.

Above all, if one would have power over men *he must himself be holy*. He must hold himself in close contact with the Source of power. A sermon may be constructed after the best models; it may conform to all the rules of homiletics; the text may be suitable and fruitful; the plan may be faultless; the execution may discover genius and judgment; there may be accurate analysis and strong reasoning; proof and motive; solidity and beauty; logic and passion; argument direct and indirect; perspicuity, purity, correctness, propriety, precision; description, antithesis, metaphor, allegory, comparison; motives from goodness, motives from happiness, motives from self-love; appeals to the sense of the beautiful, the sense of right, to the affections, the passions, the emotions – a sermon may be all this, and yet that very sermon, even though it fell from the lips of a prince of pulpit oratory, were as powerless in the renewal of a soul as in raising the dead, if unaccompanied by the *omnipotent energy of the Holy Ghost.*

"O Lord, Revive Thy Work!"

12
Prayer and Revivals

REVIVALS are born of prayer. The prayers of Elijah wrought a reformation in Israel, and prevented a perpetual going away into idolatry. Mourning over the prevailing declension, and seeing that nothing short of severe judgments would save the guilty nation, he prayed that it might not rain; and God shut up the heavens for the space of three years and six months. When the people relented and were properly humbled, he prayed again, and the awful calamity was turned back.

At a later day, the prayers of the good King Hezekiah were the means of reclaiming the nation from the brink of destruction. The monstrous impieties of his father Ahaz, had culminated in cutting to pieces the sacred utensils of the house of God, and shutting up its doors; while idol shrines were built in every city of Judah. These Hezekiah destroyed. And then he opened the house of God, and had the priests re-consecrated, and assembled all Israel, and they held a fourteen days' meeting, and separated themselves from their sins. Thus the Lord "hearkened unto Hezekiah, and healed the people."

Coming to the Pentecostal refreshing, we find it preceded by more than a week's special and earnest supplications to God for the promised Spirit.

There is also a volume of meaning in that proposal of the apostles to the first Christians, when they called them to the choice of deacons: "But we will give ourselves to *prayer* and to the ministry of the Word." Prayer, they doubtless meant, in the high and holy sense of the word. They sought strength for their work, and wisdom rightly to divide the Word of truth to every man, and holy love to give fervency, fidelity, and power to their ministrations.

The first ministers, therefore, were eminently men of prayer; they lived at the footstool of the throne of grace. Of the apostle James it is said that after his death his knees were found to be callous, like a camel's knees, from his much kneeling. The patriarchs, prophets, apostles, martyrs, reformers, were the mighty men they were because they had callous knees.

Gregory of Nazianzen speaks for the early Christians, in his exclamation touching the defeat of the emperor's wicked schemes: "How many myriads and squadrons of men were there whom we, by our simple praying, and God willing, discomfited."

"From our closet to the church: from our knees to the pulpit," was the motto of several of the Reformers.

John Knox was a man so famous for his power in prayer that bloody Queen Mary used to say she feared his prayers more than all the armies of Europe. And events showed that she had reason to do it. He often was in such an agony for the deliverance of his country that he could not sleep. He had a place in his garden where he used to go to pray. One night he and several friends were praying together, and as they prayed, Knox spoke and said that deliverance had come. He could not tell what had happened, but he felt that something had taken place, for God had heard their prayers. The next news they had was that Mary was dead.

Here is an example of how John Knox prayed: "O Lord, give me Scotland, or I die!" Then a pause of hushed stillness; when again the petition broke forth: "O Lord, give me Scotland, or I die!" Once more all was voiceless; when, with a yet intenser pathos, the thrice-repeated intercession struggled forth: "O Lord, give me Scotland, or I die!" And God gave him Scotland, a land and church of noble Christian loyalty to Christ and His crown.

Luther would sometimes pray with such humble boldness as to lead him to lay down a promise before God, and say, "Now Lord, there is Thy word; if Thou dost not keep it I will never believe Thee again!" A spy upon Luther followed him to a hotel, and slept in a room adjacent to that of the Reformer. He told his employer next day that Luther prayed nearly all night, and that he could never conquer a man who prayed like that.

On a certain occasion, a messenger was sent to Luther to inform him that Melanchthon was dying. He at once hastened to his sick-bed, and found him presenting the usual premonitory symptoms of death. He mournfully bent over him; and sobbing, gave utterance to a sorrowful exclamation. It roused Melanchthon from his stupor; he looked into the face of Luther, and said, "O Luther, is this you? Why don't you let me depart in peace?" "We can't spare you yet, Philip," was the reply. And turning round, he threw himself upon his knees, and wrestled with God for his recovery for upwards of an hour. He went from his knees to the bed, and took his friend by the hand. Again, he said, "Dear Luther, why don't you let me depart in peace?" "No, no, Philip, we cannot spare you yet from the field of labour," was the reply. He then ordered some soup, and when pressed to take it, he declined, saying again: "Dear Luther, why will you not let me go home, and be at rest?" "We cannot spare you yet, Philip," was the reply. He then added: "Philip, take this soup, or I will excommunicate you!" He took the soup, and soon commenced to grow better; and finally regained his wonted health, and laboured for years afterwards in the cause of the Reformation. When Luther returned home he said to his wife, "God gave me back my brother Melanchthon in direct answer to prayer."

The good John Welsh, of Ayr, Scotland, whose harvests of souls were so great, from the beginning of his ministry to its close, reckoned the day ill-spent if he spent less than seven or eight hours before the throne in fervent prayer. On going to rest he used to lay a plaid above his bedclothes, so that when he arose to his night-prayers he might cover himself with it. Sometimes he would retire to the church, which was at a little distance from the town, and "not find it an irksome solitude to pass the whole night there in prayer."

Mr Bruce, about the time of Welsh's removal to Ayr, commenced his ministry in Edinburgh. Kirkton describes the power of his preaching in the following words: "He made always an earthquake under his hearers, and rarely preached but to a weeping auditory." A little incident lets us at once into the secret of Bruce's power and pathos in the pulpit. At Larbot, where he frequently preached, he used after the first service to retire to a chamber near the church. Some noblemen having once come far to hear him, became impatient from his delay in returning to church, and sent the bell-man to hearken at his door if there were any appearance of his coming. The bell-man returned and said, "I think he will not come out this day, at all; for I hear him always saying to another, that he cannot go except the other go with him; and I don't hear the other answer him a word."

In other places in this book we have referred to the wonderful revival in Shotts, (Scotland), in 1630. We refer to it again for the purpose of showing the relation which *prayer* had to it. The circumstance that several of the then persecuted ministers would take a part in the solemn services having become generally known, a vast concourse of godly persons assembled on this occasion from all quarters of the country, and several days were spent in social prayer, preparatory to the service. In the evening, instead of retiring to rest, the multitude divided themselves into little bands, and spent the whole night in supplication and praise. The Monday was consecrated to thanksgiving, a practice not then common, and proved the great day of the feast. After much entreaty, John Livingston, chaplain to the Countess of Wigtown, a young man and not ordained, agreed to preach. He had spent the night in prayer and conference – but as the hour of assembling approached, his heart quailed at the thought of addressing so many aged and experienced saints, and he actually fled from the duty he had undertaken. But just as the kirk of Shotts was vanishing from his view, these words, "Was I ever a barren wilderness or a land of darkness?" were borne in upon his mind with such force as compelled him to return to the work. He took for his text *Ezekiel 36:25-26* – and discoursed with power for about two hours. Five hundred conversions were believed to have occurred under that one sermon, thus prefaced by prayer.

Of Richard Baxter it has been said that he stained his study-walls with praying breath; and after becoming thus anointed with the unction of the Holy Ghost, he sent a river of living water over Kidderminster.

Whitefield once thus prayed, "O Lord, give me souls or take my soul." After much closet-pleading "he once went to the devil's fair and took more than a thousand souls out of the paw of the lion in a single day."

In reading the marvels wrought by Whitefield, the Wesleys, and their co-workers, we do not sufficiently appreciate the straits to which they were driven, and how utterly they were thrown back on the Almighty, and made to take hold upon His strength. Denied the pulpits, and discarded by all except "the common people," their souls caught new zeal and devotion from new extremities and new trials. Wesley describes a scene which reminds us of the preparatory Pentecostal baptism by which the apostles were "endued with power from on high" for their mission. He says, January 1, 1739, that Messrs Hall, Kinchin, Ingham, Whitefield, and his brother Charles were present with him at a love-feast in Fetter Lane, with about sixty of their brethren. About *three in the morning*, as they were *continuing instant in prayer*, the power of God came mightily upon them, insomuch that many cried out for exceeding joy, and many fell to the ground. As soon as they had recovered a little from the awe and amazement which the presence of the divine Majesty had inspired, they broke out with one voice, "We praise thee, O God; we acknowledge thee to be the Lord." Whitefield exclaims: "It was a Pentecostal season, indeed." And he adds respecting these "Society meetings," that "sometimes *whole nights were spent in prayer*. Often have we been filled as with new wine, and often have I seen them overwhelmed with the divine Presence, and cry out, 'Will God, indeed, dwell with men upon earth? How dreadful is this place! This is no other than the house of God, and the gate of heaven!' "

Edwards' powerful sermon at Enfield is remarked upon in chapter 11 of this work. Bishop Simpson once asked the writer for an opinion as to the secret of that sermon's astonishing effect upon the audience. The same question has often been asked. Upon a careful analysis it is not difficult to point out several elements of the highest effectiveness. But behind this there was a mighty agency, discoverable in the fact that some Christians in the vicinity had become alarmed lest while God was blessing other places, He should in anger pass them by; and so *they met on the evening preceding the preaching of that sermon, and spent the whole night in agonising prayer.*

And Edwards himself reveals the same source of power in those days, when he says, "The spirit of those that have been in distress for the souls of others, so far as I can discern, seems not to be different from that of the apostle who travailed for souls, and was ready to wish himself accursed from Christ for them: and that of the Psalmist in saying, 'Horror hath taken hold upon me, because of the wicked that forsake thy law.' "

Prayers like these would be expected to produce astonishing results.

The connection between prayer and the more modern revivals is equally apparent. About 1795, a *quarterly concert* of prayer began to be observed by some churches in Connecticut and New Jersey. At a later period, a *family concert* of prayer was adopted somewhat extensively, and attended weekly, from September to March, on Saturday evening, the hour after sunset; and from March to September, on Sabbath evening, the hour before sunset. And later still, was observed a *sacramental concert*, which returned with the regular seasons of preparation for the Lord's Supper; and the *female prayer-meetings*, which are now so common, and which have been attended with most important results to the church. These meetings for prayer, in the forms above mentioned, were adapted to inspire Christians with that spirit which Mr Mills so often enjoined, "*Let us live looking upwards.*"

Drs Griffin, of New Jersey, Spring, of New York, and Hyde, of Montana, about this time narrate the power of prayer in connection with revivals.

Dr Lyman Beecher thus writes from Connecticut: "One day, old Deacon Miller, a holy man, sent for me. He was sick in bed. 'I am glad to see you,' he said. 'I know how you feel. You must not be discouraged. I lie on my bed at night and pray for you. I've been praying for all in the village. I begin at one end, and go into the next house, and then into the next, till I have gone round; and then I have not prayed enough, so I begin and go round again.' I went home expecting; and word was sent from the Springs that the Lord had come down on the previous Sunday, and that a meeting was appointed for Tuesday evening, and that I must not disappoint them. Then I went to the North-west, and the Lord was there; then to Ammigansett, and the Lord was there; and the flood was rolling all around. Oh what a time that was! There were a hundred converts, nearly, who most of them stood fast."

It is well-known that many of the most successful evangelists, since the time of Whitefield and the Wesleys, have been noted for their prayerfulness. One says of Nettleton that he was eminently a man of *prayer*. Entering the pulpit, or the inquiring meeting, one could witness a holy calm, and indescribable, almost unearthly solemnity and earnestness of manner, which gave evidence of his having come directly from the "mount of communion." Jabez Swan, and Jacob Knapp, and others, will recur to many minds as examples of power in *prayer.*

Rev Dr Steele, (of Boston), says of Mr Earle: "His philosophy of conversion is exactly that of Dr Durbin. No soul is ever converted except as some believer has painfully travailed in birth for that soul. Hence, there will be simultaneous conversions when many Christians are pleading with God in pain and distress of soul. The church is the bride of Christ and the mother of his children. Hence Christians are exhorted to wrestle with God till they are bowed to the dust with a burden for the salvation of lost men. They are told, even though they talk much of 'the higher life,' and 'rest in Jesus,' that there is a radical defect in their piety if they are content with easy prayers and with the delicious ecstasies of divine love, and are not in tears and pain of heart, pulling souls out of the fire. And Mr Earle himself lives in keeping with that which he enjoins upon others."

We mention several other specific cases showing how revivals originate in prayer. An aged saint once came to his pastor at night and said, "We are about to have a revival." He was asked why he knew so. His answer was, "I went into the stable, to take care of my cattle two hours ago, and there the Lord has kept me in prayer until just now. And I feel that we are going to be revived." It was the commencement of a revival. Says a pastor, "An aged man, venerated for piety, once came to my study. Though poor in this world, he was rich in faith. In prayer he seemed to converse with God. 'I have called to say to you, my dear pastor,' said he, 'that the Lord is in the midst of us, and we shall all soon see the effect of His presence.' I had observed a marked solemnity in the congregation, but nothing more. I asked the venerable man why he felt so. His reply was as follows: 'Since twelve o'clock last night the Spirit of God has been so upon me that I have been unable to do anything but pray, and to rejoice in the prospect of a blessed refreshing from the presence of the Lord.' And that was the commencement of the first revival in my present field of labour; a field which has been very often watered with the rain and dew of heaven."

Mr Finney says, "I once knew a minister who had a revival fourteen winters in succession. I did not know how to account for it till I saw one of his members get up in a prayer-meeting and make a confession. 'Brethren,' said he, 'I have been long in the habit of praying every Saturday night till after midnight, for the descent of the Holy Ghost among us. And now, brethren, (and he began to weep), I confess that I have neglected it for two or three weeks.' The secret was out. That minister had a praying church."

A minister once stated that in a certain town there had been no revival for many years, and the church was nearly run out, and desolation reigned unbroken. There lived in a retired part of the town, an aged man, a blacksmith by trade, and of so stammering a tongue that it was painful to hear him speak. On one Friday, as he was at work in his shop, his mind became greatly exercised about the state of the church, and of the impenitent. His agony became so great that he was induced to lay by his work, lock the shop door, and spend the afternoon in prayer. He prevailed, and on the Sabbath called on the minister, and desired him to appoint a conference meeting. After some hesitation the minister consented, observing, however, that he feared but few would attend. He appointed it at a large private house. When the evening came, more assembled than could be accommodated in the house. All was silent for a time, until one man broke out in tears, and said, if anyone could pray, he begged him to pray for him. Another followed, and another, and still another, until it was found that persons from every quarter of the town, were under deep conviction. And what was remarkable, they all dated their conviction at the hour when the old man was praying in his shop. A powerful revival followed. Thus this old stammering man prevailed, and, as a prince, had power with God.

A pious sick man in the western part of New York used to pray for the preachers and churches of his acquaintance daily, at set hours. In his diary were found entries like this, "Today I have been enabled to offer the prayer of faith for a revival in such a church." So through the list. It is said that each church was soon enjoying a revival, and nearly in the order of time named in the diary.

A revival often springs up without any apparent cause. But if inquiry were duly made, among perhaps the obscure members of the church, it would be found that some man or woman or child had been agonising for that revival, and was expecting it. A writer in one of the religious journals gives the following fact: "A brother in the ministry, whose parish was some ten miles from mine, once called on me and gave me an account of a remarkable revival among his people. Scores had been converted, and many were awakened. Having detailed facts and incidents full of interest, he added, "What is most singular is, the work is wholly unaccountable." He had himself felt no unusual solicitude, nor been moved to special fervour in prayer or preaching; nor did he know that any member of his church had been specially quickened. All at once this cloud overhung his people, and the rain began to descend. "I have seen," said he, "many revivals, but never one like this, preceded by no sign. It is," he added, "an unaccountable revival." The work continued and increased till more than a hundred were added to the church. From time to time I saw him, and heard of the progress of the work. Months passed away; the revival had ceased; the converts had been baptised; and that pastor called on me again. "I have found," said he, "the secret of the revival." "Ah," said I, full of curiosity; "what is it?" "There is," he replied, "a sister in my church who has been for years an invalid, confined to her bed. She lives several miles from the village, and the other day I rode out to see her. As I sat by her bed-side, she said, 'You have had a precious revival.' 'We have,' I answered. 'I knew it was coming,' said she." And then she proceeded to give her pastor an account of the burden that had been upon her heart for weeks, and of the manner in which her soul had gone forth in prayer for the unconverted, in midnight hours; and before the interview closed, the pastor felt that the unaccountable revival was accounted for.

The vital relation between prayer and revivals has often been illustrated in our institutions of learning. We have elsewhere spoken of colleges and seminaries as connected with revivals. An instance is here appended of the earnest prayers amid which such institutions were founded. It is also worthy of record as an example of the power of prayer. We find the fact stated in the life of Dr Nathaniel Kendrick, as connected with the early struggles of the institution at Hamilton, New York, now Madison University. The Board meetings were not so much seasons for the dry discussion of business as of *prayer*, inasmuch as from their great extremity they were driven to ask counsel of God, and implore deliverance from embarrassment through His interposition. At one meeting of the Board, which probably occurred in 1826, most of the time was spent in earnest prayer and strong crying to God for direction. The Board felt the need of a suitable edifice to accommodate the growing school; and besides, it was in a great measure destitute of funds to aid those whom they had received as beneficiaries. At the meeting now referred to, the only vote passed was one appointing a day of fasting and prayer some weeks from that session. It was a dark hour, but just the darkness that precedes the cheerful light of day. For those prayers were taking effect. They disturbed the sleep of Mr Nicholas Brown, of Providence, Rhode Island, and he dreamed nightly about Hamilton. And so he came to his pastor, Dr Gano, and said, 'They are in *trouble at Hamilton*, I think; for I can't sleep nights; my dreams about them disturb me; do you know their condition?' Upon being told that he was ignorant of their exact condition, Mr Brown said, 'You must go and see;' and upon this Dr Gano made the journey to Hamilton, at Mr Brown's expense; and finding out their great strait, and reporting it to Mr Brown, he at once sent them $1,000, which relieved their perplexity. Thus much for Hamilton. We mention some other cases.

Mary Lyon had faith enough to found Holyoke Seminary; and she followed it with prayer enough to secure a special revival of religion in it every year of her life. The secret of those wonderful revivals was never understood till after her death; when they were found, in almost every instance, to have been preceded by special seasons of persevering secret prayer.

In the year 1823, chiefly as the result of extensive correspondence, the last Thursday of February in each year was agreed upon "as the day for special supplication that God would pour from on high his Spirit upon our Colleges and Seminaries of learning." And what have been some of the results? In the years 1824 and 1825 revivals were experienced in five different Colleges; in 1826, in six Colleges; in 1831, in nineteen, resulting in the conversion of more than three hundred and fifty students. In one of the Colleges it is stated that a revival commenced on the very day of the Concert. In 1835, not less than eighteen revivals were reported by different Colleges, and some one hundred and fifty or two hundred hopeful conversions. Fourteen Colleges, a few years ago, experienced revivals commencing just subsequent to the last Thursday of February, and it is particularly observable that those reported, occur usually about this time. It has been estimated that fifteen hundred students were converted during the first fifteen years subsequent to the observance of the concert of prayer for Colleges and Seminaries of learning.

The *Week of Prayer*, with the beginning of every year, in which the churches throughout Christendom now quite generally unite, also furnishes most striking exemplifications of the revival results of prayer. Nothing is more obvious than the marked increase of religious interest following this worldwide concert of prayer.

The revival of 1857-8 originated and progressed, to a most remarkable extent, through the instrumentality of prayer. It was, eminently, a revival of prayer. This was perhaps the leading characteristic. It was repeatedly noticed that assemblies were more interested in the prayers than the addresses. They came together, not to hear learned, elegant, or eloquent appeals, but to unite in prayer. The great attraction was prayer. The *great business was intercession.*

We have thus noticed some few points of obvious connection between prayer and revivals; and are prepared to endorse the words of one who says, "I very much doubt whether, if we could see the connection between prayer and the glorious revivals that have blessed this land, we should find one that was not definitely prayed for by some earnest wrestlers, or wrestler, at the throne of grace."

"The conclusion is patent and important. *If there are to be more revivals there must be more prayer.* Writing of the revival of 1857-8, Dr J W Alexander says, "The lesson which it should teach us is the duty of being instant in supplication for the larger and more glorious effusion of the Holy Spirit. Acting on this, we shall behold new marvels of love." And he adds that we must pray as we have never yet prayed. "Our want of success is due to our coldness of desire and niggardliness of request. If we were but under a deep and solemn impression of the divine power, bounty, and faithfulness, how should one chase a thousand, and two put ten thousand to flight!"

We need yet to learn, for all we talk so much about it, the power there is in prayer. God indeed purposed the prevalence of revivals, but it is also His purpose to bestow these manifold blessings upon the condition of His being "inquired of" to do it for us. Prayer, thus, is of the nature of cause and effect. It enters into the plan and structure of the universe. The remark once made is not too strong, that God would as soon give rain without the clouds or the electric fluid, as revivals without the prayers of his people. To dispense with either the material or the moral instrumentality, were alike to sever the established order of sequences, and violate the ordinances of heaven.

What a privilege is here placed in the hands of believers! And what a responsibility! How awful our guilt if this power of prayer be slighted and neglected! What *right* have we to leave unappropriated and unapplied, a power which God has appointed for the salvation of men, and which heaven and earth now wait to see us put forth for the world's redemption? What "inhumanity to man," and what want of sympathy with Christ, are chargeable upon us if we fail to offer the effectual fervent prayer of the righteous in such manner and measure as God requires!

From this time forth, then, let us more than ever "give ourselves to prayer." Let us learn over again, with the teachableness of little children, what is *believing* prayer, and *persevering* prayer, and *importunate* prayer, and *united* prayer, and *consistent* prayer.

Dr Backus, former President of Hamilton College, when on his death-bed, was told that he could not live to exceed half an hour. "Is that so?" said the great and good man, "then take me out of my bed, and place me upon my knees, and let me spend that time in calling on God for the salvation of the world!" His request was complied with, and his last breath was spent in praying for the conversion of his fellow-men. He died upon his knees. This is the earnest, heart-absorbing spirit of prayer that the church needs to have. And why should not all Christians feel the same interest in a great gathering in of souls as was felt by this dying saint? Where there is such praying, a benediction is on the way.

"O Lord, Revive Thy Work!"

13

Singing and Revivals

LET it not be thought that this is an unimportant topic. Singing is an auxiliary to prayer, and to all Christian work.

The power of music all acknowledge. At a critical moment during the battle of Waterloo, Wellington discovered that the Forty-second Highlanders began to waver. On inquiry as to the cause of an occurrence so unusual, he was informed that the band had ceased to play. Instantly he gave the command that the pipes be played in full force. The effect was magical. The wavering Highlanders rallied; and solid and impregnable as the fort of Gibraltar, with tattered colours and blood-drenched swords, they went forth to win the hard-contested field.

There are reasons for the effectiveness of music. One is found in the well-known influence of mental associations. Cowper says:

> "Wherever I have heard
> A kindred melody, the scene revives,
> And with it all its pleasures and its pains."

This is not poetic exaggeration, but simple truth. The power of such associations can scarcely be overestimated. We all understand it. There are melodies which enter into the tenderest memories of childhood, and have gone singing to us in all life's way, like the airy voice of some guardian angel. They sigh in our sickness, and syllable our joy.

We could specify some special hymns which have grown in our hearts. We sang this one, perhaps, the morning that our child died.

We sang that one on the Sabbath evening, when, after many years, the family were once more all together. "There are hymns that were sung while the mother lay dying; that were sung when the child, just converted, was filling the family with the joy of Christ new-born, and laid not now in a manger, but in a heart. And thus, sprung from a wondrous life, they lead a life yet more wonderful. When they first come to us they are like the single strokes of a bell, ringing down to us from above; but, at length, a single hymn becomes a whole chime of bells, mingling and discoursing to us the harmonies of a life's Christian experience."

In this stirring of the mind by the force of mental associations, we see a reason for the power of song.

There is a deeper philosophy in it. God is pleased to accompany it with the energy of the Holy Spirit. He made us to be moved by singing. The soul is a many-stringed lyre, which He touches while working in us both to will and to do of His good pleasure. Hence, the influence of sacred song is to refresh, stimulate, and ennoble the mind. It is calculated, in a very eminent degree, to lift above mean associations, and inspire emotions which are felt in their full intensity where the Lord is worshipped in the beauty of holiness.

Moreover; God often employs it to send conviction to a soul. A wild boy in the streets of London was one day arrested by the voice of singing. He turned aside, and found two or three Christians singing religious hymns. One line struck his mind, and hung to it, so that he went away repeating it. That line was, "Stop, poor sinner, stop and think, before you farther go." Years afterward, in the city of New York, he tried to be an infidel; and for this purpose went to hear Robert Dale Owen. But still there rung in his ears, "Stop, poor sinner, stop and think." Never could he forget those words. That man is now a Christian, and an earnest worker for the souls of others.

Accordingly, God has always sanctioned the service of song. When at his fiat the world sprang into existence, "the morning stars sang together, and all the sons of God shouted for joy." When Israel had passed through the Red Sea on dry land, and saw their enemies engulfed in the returning waves, they all sang praises in an anthem composed by Miriam, the sister of Moses. On the seventh day of compassing the walls of Jericho, when the priests blew with the trumpets in an extraordinary manner, the people shouted with a great shout, and the wall of the city fell down flat. The ark was brought back from its banishment with extraordinary shouting and singing of the whole congregation of Israel.

How joyfully does David cry, "Sing praises to God, sing praises: sing praises unto our King, sing praises; for God is the King of all the earth: sing ye praises with understanding." "Let the people praise thee, O God; let all the people praise thee!" Nor did either David or Solomon, the two most illustrious monarchs that ever sat upon the Jewish throne, deem it beneath their dignity to take music under their personal management. It is plain to see what interest was attached to exercises of praise, in the dedication of the first temple. The glorious symbol of the divine presence was not given when the ark was deposited in the holy of holies, but at the glad moment when the song arose, "For his mercy endureth forever!" Then it was that the "glory of the Lord filled the house," and shone so transcendently that even "the priests could not stand to minister." This is not to be regarded merely as a part of the splendid ceremonies of a typical dispensation. There is a moral lesson in it as distinct and significant as that which attends the dedicatory prayer.

With the introduction of the new economy, most of the ancient forms of divine worship were abolished; but singing, though simplified and cast in a new mould, was still retained. Our Saviour gave it the sanction of his own example, no doubt, in his ministry; and at the institution of the Supper *they* sang a hymn, (including himself), before He went out to the agonies of the garden and the cross. "Oh! but for one moment even, to have sat transfixed, and to have listened to the hymn that Christ sang, and to the singing! But the olive trees did not hear his murmured notes more clearly than, rapt in imagination, we have heard them!"

We may be sure that there was singing at that meeting of days before the outpouring of the Pentecostal blessing. And we can see the exceeding fitness in their chanting under such circumstances, *Psalm 2*, for example: "Why do the heathen rage, and the people imagine a vain thing? The kings of the earth set themselves, and the rulers take counsel together against the Lord, and against his Anointed, *saying*, Let us break their bands asunder, and cast away their cords from us. He that sitteth in the heavens shall laugh: the Lord shall have them in derision. Then shall he speak unto them in his wrath, and vex them in his sore displeasure. Yet have I set my King upon my holy hill of Zion. I will declare the decree: the Lord hath said unto me, Thou art my Son; this day have I begotten thee. Ask of me, and I shall give thee the heathen for thine inheritance, and the uttermost parts of the earth for thy possession. Thou shalt break them with a rod of iron;thou shalt dash them in pieces like a potter's vessel. Be wise now therefore, O ye kings: be instructed, ye judges of the earth. Serve the Lord with fear, and rejoice with trembling. Kiss the Son lest he be angry, and ye perish from the way, when his wrath is kindled but a little. Blessed are all they that put their trust in him!"

After the Pentecostal effusion of the Spirit, the infant church is seen daily in the temple *praising* God. A little onward, we hear the Apostle Paul exhorting the churches "to sing with the Spirit and with the understanding;" "to be filled with the Spirit, speaking to themselves in Psalms and Hymns and Spiritual Songs, singing and making melody in their hearts unto the Lord;" and to "sing with grace in their hearts;" thus "teaching and admonishing" one another, and in "everything giving thanks."

Singing will also be prominent in heaven. There, in the world of perfection, they sing the song of Moses the servant of God, and the song of the Lamb, saying, "Great and marvellous are thy works,Lord God Almighty; just and true are thy ways, thou King of saints!" The ascriptions of rapt souls, throughout the Apocalypse, take the form of musical utterance. Those vocal acclamations of palm-bearing saints must be regarded as psalms, songs, hymns, or anthems. Thus must we judge of the Four, and the Four-and-twenty. They sing a "new song," saying, "Thou art worthy ... for thou wast slain!" The subsequent voice of the "ten thousand times ten thousand, and thousands of thousands," is the voice of song. The angels and elders, and four living ones, who fall before the throne on their faces, and worship God, cannot but utter the voice of celestial psalmody, as they say: "Amen, Blessing and glory, and wisdom, and thanksgiving, and honour, and power, and might be unto God for ever and ever."

Though we have no specimens of the Hymns and Spiritual Songs sung in the primitive times, except the occasional doxologies of the redeemed in the *Book of Revelation*, it cannot be doubted that the Christians used, not only the Psalms of the Old Testament literally, or accommodated to the circumstances of a new and rising church – but that they had original lays of their own, in which they celebrated the praises of Christ as the Saviour of the world.

In the Middle Ages, the Roman Catholic and Greek churches adopted singing as an essential part of public worship; but this, like the reading of the Scriptures, was too frequently in an unknown tongue, by an affectation of wisdom to excite the veneration of ignorance, when the learned in their craftiness taught that "Ignorance is the mother of Devotion;" and ignorance was very willing to believe it. And yet there are hymns which, (as one has it), rose up like birds in the early centuries, and have come flying and singing all the way down to us. Their wing is untired yet, nor is the voice less sweet now than it was a thousand years ago. Though they sometimes disappeared, they never sank; but as engineers for destruction send bombs that, rising high up in wide curves, overleap great spaces and drop down in a distant spot, so God, in times of darkness, seems to have caught up these hymns, spanning long periods of time, and letting them fall at distant eras, not for explosion and wounding, but for healing and consolation. There are crusaders' hymns, that rolled forth their truths upon the oriental air, while a thousand horses' hooves kept time below, and ten thousand palm-leaves whispered and kept time above! Other hymns, fulfilling the promise of God that His saints should mount up with wings as eagles, have borne up the sorrows, the desires, and the aspirations of the poor, the oppressed, and the persecuted, of Huguenots, of Covenanters, and of Puritans, and winged them to the bosom of God.

At the era of the Reformation, Psalms and Hymns in the native tongue were revived in Germany, England and elsewhere, among the other means of grace of which the *people* had been for centuries defrauded. Luther was exceedingly fond of music. He would often say to his despondent fellow-workers, "Come, brethren, let us sit down and sing the forty-sixth psalm," – "God is our refuge and strength, a very present help in trouble," etc. Bishop Jewell, (1560), speaking of the Reformation and its visible effects, says that nothing helped it more than inviting the people to sing psalms. "Sometimes at Paul's Cross, six thousand persons were sitting together, which was very grievous to the papists." Richard Baxter says, "It was not the least comfort that I had in the converse of my late dear wife, that our first exercise in the morning and the last in bed at night, was a psalm of praise, till the hearing of others interrupted it. Let those who savour not melody leave others to their different appetites, and be content to be so far strangers to their delights."

John Wesley prided himself upon the singing in his meeting-houses. His brother Charles was a born hymnist. He wrote about 7,000 hymns, nearly all for special occasions. Many were called out by some great public event, some startling religious experience, or some feeling of sorrow or joy. He was habitually indulging his love of lyric poetry. He composed immortal odes as he rode along the highways from town to town, and mob to mob. The whole soul of Charles Wesley, says one, was imbued with poetic genius. His thoughts seemed to bask and revel in rhythm. The variety of his metres, (said to be unequalled by any English writer whatever), shows how impulsive were his poetic emotions, and how wonderful his facility in their spontaneous and varied utterance. In the Wesleyan Hymnbook alone they amount to at least twenty-six, and others are found in his other productions. "They march at times like lengthened processions with solemn grandeur; they sweep at other times like chariots of fire through the heavens; they are broken like the sobs of grief at the grave-side, play like the joyful affections of childhood at the hearth, or shout like victors in the fray of the battlefield."

Dr Curry, in his *Life of John Wesley*, says, "Aware of the great advantage to be derived from psalmody, he made it an essential part of the devotional service in his chapels. He especially enjoined that the whole congregation should sing; and that, (to use his own words), not lolling at ease, or in the indecent posture of sitting, drawling out one word after another, but standing before God, and praising him lustily with a good courage."

Dr Stevens, in his *History of Methodism*, says, "It was a necessary condition of the evangelical reformation of the eighteenth century that an improved psalmody should be provided. The necessary psalmody was not only provided as a result of the new movement, but was begun even in anticipation of it. The Wesleys published their first hymnbook as early as 1738, the year in which they date their regenerated life; and the next year, the epoch of Methodism, was signalised by the appearance of their *Hymns and Sacred Poems*, two editions of which appeared before its close. And now rapidly followed, year after year, sometimes twice a year, not only new editions of these volumes but new poetic works, which were scattered more extensively than any other of their publications through England, Wales, Ireland, the British West Indies, the North American Provinces, and the United States, till not less than forty-nine poetical publications were enumerated among their literary works; and before Wesley's death a common psalmody, sung mostly to a common music, resounded through all the Methodist chapels of the English and American world. The achievement accomplished by Methodism in this respect is alone one of the most extraordinary historical facts of the eighteenth century. Its influence on the popular taste, intellectual as well as moral, could not fail to be incalculably great."

While giving the masses divine songs, continues Stevens, Wesley also endeavoured to make them sing. He was continually urging his preachers to set the example, and not only exhort the people to follow it, but to induce them to learn the science of music. "Preach frequently on singing," he said, in the Minutes of the Conference; "suit the tune to the words;" "do not suffer the people to sing too slow; let the women sing their parts alone; let no man sing with them, unless he understands the notes, and sings the bass." "Exhort everyone in the congregation to sing; in every large society let them learn to sing; recommend our Tune-book everywhere." As early as 1742 he issued *A collection of Tunes set to Music, as sung at the Foundry*. He published a small work on *The Grounds of Vocal Music*. Three other publications followed these, at intervals, on *Sacred Harmony*, adapted to "the voice, harpsichord, and organ."

This Wesleyan singing was a source of great power to early Methodism. Hundreds of hearers who cared not for the preaching, were charmed to the Methodist assemblies by their music. The singing was sometimes heard two miles off.

Whitefield, when once censured for having some of his hymns set to music which was not regarded as *sacred*, said, "Would you have the devil keep all the good tunes to himself?"

Mrs Sherwood, who knew Henry Martyn in India, says of him, "He had an uncommonly fine voice, and fine ear; he could sing many fine chants, and a vast variety of hymns and psalms. He would insist upon it that I should sing with him, and he taught me many tunes, all of which were afterwards brought into requisition; and when fatigued himself, would make me sit by his couch and practise these hymns."

Jonathan Edwards, at Northampton, writes, "There has of late been a great increase of singing." Again he says, "I believe it to have been one fruit of the extraordinary degrees of the sweet and joyful influences of the Spirit of God which have been lately given, that there has appeared such a disposition to abound in that duty, (of singing), and frequently to fall into this divine exercise, not only in appointed solemn meetings, but when Christians occasionally meet together at each other's houses." And when objectors found fault with this abounding in singing, he said, "To complain of this, is to be much like the Pharisees, who were disgusted when the multitude of the disciples began to rejoice, and with loud voices to praise God, and cry *Hosanna*, when Christ was entering into Jerusalem."

One who was a hearer at Kilsyth, (Scotland), in a revival, said, "When the notes of the congregation began to swell in a psalm of confession, I felt as if it would have *hearted* me – as if I must give way altogether."

The singing in Dr Nettleton's meetings was a marked feature. The same might be said of those of later evangelists.

Rev E P Hammond makes much of hymns. In all his meetings, hymn-singing is prominent; all of the hymns setting forth the truth. This hymn-singing attracts the young to the meetings; it rivets the truths on their minds; it adds greatly to the liveliness of the meetings.

During the revival of 1857 the demand for cheap hymnbooks was enormous; and in the meetings there was no dragging, but all sang with the Spirit; and the excellent effect was often remarked upon.

Numerous examples might be cited illustrative of the power of singing in revivals. Here is one which came under the writer's observation during a series of meetings in his church. Two worldly young men, who were acting as clerks in a post-office close to the meeting-house, often spoke to each other of the sweet music ringing out on the evening air. "Let us go in and hear the singing," said one. "Agreed," said the other; and entering, both were converted.

An actress in one of the English provincial theatres, was one day passing through the streets of the town, when her attention was attracted by the sound of voices. Curiosity prompted her to look in at an open door. It was a social meeting; and at the moment of her observation they were singing:

> "Depth of mercy! can there be
> Mercy still reserved for me?"

The tune was sweet and simple, and the words riveted her attention. She stood motionless during a prayer which was offered. But the words of the hymn followed her. She could not banish them from her mind, and at last she resolved to procure the book which contained it. She did so, and the more she read it, the more decided her serious impressions became. She attended the ministry of the gospel, read her hitherto neglected and despised Bible, and bowed herself in humility and faith before Him whose mercy she now felt she needed. She determined at once and for ever to renounce her profession; and for some little time excused herself from appearing on the stage, without, however, disclosing her change of sentiments, or making known her resolution finally to leave it. The manager of the theatre called upon her one morning, and requested her to sustain the principal character in a new play which was to be performed the next week for his benefit. Unable to resist his solicitations, she promised to appear, and on the appointed evening went to the theatre. The character she assumed required her, on her first entrance, to sing a song; and when the curtain drew up, the orchestra immediately began the accompaniment. But she stood as if lost in thought, and as one forgetting all around her, and her own situation. The music ceased, but she did not sing; and supposing her to be overcome by embarrassment, the band again commenced. A second time they paused for her to begin, and still she did not open her lips. A third time the air was played, and then, with clasped hands, and eyes suffused with tears, she sang, not the words of the song, but

> "Depth of mercy! can there be
> Mercy still reserved for me?"

The performance was suddenly ended. Many ridiculed, though some were induced from that memorable night to "consider their ways," and to reflect on the wonderful power of that religion which changed her heart and her life.

It is related that as a revival was in progress in a certain village, a profane tavern-keeper swore he would never be found among the fools who were running to the meetings. On hearing, however, of the particularly pleasing mode of singing, his curiosity was excited, and he said he did not know but he might go and hear the singing, but, with an imprecation, that he would never hear a word of the sermon. As soon as the hymn before the sermon was sung, he leaned forward and secured both ears against the sermon with his forefingers. Happening to withdraw one of his fingers, the words, "He that hath ears to hear let him hear," pronounced with great solemnity, entered the ear that was open and struck him with irresistible force. He kept his hand from returning to the ear, and, feeling an impression he had never known before, presently withdrew the other finger, and hearkened with deep attention to the discourse which followed. He became truly pious, and after some years' faithful service, died rejoicing in the hope of glory.

While a powerful revival meeting was progressing in the main room of "Burton's Theatre," New York, and just as the prayer had concluded, and all was silence, the sound of distant *singing* was heard; when the leader, (Mr Beecher), said, "Brethren, do you hear that? Stop a moment and listen to that: that is the singing in the old bar-room of this theatre! Let us spend two minutes in silent prayer and thanksgiving!" With one accord 3,000 heads were bowed; and for two minutes no sound was heard save the singing from the old bar-room, and the ripple of the gas at the footlights. No more impressive scene was ever witnessed within those walls.

It is probable that during the revival of 1857-8, the hymn beginning,

> "Just as I am, without one plea,"

was the means of bringing peace to many hundreds of troubled souls. In Mr Hammond's meetings, the hymn,

> "Nothing either great or small.
> Nothing, sinner, no,"

has been equally blessed of the Spirit.

Probably there are thousands in our churches who can recall the effect upon their minds, many years ago, of the singing of such hymns as these:

> "O turn ye, O turn ye, for why will ye die:"
> "Now the Saviour standeth pleading:"

"O, there will be mourning:"
"Come trembling sinner, in whose breast," etc.

Who can estimate the influence, in seasons of declension, of such hymns as the following:

"Saviour, visit thy plantation;"
"The Lord into his garden comes:"
"Is this the kind return;"
"Return, O wanderer, to thy home."

Of more modern hymns, mention may be made of such as these, which have been greatly beneficial in the awakening or guidance of souls;

"Lord, I hear of showers of blessings:"
"Come to Jesus:"
"I am coming to the cross:"
"Weeping soul, no longer mourn:"
"What means this eager anxious throng;"
"Today the Saviour calls."

We answer a few questions which may arise as to singing in revivals.

Should there be much singing in the incipient stages of a revival? No. The meetings then are for confession and contrition. A bowed, self-abased, aching heart cannot sing. Neither can one that is in an agony for the souls of others. Singing then is an impertinence. In Gethsemane there were but tears, and sighs and groans. Mr Finney has some excellent remarks here: "I never knew a singing revival to amount to much. It dissipates feeling. The agonising spirit of prayer does not lead people to sing. There is a time for everything; a time to sing, and a time to pray. But if I know what it is to travail in birth for souls, Christians never feel less like singing than when they have the spirit of prayer for sinners."

Are special singing-books desirable? On some accounts they are. All the congregation should be supplied with the hymns and tunes, and it can be done more cheaply by little books. The particular hymn, too, is readily and quickly found; which is quite important.

Should the choir be expected to sing? If the services are in the main audience-room, it may be desirable. But they should act only as leaders of the congregation – *not* as monopolisers of the singing. The leader, also, should be thoroughly in sympathy with the preacher, and discard all idea of exhibitions of skill. It is important, in all revival meetings, that at the outset there should be a mutual understanding as to the matter of choir-help.

Should the organ be used? A melodeon is better, as being generally closer to the audience, and more readily handled. As a rule, perhaps, it is better to dispense with instrumental music.

What should be the character of the singing? This depends much upon the circumstances. If it is in a low state of the church, it should generally be grave, penitential and subdued. If the feeling is high, and converts are multiplying, it may be more joyous and demonstrative. It should always, however, be prompt and spirited, never dull and prosy. Above all, let those who sing *feel* what they utter, and so *plainly speak the words* as to edify one another – as Paul says, singing "with the understanding;" that is, so as to be understood. We append a few other hints.

Let the leader be in front of the congregation, before the pulpit, and nearly on a level with the pews.

Use a given hymn always with the same tune.

Use a book in which the hymn and tune are upon one page.

The connection of the hymn should not be broken by interludes, or long pauses.

The verses in any one singing should be few; seldom more than two or three.

The singing of a familiar hymn will often be more spirited if the reading of it be omitted.

Use tunes that are strictly congregational in their structure.

If new tunes cannot be learned, use such as are already familiar.

Let the sentiment of the hymns, in any given meeting, be uniform from beginning to end. Keep to the "key-note," in this respect, throughout; otherwise the mind is turned off from the main point of the meeting.

Let everything bend to the one object of awakening, edifying and saving men; and do it "heartily, as unto the Lord."

"O Lord, Revive Thy Work!"

14

Personal Effort and Revivals

EVERY attentive reader of the New Testament perceives how the gospel at first won its way. The converts told the good news to their friends, who, in turn, believed and influenced others.

Take this narrative: "John stood, and two of his disciples; and looking upon Jesus as he walked, he saith, Behold the Lamb of God! and they followed Jesus. One of the two which heard John speak, and followed him, was Andrew, Simon Peter's brother. He first findeth his own brother Simon, and saith unto him, We have found the Messias, which is, being interpreted, the Christ. And he brought him to Jesus. The day following Jesus would go forth into Galilee, and findeth Philip, and saith unto him, Follow me. Philip findeth Nathanael and saith unto him, We have found him of whom Moses in the law, and the prophets, did write, Jesus of Nazareth, the son of Joseph. And Nathaniel said unto him, Can there any good thing come out of Nazareth? Philip saith unto him, Come and see." (*John 1:35-46*).

Thus a company of believers gathered about our Lord Jesus, and from Him radiated abroad throughout Judea. The absence of any distinct organisation is most observable. And in the formation of the church at Jerusalem, how plain that everything centred, not in an organic body, but in the individual convert.

Speaking of this first church organisation. Dr William Adams says, "It formed itself, as it were. It was a collection of believing men and women who were baptised in testimony of their Christian belief. All the organisation there was about it, appears to have been as exigencies arose, necessities required, and proprieties prompted. What

Christ enjoined, was that every creature should believe on Him as a personal Redeemer; and that all who believe on Him should observe His ordinances, baptism and the Lord's Supper. Nothing beyond this do we find in the record. Our Lord always individualises men. Faith in the heart of the particular man is the essential thing. All those who believed on Him after this manner, gravitating towards a common centre, naturally and voluntarily associated together; and so particular churches were formed and organised, by the election of their own officials, and the administration of their own rules. So simply lies the whole matter in the New Testament. The first Christian church was in that city where the gospel was first preached. It consisted of those resident in that place who, in the comprehensive but laconic phrase of Scripture, called on the name of the Lord Jesus."

When persecution burst upon this society of believers, they were all scattered abroad *except the apostles*, who remained at Jerusalem. And we read that "they that were scattered abroad went everywhere *preaching the word.*" We are also told of a few years' results of this individual heralding of the new faith. "Now they which were scattered abroad upon the persecution that arose about Stephen travelled as far as Phenice, and Cyprus, and Antioch, preaching the word to none but unto the Jews only. And some of them were men of Cyprus and Cyrene, which, when they were come to Antioch, spake unto the Grecians, preaching the Lord Jesus. And the hand of the Lord was with them: and a great number believed, and turned unto the Lord." (*Acts 11:19-21*).

The great commission is virtually repeated in *Revelation 22*, and in how broad a form! "The Spirit and the bride say, Come; and *let him that heareth* say, Come." The idea is that of a crier, proclaiming good news as he runs; and everyone that hears, takes up and repeats the tidings, the sound echoing from hill to valley, till all do hear. Here, then, is a universal command to everyone that receives the gospel, to make it known to others.

Soon after this, the simple apostolic idea of an associated company of believers, was lost in a "*clergy-church.*" The church idea of Christianity culminated in ripe Romanism. Henceforward, religion was sacerdotal; and there was a *monopoly* of the word of life. Ecclesiastics were everything; the laity nothing. A masterpiece of organism, known as THE CHURCH, assumes the care of souls, and dispenses salvation. As Isaac Taylor has it, this "church idea," lays its hold on all that are born within its circle, and it seals them as the property of the church, and treats them as passive subjects – not individually indeed, but *seriatim* rather – in its own appointed manner, as they arrive at each epoch of their mortal journey from the womb to the grave. It daily engages for their safety and welfare, (certain conditions complied with), and it sends them along authoritatively countersigned and endorsed, into the unseen world.

With the first of the revival periods which we have chronicled, there was a return, in part, to the primitive idea of a church of Christ. Individual Christians began again to stand forth. After a while, however, Protestantism crystallised into Formalism; and "*Church*-ianity" instead of *Christ*-ianity again prevailed. Then came the reformers of the Reformation; and a religion began to be preached, by which *individuals* should be saved, instead of being "left to freeze to death in the arms of an establishment."

Here, as one has remarked, is the core of all modern evangelism: self-conviction on the part of individual members of Christ's church, prompting to produce the same convictions in others. And from this centre have sprung all those achievements by which Christianity has been so rapidly and extensively diffused in our times. Two things cannot be conceived in more decided contrast than the *church idea* of Christianity in medieval history, and the *true idea* so potent in the primitive churches, and greatly restored in these last days.

Nor can one fail to see a deep divine philosophy in the arrangement by which men are *individualised* in all the things of salvation. Plainly this is after God's order. It is no disparagement of the ministry to make prominent the laity. True, the churches must have leaders; but a general is not to be left to fight alone. Men must be specially *commissioned* and ordained to dispense the Word and ordinances; but there is abundant room for all non-commissioned officers – the great body of believers. When a house is on fire, it were a poor plea for inaction in a bystander to say, "I am not a regular fireman; I have no commission; putting out fires does not devolve on *me*." His business is to rush in and by all means deliver those in peril.

The truth is, since a church is only a company of individuals, the obligation to reclaim a lost world presses on all alike. It is not the work of a great corporate body, but of believers personally. The pastor is to act; but so must the church members. Each one is responsible for the duties of the station where he is placed. He cannot work by proxy. His own growth in grace and spiritual enjoyment depend upon his fidelity and activity. The eye and the hand, the brain and the lungs, have different offices. But by what reason or law is the hand expected to be more faithful than the foot, or the ear, or the tongue? And there is no reason why an apostle, an evangelist, a pastor should be more faithful in his official way than a merchant, a physician, a lawyer, a housewife should be in their sphere. All alike are to act with prime reference to the honour of Christ in the extension of His church through the earth.

In all the revivals which we have sketched, this lay element was effective. Is it to be supposed that Baxter accomplished the great work we have spoken of without helpers? Let him speak on this point: "One *advantage* which I had was through the zeal and diligence of the *godly people of the place who thirsted after the salvation of their neighbours, and were in private my assistants;* and being dispersed through the town, they were ready in almost all companies, to repress seducing words, and to justify godliness, and convince, reprove, and exhort men according to their needs; and also to teach them how to pray, and to help them to sanctify the Lord's Day. Those people that had none in their families who could pray or repeat the sermons, went to the houses of their neighbours who could do it, and joined with them." Should we expect anything less than a great work in such a case?

What worlds of self-help were in those words which formed the hope and motto of the first Methodists: – "*All at it; always at it; altogether at it!*" It has often been observed that a chief element in John Wesley's power was in organising and inspiring his fellow helpers. What could he have done without them? Stevens says, with reference to the year 1742: "The *evangelical itinerants* directed their course toward the mining populations of the north and west, prepared for mobs, and, if need be, for martyrdom. Hitherto Wesley's lay '*helpers*' had been but '*exhorters,*' and '*readers,*' and '*expounders,*' of the Scriptures; but '*lay preaching*' was now formally begun."

Half a century later, we meet a fine example in the unofficial personal exertion of the brothers Robert and James Alexander Haldane, of Scotland. Robert sold his princely estate for seventy thousand guineas, and appropriated the avails to the promotion of religion, excepting only his family expenses, which he limited to five hundred pounds annually.

In May, 1801, James Haldane proceeded on a preaching tour in the south of Scotland, and for four months preached every Lord's Day to large congregations in the open air, and under a tent, and every day in the neighbouring towns and villages. And everywhere his preaching was acceptable, and often was it seen that the Word was with power. He was for half a century a revival lay-preacher, in the best sense of the term. Eternity alone will disclose the fruits of the loving spontaneous labours of these men.

In more modern revivals this element of voluntary effort is observable. Dr E Porter, in his *Letters on Revivals*, says: – "During the revivals of religion which prevailed at the beginning of this century, there was but *one sentiment* among ministers respecting the indispensable importance of using more than the 'ordinary means' for the conversion of sinners. In Connecticut several intelligent and pious laymen, fired with a passion for saving souls, united and went from town to town holding protracted meetings for prayer and exhortation, several days in a place. They visited fifty places, in each of which a precious work of grace followed, and many souls were hopefully converted."

The lay element may be said to have been *the* feature of the revival of 1857-60. In a letter from Scotland, Rev A Robinson has the following: "It has been said that lay agency has done more harm than good in the successful promotion of revival work. My experience is the reverse. I have seen indisputable proof that the Lord greatly honoured and blessed the zealous self-denying efforts of the Christian people. These young men deserve the highest praise, and I bear this testimony, that I have seen literally nothing of that overweening conceit and spiritual pride, so natural, and so much feared by some good men. It was said that the church would be inundated by a very deluge of heresies, as the fruit of such promiscuous and uneducated exhortation. It was more practised here than elsewhere, and yet we have been troubled with no heresies."

It is well known that the Fulton Street prayer-meeting, New York, was a movement of businessmen, the same being true of similar meetings all through the land.

In a letter of that date, Rev Theophilus L Cuyler thus refers to another form of lay-work, which was common: "Since the revival commenced, our active members have arranged a systematic visiting of the impenitent, conversing with them or addressing them by kind letters. Each one selects one or more to look after. He makes himself *responsible* for those persons. The best Sunday School teachers visit their scholars during the week. In this way the pastor is powerfully aided – the working piety of the church is developed, and many are reached and brought to the evening services for prayer. Every evening meeting witnesses new cases of inquiry, and new converts to Christ. I earnestly wish that every church would adopt these two lines of action and carry them both out far more thoroughly than we have done. Are not *fighting sin and saving souls* the two great purposes for which churches exist?"

It is important to remark that lay-effort ought to be *intelligently* employed. It is everyone's duty to be "wise" in winning souls, to the greatest possible extent.

We give a few hints and suggestions which may help those anxious to do most good in the Master's work.

Parents should influence their children. Especially in a revival should they earnestly and lovingly converse and pray with them. If they show anxiety, they should carefully guard it from being dissipated. If they rejoice in hope, they should instruct and encourage them. Never is paternal neglect more culpable than during a revival of religion.

Sisters and brothers may exert a blessed influence. A young man on examination for ordination, stated that he was converted in a revival. Upon being asked as to the special means, he replied: "My sister's tears broke my heart; she was so anxious for my salvation."

Family visitation is another means of usefulness. Even the apostles "ceased not to teach and to preach in every house," as well as "in the temple."

Religious conversation is a means which all can use. And the power of "words fitly spoken" is often exemplified in revivals of religion.

Prayer is an instrumentality available to all. A feeble sick man, on his bed, can draw down a revival. When every other expedient fails, supplications to the Almighty are still left to us.

Watch the best opportunity to approach someone; especially waiting till disengaged from any employment, so as not to be deemed obtrusive; and when the person is in a good temper.

In the main, *speak to one when alone.* Most persons are timid, or too proud, to converse on religion in the company of others.

Seize the time when *some providence* favours your designs; as sickness, or any affliction.

Do not procrastinate. Make an opportunity if you cannot find one. Death, and God's blessed Spirit, may not wait for your "right time" to come.

Aim constantly at saving men. It is a great enterprise to *win souls* to Christ; and when it ceases to be of secondary importance to the mass of professing Christians, salvation will come out of Zion.

Realise the worth of souls. A soul! a soul! Think of its capacity, duration, value. Look upon sinners as under sentence of death. Ask when you see the vast procession of mankind moving toward the grave, where will they be a few years hence? – and then go out to try to save them.

Be filled with the Spirit. This will make one's face to shine as did Moses'. Men will see and feel that we have been with God. A man once went from a revival-meeting into a manufactory, to speak to some of the operatives. All *felt* that he was there on solemn business. A young lady made a trifling remark, and laughed. He looked at her with a feeling of grief. She stopped, her thread broke, she became agitated, and soon sat down overcome with emotion. She had been stricken with a sense of sin; and conviction seized the rest of the hands, so that the astonished owner proposed to stop work and have a prayer-meeting; and nearly all in the establishment were converted.

Especially work while the Lord works. President Edwards says of the revival in his time, that more was done in one week then, than in seven years before.

And yet, if believers will but arouse themselves to God's work, the lack of revivals will not be complained of. They will exist already.

This lack of personal exertion, is the great want of the time. The vast majority of professors of religion are ready to fortify themselves with excuses against all appeals to a positive Christian life. A minister once urged a good farmer in his church to come out and co-operate in the meetings; and now, particularly, to be at one of special appointment. He assented; and as the pastor left, thinking he had gained a point, the farmer shouted, "If I do not come I'll send a hand!" This suits very many. Here is a man who has plenty of money, and is disposed to take life easy; and he says "I'll give money; but you do the work: – I'll *send a hand.*" Here is a woman with plenty of time at her command, and when you urge her to visit the poor and sick, she says, "O, I do not exactly like to go myself; I'll subscribe – I'll send a hand!" Christian parents lay over on the Sunday School teachers the work of praying with and for their children: saying, "It's a trial to me; a cross; but *you* do it. – I'll send a hand." And here is a man of wealth whose son God evidently calls to preach, or to go a missionary: but the fatherly pride choosing for that son some lucrative profession, the parent answers, "I cannot give up my son; but I'll give money to educate some *other one* for the ministry: – I'll send a hand." And so this excusing goes on; forgetful of the fact that God never yet *delegated* one man to do another's work; but everywhere, and in every way, calls for personal service.

The most frequent plea is want of *ability;* to which we answer, there are many ways in which you can exert a positive influence for Christ, and within your present capacity. In the days of Bonaparte the yeomanry of a certain district of France came together with their muskets and swords to repel an invasion; and an old woman was seen among them with a broomstick. "Janet," said the colonel, "what are you doing here with that?" She replied, "I am come to take part with the volunteers." "But how can you take part with a broomstick?" inquired the colonel. "Sir," said she, "I can show which side I am on."

Who has not the ability in many ways of showing what side he is on?

It is worthwhile for the reader to ask, "Is my influence *for* or *against* a revival?" Mr Cuyler somewhere asks, "Who *votes against a revival?*" And this is his forcible answer: The Christian who neglects his duty practically votes against a revival. He who is more busy in making money than in doing good, is opposing the advent of Christ into our churches. When I see a vacant seat in the prayer-meeting, or an empty pew on an unpleasant Sabbath, I say to myself, "There is a vote against a revival." When I see a Sunday School class left without a teacher, I say, "There is a vote against a revival!" When I hear of church-members quitting their places of prayer for the opera-house or the ball-room, I count up so many votes against God's coming among us. Drinking usages hinder revivals. Injustice to God's poor hinders a revival. Inconsistent Christians are just so many dams to obstruct the river of salvation. O, for less voting against revivals, and more of decided purpose, under God, to turn many unto righteousness!

"O Lord, Revive Thy Work!"

15

The Sunday School and Revivals

SUNDAY SCHOOLS are the most encouraging fields of revival effort. They have been so regarded from the date of their origin.

During the last half of the 18th century they arose in England, and became an ally in evangelistic movements. As early as 1769, a young Methodist, Hannah Ball, established a Sunday School in Wycombe, and was instrumental in training many children in the knowledge of the Holy Scriptures. Doubtless similar attempts were made before that time, but they were only anticipations of the modern institution of Sunday Schools. In 1781, while another Methodist young woman, (afterwards the wife of the celebrated lay preacher, Samuel Bradburn), was conversing in Gloucester with Robert Raikes, (a benevolent citizen of that town and publisher of the *Gloucester Journal*), he pointed to groups of neglected children in the street, and asked: "What can we do for them?" She answered: "Let us teach them to read, and take them to church!" They immediately proceeded to try the suggestion, and he and his female friend attended the first company of Sunday scholars to the church, exposed to the comments and laughter of the populace as they passed along with their ragged procession.

Wesley's earliest notice of Sunday Schools is in his *Journal* for July 18, 1784, the year of Raikes' published account of them. He speaks of them prophetically: "I find these schools springing up wherever I go; perhaps God may have a deeper end therein than men are aware of; who knows but some of these schools may be nurseries for Christians?" They were introduced into the metropolis by Rowland Hill, in 1786. Wesley mentions in 1786, that five hundred and fifty children were taught in the Sunday School of his society at Bolton, and the next year he found there eight hundred, taught by eighty "masters." Richard Rodda, one of his preachers, records that, in 1786, he formed a Sunday School in Chester, and soon had nearly seven hundred children "under regular masters." Wesley wrote to him in the beginning of 1787: "I am glad you have taken in hand that blessed work of setting up Sunday Schools in Chester. It seems these will be *one great means of reviving religion throughout the nation*. I wonder Satan has not yet sent out some able champion against them."

A Presbyterian minister in Scotland, narrating the means blessed in the modern revivals there, says, with reference to Sunday Schools, "On these the blessing of God has abundantly rested. Frequently has it been observed that in revivals the Bible classes and Sunday Schools have been deeply affected; *they* have felt the *first* influence of God's grace, and the great work has sometimes commenced with them."

Dr Stephen H Tyng, in his *Forty Years in Sunday Schools*, has furnished some very interesting facts as to the agency of Sunday Schools in gathering souls to Christ. Looking back to the commencement of his ministry in Philadelphia, he says, "five years' ministry at St Paul's prepared me with a knowledge and experience which were brought into operation in the successful founding and establishment of the Church of the Epiphany in the same city. That church was founded upon the Sunday School. Its energy and strength were given to the schools. And they were blessed with many very precious evidences of the Lord's presence and grace, and large numbers from them were gathered to the table of the Lord, and already many young ministers are in the Lord's work who have gone forth from them."

He further says: "In the 31 years that I have been a city pastor, I have received to the Lord's Table over three hundred youth of both sexes directly from the Sunday School. And I have no doubt I might with equal truth add two hundred more, uniting with us from the resulting influence of previous Sunday School instruction. An early revival in St Paul's church in Philadelphia commenced in our weekly Sunday School prayer-meeting. The exercises closed, and the people were dismissed, when, rising from my place, I counted sixteen of our youth still on their knees on the floor. I went from one to the other with a few words of affectionate and pastoral conversation, and appointed Monday evening as an occasion for their special assembly. On the next day I gave notice of this appointment, and over seventy youth met me for instruction and prayer. It was the divine commencement of a very remarkable work of mercy. The result was the addition of over one hundred, mostly from the Sunday School, to the communion of the church. The subjects of that work are now active and earnest Christians, in the maturity of grace."

In the United States the wonderful revivals at the beginning of the present century were closely identified with Sunday Schools. Rev Archibald Maclay, pastor of the Mulberry Street Baptist church, New York, states that a year after that church was formed, (in 1809), a Sunday School was established; and a little later three others. He says that for ten years they had almost a perpetual revival, and that at least 500 souls were hopefully converted during that time. The connection between this Sunday School movement and the large ingathering is most suggestive. *Eighteen of the converts from the school were licensed to preach, and became ministers of the gospel.*

Dr Francis Wayland wrote, in 1842, "Perhaps few means have been attended with more invariably good effect than the establishment of Bible classes. I perhaps should not err in saying that revivals have more commonly commenced in Bible classes than anywhere else."

Dr W B Sprague, about the same time says, "Revivals have of late more frequently commenced in Bible classes and Sunday Schools than anywhere else; and not a few instances have occurred, in which all or nearly all the members of a class have become hopefully the subjects of renewing grace; while the work, which had its beginning here, has extended on the right hand and on the left, till multitudes have experienced its quickening and renovating influence." "It is a well-known fact," he adds, "that the records of Sunday Schools and the records of revivals are to a great extent identified – that the noblest triumphs of God's grace have often been found in these nurseries of knowledge, virtue and piety."

In a certain school in New England, in 1832, *sixty-one* out of fifteen classes of 160 pupils under sixteen years of age, became hopefully pious. In six classes, embracing seventy-one young persons over sixteen years of age, *sixty* indulged hope that they had passed from death unto life, making in all one hundred and twenty-one who became hopefully pious in a school of 231 scholars. In a County Sunday School Society, in Massachusetts, embracing ten parishes, and the same number of schools, the Lord smiled upon this institution, in 1834-5, and shed down upon it the influence of His Holy Spirit. Six schools were blessed with powerful revivals of religion. Three hundred scholars from these ten schools made a profession during the year. It was supposed that the whole number that passed from death to life was over four hundred.

It is an interesting circumstance that special efforts to establish Sunday Schools all through New York and Brooklyn, were in active progress when the revival of 1857 and 1858 commenced. Up to this time there was no organised systematic effort to establish and sustain mission schools. It was the spontaneous effort of individuals. A Sunday School Union had existed for years; but it contemplated little more than a bond of union among the schools, and made no aggressive movements. Early in the year 1855, this organisation was given up, and a new one formed, with special reference to the missionary work; and it became an important element in the revival that soon followed.

The intimate connection between Sunday Schools and revivals is obvious upon the least reflection. Probably there are in the United States some *four million* scholars in Sunday Schools, with some *eight hundred thousand* teachers. Can anything be more important for the cause of the Redeemer than revivals of pure religion among these mighty hosts of children and youth? What an amount of sanctified influence were thereby secured!

Several things are necessary in order to the greatest efficiency of the Sunday School movement. There must be an adequate teaching force; the attendance and improvement of the young; and purity of doctrine in the instruction given. Now *only by revivals* can we have a sufficient number of competent teachers – themselves taught of God, and full of the Spirit, able and willing to discharge their high trusts. Revivals give to teachers a tender concern for their pupils, right views of their relations, and the power of a constraining love.

They also serve greatly to increase the number of those taught. Under a strong heavenly influence, teachers go out into the highways and hedges and compel the wanderers to come in; and parents gladly co-operate in filling up the school; while the true end of all instruction, the conversion and sanctification of those who are taught, is gained by the mighty power of the Holy Spirit. At the same time, the truth "as it is in Jesus" is imparted; for it is in a cold, not a revived state of the churches, that doctrines are corrupted.

It must also be remembered, that the pupils in the Sunday Schools are generally in the morning of life, and that a revival in numbering them as its subjects, secures the influence of nearly a whole life to the cause of truth and piety. When an individual comes into the kingdom with the full freshness and vigour of youth, there is occasion for joy not merely because, from an heir of hell one has become an heir of heaven, but because there is reason to hope for a useful life in the advancement of the cause of Christ. When, therefore, the dews of divine grace descend copiously upon Sunday Schools, there is an amount of influence secured in favour of the interests of the church which outruns all calculation.

Then look upon the Sunday School as an auxiliary in the cause of revivals. We hesitate not to say that a more important influence for good, or one more actually effective upon the character of men, (except always the ministry and the churches, as such), cannot be found than is seen today in the organised and active Sunday School forces of Christendom. Here is at once the material and the enginery of revivals.

What wise pastor, if he desires a revival, does not look *first* to his Sunday School? *There* are the hearts most apt to catch anew the heavenly flame, and hands most ready for sanctified service. And there are found scores and hundreds of souls in the most impressible and hopeful condition of life. The present generation of youthful pastors, missionaries, teachers, and earnest workers of any kind, are chiefly the precious fruits of that which was scattered as a handful of corn in early Sunday School efforts.

There is another point of view in which the influence of Sunday Schools is helpful to revivals. We refer to the fact that they contribute to right views of religious truth, and to the purity of revivals. Dr Archibald Alexander has somewhere said: "In a revival, it makes the greatest difference in the world whether the people have been carefully taught, or are ignorant of the truths of the Bible. The impression on the minds of the people in such a work is the exact counterpart of the truth; just as the impression on the wax corresponds to the seal." In this respect the results of Sunday Schools are invaluable.

Viewed in whatever light, then, who can resist the conviction that through our Sunday Schools are to be gathered the largest harvests of glory in the salvation of men? There is no rival operation. There is no comparable instrument. There is no agency to take the place of this great work, even in the most partial degree.

As to the *conditions of increased effectiveness in soul-saving*, on the part of the Sunday School, several things must be secured.

First of all, *ministers and churches must have a more lively interest* in this department of Christian activity. The churches, as such, must come to feel that this is the most hopeful scheme for the welfare of the people; and so give to it their sympathies, prayers and co-operation.

And ministers must view Sunday School work as not separable from, but a part of their appointed ministry. "The teachers of my school," remarked a pastor, "are but parts of myself: like the fingers of a power-press, they take up the very pages which I desire to impress, and smoothly and quietly spread them out before me, prepared to receive the blessed communications from on high which I long to stamp on their minds and hearts forever." This is a correct view. Thus the minister reaches out the arms of his strength over his congregation, inciting all the members to activity, and bringing them into harmony and mutual affection.

Thus, too, is the minister himself benefitted. There is great force in what has been remarked as to the personal advantage coming to the pastor who is closely linked with his school. It makes him more effective and real in every other department of his duty. It is the very manufacture which the raw material of a multitude of ministers requires to transform them into useful, appropriate, and practical agents in the Lord's house. It mortalises their ministry, by bringing them down to a practical shape and compelling the cultivation of a common-sense habit of teaching and address. It converts their abstractions into realities, and by making them the "teachers of babes" makes them the more intelligible and useful teachers for all. "When will ministers cease to try to feed their sheep out of horse-racks?" said a plain man once, in expressing his dissatisfaction with a sermon which he could not understand. There would be less of this if they were used to feeding the lambs.

There must be more of the aggressive spirit in our Sunday Schools. It is too often the case that a school is making no earnest efforts, to lengthen its borders; it is content in its own sweet enjoyment, which is foreign to the spirit of the gospel.

Every Sunday School should feel bound to "go up and possess the land," and rest not so long as one child is unembraced in the arms of this comprehensive effort. Where children cannot be gathered into the church schools proper, *mission* schools should be established. Indeed, this is a mighty Sunday School agency, and not yet half developed.

Were the *aggressive* spirit fully to seize our schools, what extensive revivals would follow!

As another condition of increased efficiency, *doctrinal truth must be more thoroughly* taught in our schools. It is alarming to think what an amount of crude and false instruction is given to classes every week. We fear that even the *three 'Rs'* of William Jay, are not insisted upon – R – *Ruined* by sin: R – *Redeemed* by Christ: R – *Regenerated* by the Spirit.

At a Sunday School Convention the following conversation occurred between Mr A and Mr B.

A. What does that text, "Feeding lambs," mean?

B. I suppose it refers to the little children.

A. To all little children?

B. Yes, I have so regarded it.

A. If you call them the lambs of Christ, do you not imply that they are either *regenerate* ones, or that they are holy, or in a saved state, without regeneration?

B. It strikes me you are correct.

A. Lambs are simply young sheep: they *are* sheep, and Christ applies that term to regenerate ones. You might call children *kids*, but certainly until made Christians by God's renewing spirit, they are not lambs.

B. What, then, did Christ mean when he directed Peter to feed his lambs?

A. Evidently the weak, uninstructed, inexperienced ones of his flock, including of course those of tender years. One *recently converted* is a lamb, be the age what it may. A lamb is one young in experience – not necessarily young in years.

Here the conversation ended. Mr A was correct; but how often does Mr B find embodiment in Sunday School "talks," not to say *instructions*, even from those who are "leaders" in this branch of effort! How easy, as we see from this, to inculcate the idea that children are little "innocent" things, and not needing conversion! And worse yet, that if they are "good" they will go to heaven! – *pure legalism!*

Just now doctrinal teaching is decried, and the demand is, "Teach practical truths!" But what reliance can be placed upon practical teaching that has not its origin in a clear, strong, sharply cut system of doctrine? Who will vouch for its orthodoxy?

And all this outcry against teaching the "dry dogmas" of religion is as utterly unphilosophical as it is mischievous. As Dr Gulliver remarks, if this talk were to be taken literally, it would show about as much sense as a demand that shipmasters should never be taught the principles of navigation; that farmers should only be anxious to learn what their grandfathers did; that physicians should practise by a "Dispensatory;" and parents govern their children according to *The Mother's Own Book*.

Dr Arnot, of Scotland, in his Evangelical Alliance address, in New York in 1873, says with reference to the modern theorisers, "For our convenience they have compressed the essence of their system into a phrase that is compact and portable. 'A grain of charity is worth a ton of dogma.' The maxim is well constructed, and its meaning is by no means obscure. If it were true I should have no fault to find with it. But as I have seen a mechanic, after the rule applied to his work gave unequivocal decision on its form, turning the rule round and trying it the other way, lest some mistake should occur; so in this important matter before us, it may be of use to express the same maxim in another form, lest any fallacy should be left lurking unobserved in its folds; thus 'a small stream flowing on the ground is worth acres of clouds careering in the sky.' In this form the maxim is arrant nonsense; but the two forms express an identical meaning, like the opposite terms of an algebraic equation. Wanting clouds above us, there could be no streams, great or small, flowing at our feet; so, wanting dogma – that is, doctrine revealed by God and received by man – there could be no charity. They scorn dogma and laud charity – that is, they vilify the clouds and sing paeans to running streams!"

Again; there must be *better aims and the wiser use of means*, in our Sunday Schools in order to their greater effectiveness in soul-saving. The teacher's thought and plan must be that of a real and living messenger of Christ to a little congregation, whose eternity may depend upon this immediate relation and opportunity.

And the *expectation* should be that the pupil will be converted. This expectation is the teacher's right; because it is the subject of the divine promise; and what God has promised, we have a right to expect.

Of course this assumes the piety, and the deep piety, of the teacher. The piety, we say, for what is a Sunday School teacher but a minister of God? In the very nature of the employment it is a work for Christians and for them alone. It is really a ministry for souls in eternal things, and at a period of life when the impressions received are very permanent and effectual. As well have unconverted ministers as unconverted Sunday School teachers. In either case it would be the blind leading the blind. Of all qualifications in a teacher, certainly the *essential* one is regeneration.

It also assumes that there is *deep* piety on the part of the teacher. Teachers should not only be alive to God, but *lively for God*. They imperatively need a real living experience of the *power of the truth*, and the love of the Word of God, and an earnest desire for the salvation of those to whom it is offered, with a real belief that they *can be*, and *ought to be* saved, under its ministration. This constitutes the adaptation of the ministry in the pulpit, and is equally the instrument of blessing for precious souls in the Sunday School.

Besides this right aim, there must be *the wise use of means* for the conversion of the unrenewed.

Personal conversation is one of these means. There is much talking at scholars that is not adapted to their conversion; but the wise use of personal appeal is a most cogent and effective agency.

Letter writing is often still better. Where, from many causes, conversation cannot be had under favourable circumstances, a loving, earnest, tender epistle directed to the pupil will produce the desired result. No teacher should leave this method untried.

Visiting from house to house, not only their own scholars, but the family and the neighbours also, is a method which wise and earnest teachers will not neglect. There are hundreds upon hundreds of country towns, thinly settled, and with perhaps not population enough to sustain preaching, where Sunday School teachers are the *only human reliance* for the salvation of the inhabitants. God grant them grace to be *missionaries to the destitute!*

Positive identification with the pupils is a mighty advantage. The scholars will then feel that their teachers are their true friends, and will be ready to yield to their influence.

Prayer with the classes is a powerful instrumentality. Are there not many classes who never heard the voice of their teacher in supplication on their behalf? Are there not many pastors who never knelt with their Sunday School classes and prayed with them? What an agency is here unused! The writer of this work has few more pleasant memories than of those seasons when he has bowed with his Sunday School, class by class, so far as time would allow, while they knelt around him. At times he has requested the scholars, at the close of the lesson, to come around him near the platform, and kneel in prayer, almost the whole school complying with the request. On such occasions heaven has come nigh to earth!

Bringing the scholars to the pastor is an incalculable advantage. Especially in times of a revival, when many are awakened, is the pastor by this means very greatly assisted, and the teacher's influence is greatly extended. A good minister will always encourage this practice, and wise teachers will use their best endeavours towards the same end.

Meetings for conversation and prayer can hardly be held too often. Frequently, when it is not suspected, religious concern is felt by a scholar; and in this way it is developed. Many a revival in the writer's congregation has begun thus. At first, perhaps, there was but one inquirer; but that was a living coal, and though a little matter, it kindled a great fire.

The Sunday School and Revivals! How interesting a topic! What glory from thence already fills the heavenly courts! What numbers of teachers and scholars are there rejoicing together before God! What numbers are on their way thither! And what encouragements to hope that, as the ages go on, the church of Christ will more and more, through this source, clothe herself with souls "as with an ornament, and bind them on her as a bride doeth!"

"O Lord, Revive Thy Work!"

16

Treatment of Inquirers

PASTORS of inexperience, and even skilled workers, are often perplexed as to the treatment of inquirers. And the matter is one of exceeding importance. Most responsible is the office of an adviser under such interesting circumstances. It is perhaps the crisis of a soul. The mind is in a state to be easily influenced, and the subject is one involving all the interests of eternity. Of what vast consequence may a word, a suggestion, an item of advice now be!

The condition of a soul then is like that of a sick person when in the critical period, and the case is balancing between life and death. And the concern of the spiritual adviser may well be greater than that of the physician, who watches each symptom, and anxiously counts the number of the pulse-beats in a minute!

Nor can it be doubted that false instruction is often given, even by those who have been taught of God. Not every Christian is fit to talk to inquirers. The warm-hearted and enthusiastic may mislead; and if inexperienced and unintelligent, it were well for them to leave this service to other hands. A master workman in spiritual things, once said, "The more experience I have, and the more I observe the workings of things, the more suspicious I am of the attempts of even good people to direct their anxious friends."

Yet directions to inquirers should be given. It is an error of some to limit all advice to this: "Repent and believe." Can the sinner do this before understanding at least something of what it is? A large part of the conduct of a revival consists in counselling the awakened; and on the manner in which this duty is performed, as much as anything, depend both the character of the work and its results. How important, therefore, that ministers and members be so enlightened as to be safe guides on this momentous subject; that thus they may never put in jeopardy the interests of those whom they attempt to direct.

Perhaps we can best discuss the subject by proposing and answering several questions.

1. *What are some of the methods of ascertaining and approaching inquirers?*

Requesting them to call upon the pastor is one of these. Good ministers have always encouraged the anxious to make it known by coming to them for conversation and advice, either singly or together. The practice is every way desirable.

Written requests for prayer, either sent to the pastor at his home, or handed in for presentation at meetings, is another method. This does not identify the inquirers, to a great extent, but it is a useful custom, and greatly resorted to of late in almost all revival meetings. Dr Payson adopted the plan of having a box at the church-door, in which written requests for prayer were deposited.

Rising for prayer is another method. Half a century ago this became quite common, though some strongly objected to it, especially in large assemblies. The practice, however, has secured quite general sanction, and is common in almost all meetings in times of special interest.

Anxious seats, (as they were unfortunately called), became common about the same time. It cannot be said that they met with general approval; and the more conservative pastors strongly discountenanced them.

Coming forward for prayer, (which, is little else than the above), is very general in revival meetings. We do not see that exception can be taken to the thing itself, though methods sometimes used to persuade, urge, and almost force attendants thus to present themselves, should not be countenanced. The advantage here claimed is that the person is thus *committed* to serious things. The objection that "there is great danger, when you persuade a man who is not yet converted, publicly to commit himself, that he will be induced by other than religious feelings and motives to persevere and come into the church, and hang as a dead weight upon the cause," does not seem to have force. Nor yet again, another, sometimes urged, that this encourages forwardness, ostentation, and rashness. Where discretion is used, we do not see how harm can come from the practice, provided the state of things seems to call for it. It is in place to state that Dr Nettleton never adopted the anxious seat, nor requested persons to rise in the assembly to be prayed for, or to signify that they had given their hearts to God, or that they had made up their minds to attend to the subject of religion.

Inquiry meetings are now almost universally approved. Dr Humphrey writes thus: "Among the means which God has signally blessed in carrying forward revivals of religion, meetings for personal conversation with the awakened are found to hold an important place. These meetings are by common consent called *Inquiry* meetings, in distinction from all others – a better name, I think, could not be given them. And in the progress of a powerful revival, when large numbers are in the several stages of alarm and inquiry, they are so essential, that no pastor who would make the most of his strength, can dispense with them. When they were first introduced among the means which God has been pleased to own in the glorious 'times of refreshing from His presence,' I do not know. In the great revivals at the beginning of the nineteenth century, I neither saw nor heard of such inquiry meetings. Indeed, my first acquaintance with them was about 1817, it might be a little earlier, when Mr Nettleton was in the midst of his remarkable career, going from place to place in the shining armour of his mission, 'the Lord working mightily with him,' wherever he went. He held inquiry meetings, (*anxious* meetings as he called them), and felt that in the midst of a large revival he could not do without them. Other highly favoured servants of the Lord, ever since his day, have felt so; and such inquiry meetings as he held are now almost as firmly established, where God pours out his Spirit, as special meetings for prayer.

"The two great objects of an inquiry meeting are, to ascertain the actual state of the revival, and in a very few words to drop into the ear of the inquirer, such advice as seems to be wanted at the moment. Where the number is large, there is no time for extended conversation; but as he passes round, the pastor will ascertain where it is needed, and will reserve such cases for personal interviews elsewhere. The meeting should always be opened with a short prayer, and all should be requested to *kneel.* Some may regard the posture as a matter of very little consequence; but it is 'much every way.' It brings down stiff knees, that perhaps have never kneeled before; begets a sacred awe and reverence which pertains to no other posture; and no other posture should be encouraged at such a meeting, where there is room to kneel. In passing round, the minister may either speak to each individual, in a voice not so low but that those who sit next can hear at least a part of what is said, or lower it down to a whisper, so that the individual alone can hear."

What we consider the best method of conducting inquiry meetings is brought out in the above. We add an item or two. The pastor, in these meetings may well make a memorandum of the *names* of the inquirers; and endeavour to be able to *identify* each one. It is also an excellent practice when all are kneeling, for the leader to give to the inquirers words to repeat after him, in the simplest and most direct form of supplication, confession, and self-dedication. We have found this of very great advantage. When any important thought is suggested by the answers elicited, it is well to throw it out to the meeting, as briefly as possible, and then pass on. We always make it a practice, too, to give to inquirers *tracts*, or pamphlets, adapted either to awaken, or direct, as the case may seem to require. This is of great importance; as reading will tend to fix upon the mind the impression which the conversation may have made, and lead to clearer views of truth and duty.

Invitations to remain after the assembly is dismissed, is another method of access to inquirers; though it is apt to lead to the continuance of meetings to unreasonable hours, which, except in the most extreme cases, should be avoided.

The above are some available methods of coming into contact with inquirers.

2. *What should be some of the primary objects in dealing with inquirers?*

First of all to *obtain an exact knowledge of their mental condition.* Such points as these should receive attention: What is the true cause of the apparent concern? What has produced it? How long has it been felt? Is there real sincerity? Is there a sense of sin? How much knowledge has this person of Scripture truth? Upon what subject is light most needed? Is there genuine conviction, or is it only the temporary excitement of the sympathies and feelings? And is there a fixed determination, or otherwise?

Careful instruction should be another chief object. Truth is the instrument in conversion. Therefore the great thing is to bring truth to bear upon the mind. Difficulties must be cleared up; darkness dissipated; errors removed. Light, light – this is the great thing required.

Genuine conviction should be a chief object aimed at. There may be conviction enough to bring the sinner to you for counsel, when there is not enough to bring him to Christ for salvation. There should be no superficial work here. Let sin be spread out before the mind. Let the length and breadth of the law be enlarged upon. Get at the conscience; never be drawn aside into either speculations, or doctrinal discussions. Charge home guilt. Show a present condemnation, and an impending peril. Press the duty of immediate repentance, and set forth the awful guilt of unbelief and the rejection of Christ.

The following statement by Dr Payson, of his aims in meeting inquirers, answers very happily, in its main aspects, the question under consideration. He says: "We should endeavour to bring sinners to the same point to which God would bring them. This point is a complete self-despair and hope in Christ. The former is a pre-requisite to the latter. I therefore aim in the first place to increase their convictions of sins, especially of the great damning sin of unbelief. If they ask, What shall we do? I never dare give them any other answer than that given by Christ, and his apostles: 'Repent, and believe the Gospel.' I insist much on the character of God; the strictness, extent, and spirituality of his law; the various artifices, deceptions, and excuses of the heart; the false hopes of sinners and hypocrites; the nature of true and false conversion; and the great danger of being deceived. I also frequently warn them of the dreadful consequences of delaying repentance, grieving the Spirit, losing their convictions, or resting on false hopes, like the stony-ground hearers. I labour especially to convince them that all the difficulties which oppose their salvation lie in their own hearts – that Christ is willing to save them – but they are unwilling to be saved in His way and are therefore without excuse. This is a very important point. I have seen none go back who appeared to be truly convinced of this. In addition to this, I say much of the glory, beauty, and sufficiency of Christ, and of the perfect freeness of the blessings which He offers, and endeavour to show them the horrid pride and ingratitude, of neglecting to accept of them."

3. *What are some of the errors and obstacles common to inquirers?* A prominent one is, *that they must make themselves better*, and so recommend themselves, in some sense, to the favour of God. They are slow to apprehend that they have but to accept the proffers made in the Gospel.

Hence the *legal way of seeking salvation* is universal in the early stages of awakening. For this reason inquirers must be shown the utter futility of their works, and the duty of accepting the finished work of Christ.

Waiting for feeling is another error with inquirers. They often imagine that if only they could have some overwhelming sense of sin, some awful terror, and shed copious tears, then they would be saved. Hence they must be shown that there is no virtue whatever in all their bad feelings. We sometimes put it in this way: Were you in a house on fire, would you make no effort to escape from the devouring element until you *felt* the flames? If bitten by a rabid animal, would you wait until you *felt* the spasms before you sought a remedy? If a sick man has enough of pain and a sense of danger to make him willing to take the proffered remedy, he has feeling enough. So if you have feeling enough to cause you to wish to be a Christian, to feel your need of a Saviour, that is feeling enough.

Desiring deeper convictions is similar to the above. And here the sinner must be made to see that all this is but a species of self-righteousness: that he fancies, perhaps unconsciously, that there is some merit in pangs of repentance. Should a stubborn child imagine he is gaining anything by his agony? Shall he pray for more conviction? Does that make him any better? Does his father pity him any more because he stands out?

Protracted sorrows of mind are often considered necessary by inquirers. They are fearful of finding salvation too soon. It is well, then, to point to the Scriptures, and ask: Did you ever find in the Bible a command that you must have this feeling or that feeling before you could believe on Christ? Did our Lord tell Nicodemus to go home and wait until his heart was broken, and then come again and receive life? Did the apostles tell the thousands who were awakened by Peter's sermon on the day of Pentecost, to wait for further light or further conviction? And have you not erred in supposing that salvation is an emotion, or a feeling, or a series of these, rather than a new life begun in faith?

Waiting for the heart to be changed is much the same thing, "What?" say they, "am I to repent and believe in Christ before my heart is changed?" Now the simple answer is, that the change of heart is the very thing in question. God requires sinners to love him. *That* is a change of heart. God requires them to repent. *That* is a change of heart. God requires the sinner to believe the Gospel. *That is* a change of heart. God does not tell us to wait till the heart is changed. The very word itself, *repent*, signifies a change of mind or heart.

Laying out some plan for God to change them in is a frequent thing with inquirers. It must be made plain that this is all wrong; that they must not lay out a path beforehand, but let God lead them as He sees to be best; and that He always leads the blind by a way they know not. Never was a sinner brought into the kingdom through such a course of feeling as he expected.

Among the obstacles often lying in the way of the progress of inquirers are the following:

Expecting some marvellous and sudden change. Often they are anticipating some wondrous appearance, or some tangible impression, as if God would speak to them, or lay hold upon them, or prostrate them, like Saul, to the earth; or something of this kind. They must be told that some have more marked views and exercises than others: but that nothing of this kind is to be expected; and that most often the Spirit comes as the "still small voice." The transition may be like ushering from midnight darkness into noon. But most often, the light comes as that of the rising sun: first whitening, and then reddening the eastern sky; and so, little by little, approaching the perfect day.

Dread of having committed the unpardonable sin may hold one back from comfort. In such a case it must be shown that the fact of their concern is evidence of not having thus sinned. Where this sin is committed God has said, "Let him alone," and since you are not let alone, it is proof that mercy is still proffered.

Trying to do too much is a frequent obstacle. Let it be inquired: "In what manner are you striving? Is it not in a self-righteous spirit? And will you not now stop trying to save yourself, and simply lay hold of the arm of Christ?"

A supposed willingness to be saved is often entertained. They say: "Oh, yes, I am perfectly willing to do this, or that; I wish I could do it; I would give anything if I could do it." They must then be made to see that being truly *willing* is doing it; but there is a difference between willing and desiring. People often *desire* to be Christians, when they are wholly *unwilling* to be so.

Leaning upon the minister, or someone else for help, is sometimes a bar to progress. In that case stand out of the way: withdraw for a season, until it is felt that every prop has failed, and that no finite power in the universe can help.

Failing to relinquish what is demanded frequently stands in the way of peace. Ascertain the truth on these points: Is there not some idol, some darling object, some indulgence, that you are not willing to give up? Are you not retaining a prejudice, or ill-will, or an angry and unforgiving spirit toward someone? Or is there not some redress or confession to an injured person which you refuse to make?

An idea that they are not converted often prevents peace on the part of those truly changed. Edwards says of some of the converts under his eye: "It does not so much as come into their minds that they are converted: and very often the reason is that they do not see that they do accept of this sufficiency of salvation which they behold in Christ, having entertained a wrong notion of acceptance." And Dr Hallock remarks, "During my experience in revivals, I have often found that a man who is but recently born of the Spirit would often say, 'No, Sir,' should you ask him if he is converted; and yet I may have much better evidence of his real change than I have of another, who has an early and confident hope." Says Henry Ward Beecher, "A disease may pass its crisis, and for hours and days one may not be conscious of it. My own observation has led me to the conclusion that more persons become true Christians without sudden joy, and without the consciousness, at the time, of transition, or a great change, than with it."

4. *What are some of the counsels which are unwisely and injudiciously given to inquirers?* We specify the following:

"*Be patient and wait God's time.*" God's time is *now*. And is one to be "*patient*" in his sins? Telling the sinner to wait for God to convert him is telling him to continue in sin a while longer. Any direction given to sinners that does not require them *immediately* to obey God is an indulgence to sin. It is in effect giving them liberty still to fight against God. Such directions are wicked and cruel. It is pleading the sinner's cause against God.

"*Continue to use the means and strive on,*" is of the same nature. By no means discourage, but rather enjoin, the use of the means of grace; but *insist upon an instantaneous surrender to God's claims.* To direct one to keep on using the means is to abate the sense of guilt, and lull the soul into stupidity, or else, to put the inquirer upon a course of self-righteous effort. God calls the sinner to repent; He threatens him; He persuades him; He uses motives; and the sinner is distressed to agony because he sees himself driven to the dreadful alternative of giving up his sins or going to hell. He ought instantly to relent and lay down his weapons. But he resists, and struggles against conviction, and that creates his distress. Now will you tell him to *persevere?* Persevere in what? In struggling against God? That is just the direction Satan would give. All he wants is to see him persevere in just the way he is going on, and his destruction is sure. The seat of all the trouble is in his own *will.*

A venerable minister in the West, now in glory, used to relate the following incident with bitter tears: "In my early ministry, a woman came to me to inquire what she should do to be saved. I told her to go home and read the Bible and pray, be careful of her conduct, and attend upon all the means of grace. Some time after, I saw her, and inquired if she had followed my directions. She said she had, and felt better. But she had settled down into a state of quiet security, from which I could never awaken her. I felt that I had murdered her soul; and I determined from that day forward, that I would never again give a direction to an inquiring sinner, which, if followed, would not save his soul."

"*Your condition is encouraging; I hope you will soon be rejoicing,*" is dangerous language to a distressed soul. Of Dr Nettleton it is said, he was careful never to allay the fears of inquirers. He never expressed to them the opinion that their condition was hopeful. On the contrary, he gave them to understand, that while they remained impenitent, there was an awful uncertainty whether they would be saved. He urged the duty of immediate repentance, and showed them that they could do nothing short of repentance which would in the least degree improve their condition.

"*Try to repent and give your heart to God, and ask him to help you,*" is objectionable language. "I am willing to try; I have tried, and what more can I do?" is the answer to your counsel. All this is just what a rebellious heart wants. It relaxes the pressure of present obligation, and helps to cast the blame of continued impenitence on God.

Besides the above, there are expressions used in prayer liable to mislead inquirers – such as these: "Have mercy on these *penitent ones,*" or, "on those *seeking thy love to know,*" or, "those who are *seeking thee sorrowing,*" and the like. It is better, on several accounts, to refrain from the use of set phrases like these.

5. *What specific directions may with safety be given to inquirers?*

It is always safe to urge the sinner to *repent.* And it should be shown that this is the exercise of godly sorrow for sin. When one truly repents, he sees that God has been in the right, and he in the wrong; that His laws are holy, just, and good, and by those laws he is justly condemned. A sense of the goodness of God affects him; he is ready to cry out, "How could I sin against One so kind, so loving, so patient, so forbearing! Ah, me! wretch that I am! I am undone, I deserve the lowest hell! 'God be merciful to me a sinner!' "

It is always safe to urge one to *believe on the Lord Jesus Christ.* And it is important to show what true gospel faith is. The things to be believed must be set before the mind – particularly, what God has said concerning the work and deservings of His Son. "You are to believe that He satisfied divine justice for human guilt; that He became a propitiation for our sins; that what He did and suffered, is a ground for pardon to sinners; that since He died they need not die; and that however guilty you may be, yet, repenting of sin, and trusting in Him, His merit becomes, as it were, yours; and by it you are saved."

Also the act of believing is to be explained – that it is *receiving* Christ; *trusting* in him; *fleeing* to him; *coming* to him; *looking* to him, and the like. Particularly, must appropriating faith be made plain. "It is the *ear* of the soul whereby the sinner 'hears the voice of the Son of God and lives;' the *palate* of the soul whereby he 'tastes the good word of God and the powers of the world to come;' the *feeling* of the soul, whereby he perceives the presence of Him whom he seeks; the *hand* of the soul whereby he reaches forth and takes all the fulness of Christ to himself."

It is always safe to exhort one *to confess and forsake sin* – to confess it on the knees before God, with all honestness and earnestness, and to loathe *and turn away from it.*

It is always safe to urge *submission to God.* "Suppose a rebel in arms against a king was called on to submit. What would he understand by it? Why, that he should yield the point, and lay down his arms. That is just what it means for a sinner to submit to God. He must cease his strife and conflict against his Maker, and be at peace with Him."

It is always safe to urge *the present as the best time* for making salvation sure. "There is a special energy and efficiency in the means of grace: the Spirit is near: ministers preach and Christians pray with unwonted earnestness; and from many causes you may never see so favourable a moment as now."

It is always safe to warn against *seeking salvation in a self-righteous spirit.* This is so natural, and so subtle a thing, that it should be guarded against at every point.

It is always safe to set forth *Christ's willingness and the extreme simplicity of the plan of salvation.* During a religious awakening in a factory village in New England, a foreman was awakened, but he could not find peace. His superior sent him a letter, requesting him to call at six o'clock. Promptly he came. "I see you believe *me*," said his master. The foreman assented. "Well, see; here is another letter sending for you by One who is equally in earnest," said his master, holding up a slip of paper with some texts of Scripture written on it. He took the paper and began to read it slowly, "*Come – unto – me – all – ye – that – labour,*" etc. His lips quivered, his eyes filled with tears, and he joyfully said, "I see it: I am to believe *that* in the same way I believed your letter!"

It is always safe to urge *an immediate coming to Christ.* "No reformation can be genuine till you come to Christ. No preparation is needed for coming to him; and none can be made."

It is always safe to tell of *Jesus and his dying love.* We are told of an old emblem in the shape of a lock, constructed of rings, on each of which was a letter, and which would unlock only when those rings were so arranged as to spell the word Jesus. Apt emblem of the human heart in yielding to the power of the cross! Was one ever known to open except to the name of JESUS?

It is always safe to state that *an actual sense of unfitness is true fitness.* Mr Whitefield, brother of the noted preacher, had fallen into a desponding state. In conversation with the Countess of Huntingdon one day, he said, "My lady, I know what you say is true: the mercy of God is infinite: I see it clearly. But, ah! my lady, there is no mercy for me – I am a wretch, entirely lost." "I am glad to hear it, Mr Whitefield," said Lady Huntingdon. "I am glad at my heart that you are a lost man." He looked with great surprise. "What, my lady, glad! glad at your heart that I am a lost man?" "Yes, Mr Whitefield, truly glad; for Jesus Christ came into the world to save the lost!" He laid down his cup of tea on the table. "Blessed be God for that," "Glory to God for that word," he exclaimed. "Jesus Christ came to save the lost! then I have a ray of hope!"

It is always safe to urge a *perpetual looking to Christ.* Mr Spurgeon tells how when in trouble about his soul he heard a sermon on the text "Look unto me, etc." – "Fixing his eyes on me, as I thought, before he began to preach to others, he said: 'Young man! look! look! look! You are one of the ends of the earth; you feel you are; you know your need of a Saviour; you are trembling because you think he will never save you. He says this morning, "Look!"' O how my soul was shaken within me then! What! thought I, does that man know me, and all about me? He seemed as if he did. And it made me 'look!' Well, I thought, lost or saved, I will try; sink or swim, I will run the risk of it; and in that moment I hope by His grace I looked upon Jesus, and though desponding, downcast, and ready to despair, and feeling that I could rather die than live as I had lived, at that very moment it seemed as if a young heaven had had its birth within my conscience."

It is always safe to urge *approach to God in Christ's name.* "A beggar comes to you for charity. You have no ready money, but you give him a cheque on the bank. He enters the door, the bank officers stare at him as he enters – poor, ragged, filthy, wretched – they think that he is nothing but a common beggar seeking alms, perhaps, but he goes to the counter, he presents his cheque. The cashier does not look at the beggar or his rags any more; he looks at the name at the bottom of the cheque, and if that is genuine the money is handed to the bearer. It is the name that does it – that and nothing more. So it is in salvation."

It is always safe to set forth *the freeness and fulness of Christ's righteousness.* As John Wesley had come to life's close, a group of friends around him knelt in prayer. He responded the 'Amen' with unusual fervour. Soon after he exclaimed: "There is no need for more than what I said at Bristol; my words then were:

> 'I the chief of sinners am,
> But Jesus died for me.'"

"Is this the present language of your heart?" asked one of his friends, "and do you now feel as you did then?" "Yes," he replied. "'Tis enough," rejoined his friend; "He, our precious Immanuel, has purchased, has promised all." "He is all! He is all! I will go!" responded the dying man.

6. *What are the evidences of conversion that may safely be put before inquirers?* No question could be more momentous. Oh, what a responsibility to undertake to give directions here! Never was an angel employed in a more solemn work than are we in telling a sinner when he may safely entertain a hope! The judgment fires will reveal our work, of what sort it is! One thing it is always safe to do, namely, to be *sure* that the work is deep and thorough. Our fathers and mothers used to talk of "experiencing religion," and no term could be better. Today we hear the objectionable expression, "getting religion," or, "has got religion." Let us be satisfied that there is a real *experience* of the change of heart by the power of God.

Mr Earle has given away many thousands of little cards on which are printed the following *Evidences of conversion for young Christians.*

1. A full surrender of the will to God.
2. The removal of a burden of sin gradually or suddenly.
3. A new love to Christians and to Jesus.
4. A new relish for the Word of God.
5. Pleasure in secret prayer, at least at times.
6. Sin or sinful thoughts will cause pain.
7. Desire and efforts for the salvation of others.

8. A desire to obey Christ in his commands and ordinances.
9. Deep humility and self-abasement.
10. A growing desire to be holy and like Christ.

It is safe to hold such language as this in conversation with those inclined to entertain a hope: "By fervent prayer for divine illumination, and by searching the Scriptures, you may know in whom you have believed. You may have the witness in yourselves, more or less clear according to the earnestness of your seeking in reliance upon the aid of the Holy Spirit, who alone can take of the things of Christ, and show them unto you. What, then, do you say for yourself? You know where you were once, sinking in the horrible pit and the miry clay. Where do you now stand? Has Christ brought you up and placed your feet upon a rock? Do you begin to feel its firmness, and rest upon it? Can you say, 'One thing I know, that whereas I was blind, now I see?' Have you seen the plague of your own heart, and heartily repented of all your sins? Have you new views and new desires? Do you approve of the law of God, which is holy, just, and good? Have you been brought to see the impossibility of saving yourselves, and have you, by the grace of God, fled for refuge to lay hold on the hope set before you in the gospel? Has your mind within these few weeks passed through a great change? Do you love that which you before hated, and hate that which you loved? Do you love the Bible; do you love the prayer-meeting; do you love the house of God; do you love the brethren? Time was when you saw no beauty in the Saviour, that you should desire Him. How is it now? Is He precious to your soul? And on Him do you rest all your hope?"

"O Lord, Revive Thy Work!"

17
Training the Converts

GAINING converts is one thing; *training* them is another thing. Failing properly to appreciate this fact, many pastors fail to build up the churches. The list of communicants is not always an index of church-power. Strength consists not in numbers, but in character. When Gideon had mustered all his soldiers for the war with Midian and Amalek, "The Lord said unto him, The people that are with thee are too many." With the number reduced there was more effectiveness.

A revival brings with it tremendous responsibilities. It loads the pastor and members with new obligations. With the accession of converts there come the questions, "What is to be done with these fresh professors? How much of this material shall turn out to be little less than dross and chaff, and how much of it solid substance?"

If revivals are graduated in their value only by the number of supposed *converts;* if all the attention of the church is drawn to the single point of securing conversions, without any regard to the ripening of them; if it be supposed that nothing is happening when there are no conversions; if there is no thought of cultivation, no valuation of knowledge and character, no conviction of the fact that one Christian well taken care of and developed is worth a hundred mere beginners, a most inadequate and pernicious opinion prevails.

Indeed, as a matter of fact, how distressing is the picture which often forces itself upon the mind, where multitudes are hopefully converted, and yet so little pains taken with the converts, that in a single year one can hardly tell them from those not professing conversion!

On this very account the whole theory of revivals is reproached. And if we answer, "It is not the fault of the *revival* that the fruits are not permanently good, but because there is lack of *cultivation,*" still, the circumstance has its influence, and operates to produce a suspicion of all special ingatherings.

It will hardly be too much to say, that if the churches had done their full duty to the converts, the world would have been given to Christ before now. "Feed my sheep; feed my lambs," – that is, 'act toward them the part of the shepherd – guiding them, protecting them, nourishing them,' – this is a command to all Christian leaders. And we question whether the churches yet fairly begin to apprehend the duty of bestowing culture upon the young members of the flock – the lambs of Jesus. From this cause half the benefit of revivals is lost.

The force of this thought is enhanced by considering that the convert alone is in the ductile, shapeable period. The wax is now warm, and readily takes the seal; the clay is moist, and the hand of the potter may form it as he wills. There is but one convert-period, as there is but one child-period, and whatever is done *then* to mould the character, will exert a far more decisive influence than anything done at a future period; and upon the counsels and directions which an individual receives at such a moment, depends in a very great degree the amount of good which he is to accomplish during his whole life.

We condense what is to be said here into a few suggestions, suitable, first, for instructors; second, for converts themselves.

I. *Duties on the part of pastor and people.*

Acquaintanceship is a first duty. In large congregations, especially in cities, it is not easy to know intimately a company of newcomers. Shall we say that to a great extent such acquaintance is never formed? Shall we say that members of the same church do not know each other – not even sufficiently to recognise one another on the street? Such is the case; and if the church is a family, what a strange family that is, and how is it possible that there be reciprocal duties and affections?

The pastor then, especially, will seek an acquaintance with all the converts, and the more intimate the better. It will be well to carry with him a list of the names of these, which he will look over occasionally to facilitate identification and recognition. And the same should be true of the older members generally, as far as possible.

Instruction is another duty. The babes need teaching; and the church is the appointed teacher, particularly through the pastor. Converts' meetings will therefore be held; not only for their own mutual edification, but for pastoral counsel and direction. It is the sacred duty of the minister to meet the young disciples there, and instruct them fully in the things of the kingdom. He will also see that they are in the Sunday School, or in Bible classes, still further to be taught. We always enjoin this upon converts, and *see that it is done!* If not already in the Sunday School, the right time to introduce them is when they are setting out in the new life. It is said of Nettleton that he took great pains to instruct young converts in the fundamental principles of the Christian religion. He would often appoint meetings for their special benefit. In these meetings he was wont to explain and enforce in a familiar manner, the doctrines of the gospel. Hence the young converts became rooted and grounded in the truth and continued steadfast in the faith. In this way also, they became acquainted with one another, and receiving the same doctrines and drinking into the same spirit, they became united as a band of brethren.

The remark was made by Rev Daniel A Clark, as to some converts, that "they would not have known when they were converted, who converted them, or what they were converted for." Accessions of this sort, certainly if allowed to remain such, would only weaken a church. Defective instruction must dwarf the new nature, since *truth* is the food upon which it grows. Where religious character is feeble, it is generally because neglected, or wrongly instructed, at the outset. And there is an awful criminality here, on the part of very many pastors. It is simply alarming to see how little careful instruction is given to converts.

It were well if pastors, subsequent to revival ingatherings, should lay out and pursue a *plan of systematic instruction* for the converts, embracing the evidences of Christianity, the principal Scripture doctrines, the confession or articles of faith held by the church, and the covenant engagements entered into upon profession. No member of a church should have it in his power to say, "The confession of faith was never explained to me before I joined the church.

There are some things in it which I do not believe; and if I had known how they were understood by the church, I should not have come in."

Reception to membership is another duty on the part of the church. Every convert should be encouraged, at a proper time, to make a public profession of religion. Opinion differs as to *how soon* after hopeful conversion a profession should generally be made. That is a question for each church to decide for itself, and no one rule is applicable in all cases. There may be rash and premature admissions; and there may be too much delay.

Watch care is another duty. A church should watch over all the interests of her young members; know where they are; and what are their habits, temptations, dangers, privileges, state of religion in their hearts, spirit of prayer, and the like. If they are seen to be going astray, they are to be exhorted and admonished. But this should be done with all kindness, considerateness, and affection. The heart of a young convert is tender and easily grieved, and sometimes a single unkind look or word will cast a cloud over the mind, and throw one back for a lifetime.

As a rule, sufficient allowance is not made for those young in experience; and the too frequent habit of *complaining* of them, is much to be regretted. Converts are but children, at best, and if those who are ever ready to speak of the deficiencies of the "young members of the church," were as attentive to watch over and help them, as they are to condemn them, it were at once more beneficial and more pleasing to God.

II. *Things profitable to be kept before the mind of converts.*

1. That the religious character is now taking shape. First steps are usually most decisive. Urge upon them this thought – that the tone of piety and of action which they adopt during the first few months will likely go with them through life. *The first six months of a convert's experience generally tells what he is to be.* "Answer to me for his being right that time, and I will answer for the rest."

2. That he should be in the Sunday School.

3. That the beginning of decline be watched against.

4. That besetting sins, from former bad habits, be particularly guarded against.

5. That *growth* is the great law of life, animal or vegetable; and that *he* is to "grow in grace and the knowledge of Jesus Christ." At conversion the great work is but *begun;* and it is the *growing* of the new life which proves the new birth a real birth, and not an abortion; a birth of life, and not of death. And this growth must continue day by day, and year by year. "It is not a dead past, but a living present which must testify for you before God."

6. That self-denial is to be exercised. "The sins which most easily beset you will again lift their bruised heads; broken tempers will again clamour for mastery; your weak points will again be assailed by the great enemy of souls; duty-posts will again look dangerous and forbidding; ease will beckon you to her flowery beds, and to the Lord's calls unbelieving timidity will whisper her excusing petitions."

7. That they have been converted for *usefulness*, for *work*, for *bringing others to Christ.* "A profession of religion is no sinecure. If Christ in the abounding riches of His grace has called you into His kingdom, it is that you at once enter into His service; and your first inquiry should be, *Lord, what wilt Thou have me to do?* He wants no idlers among his professed followers; and other professors are no standard for you."

8. They are to *aim high.* They should look to the Scriptures for their standard, and to Christ for their model. "If, having got into the church, you take a low stand at first, instead of rising you will invariably decline, till your brethren will be constrained to stand in doubt of you, and the world will ask, What do ye more than others? But if you set your mark high, remembering that 'ye are not your own,' but 'bought with a price,' even the precious blood of Christ, you will, by the aid of the Holy Spirit, witness a good profession, and bring forth much fruit to God's glory."

9. That *principle, not feeling, or emotion*, is to govern them. Many will be zealous in religion when they feel like it, when their emotions are warm and lively; but they will not act out religion consistently, and carry it into all the concerns of life. They are religious only as they are impelled by a gush of feeling. This is not true religion. Let the converts be taught that true piety does not consist, chiefly, in high-wrought frames of feeling, but that it consists rather, in a fixed choice and purpose of heart to serve God; in a settled principle of obedience to His will.

10. That they have renounced all ownership of themselves or their possessions. They should not be left to think that anything is their own, their time, property, influence, faculties, bodies or souls. "When you submitted to God, you made a free surrender of all to Him, to be ruled and disposed of at His pleasure. You have no right to spend one hour as if your time was your own; no right to go anywhere, or do anything, for yourselves, but should hold all at the disposal of God, and employ all for His glory. If you do not, you rob God, and cannot be expected to prosper in the divine life."

11. That they should keep their consciences just as tender as they are now. In a few months, if properly taught and attended to, young converts may have a conscience so delicately poised that the weight of a feather will turn them. Only bring a "Thus saith the Lord," and they will be always ready to do that, be it what it may.

12. That they should be "temperate in all things" – It were better to give up, (if used), tobacco; certainly all strong drinks. Dr Nettleton said: "I have made particular inquiry, and find that the declension of some has commenced with an undue conformity to the world. But the sin of intemperance has caused more trouble, and done more dishonour to the cause of Christ than any other that can be named." By all means induce converts to "sign the pledge," if they have not already done it. If pastors begin right just here, wrong habits can be rooted out thoroughly. If they neglect it now, they may lament it when it is too late.

13. That they should carry their religion into their business. "You should be just as holy, just as watchful, aim just as singly at the glory of God, and be just as sincere and solemn in all your daily employments, as in the act of coming to the throne of grace. This God demands."

14. That they be regular in all the church services; on Sunday, and the weekly meetings.

15. That they should allow no day to pass without secret prayer. "In the closet, the battle is lost or won."

16. That they take heed as to worldly companionship, and worldly amusements – "Can one take coals of fire in his bosom and not be burned?"

17. That they be not conformed to the world.

18. That they neglect not to search the Scriptures. "Christ is now putting you to school, not under the law, but under the Gospel, that you may be trained up for His service. And the Bible is your text-book. Read it. Study it. It will take but a moment or two to *commit* a text to memory every morning, which may be kept in mind through the day. Do this, and you will have treasured up three hundred and sixty-five verses at the end of the year. How many in ten years? No less than three thousand six hundred and fifty!"

We are happy in being able to append here the views of two ministers of the gospel, of ripe experience and sound judgment, in a matter of such moment as the training of converts. The first of the two has been in the ministry sixteen years – a quarter part of which has been passed in revivals: and the topic of his letter is one in which he has very great interest. The writer of the second letter is widely known for his ability, and the wisdom of his opinions.

From Rev E S Atwood, Salem, Massachusetts,

My Dear Brother:

I have a firm belief in the necessity and helpfulness of the *systematic religious culture of the converts*, and if I have had any success in revivals it is mainly owing to the time and effort spent in this direction.

A competent gardener, when his choice seeds have germinated, and the shoots are fairly above ground, feels that the real difficulties of his work have only just commenced. Possibly the very *life* of the plants, certainly the *symmetry* of their growth and blossoming, depends upon the care and culture which they now receive. Nature has done her part well, as she always does; the question of further success is conditioned upon the fidelity and skill with which man discharges his share of the responsibility which now accrues.

Practically, this element essential to success in revival work, is largely overlooked. It is a common odium cast upon revival measures, that their results are largely evanescent; that the ultimate and permanent receipts are lamentably meagre when compared with the effort expended, and the promise which the work gave at certain stages of its progress. As the easiest way out of the difficulty, the responsibility for this unsatisfactory state of things is laid upon revival preachers and their "injudicious" methods. A great deal of cheap sarcasm is wasted upon the folly of religious spasms. The evangelist, or the earnest pastor, is characterised as a mountebank, who succeeds only in stirring up a little whirl of excitement, that very soon subsides into more complete stagnation than before: and the world, and too often the church, furnishes itself with a new argument against revival measures.

Now this commonly accepted explanation of the comparative fruitlessness of revivals, is utterly baseless and bad. Let the responsibility rest where it belongs. The mischief does not have its root in the unusual fervency with which truth is pressed by the preacher – nor in the unusual methods which are employed to drive men to religious decisions. If the truth lay here, the criticism would hold with vastly more force against the day of Pentecost and the day of Judgment, as having a tendency to blunt the religious sensibilities of men and stale the power of the great truths of God. No exception can rightly be taken to fiery preaching, or to the most intense pressure brought to bear upon the soul to force it to decision. Excitement produced in this way is neither delirium nor intoxication. If it comes to nothing, or worse than nothing, the fault lies with those who neglect the work, or do not know how to push it to its legitimate issue. The processes of religious life, in many important particulars, are so identical with the processes of natural growth, that what is imperative in one case is equally imperative in the other. What would be folly in the management of a garden, is a similar and a greater folly in the training of a soul.

Convert-culture ought to be recognised as a distinct and indispensable department of revival work. Every minister who has had much experience in revivals, notices that after a season of religious interest, he generally finds himself with three distinct classes of hopeful cases on his hands. There is, first, a small number who have been quietly led of the Spirit to an intelligent comprehension of their spiritual wants, and an intelligent acceptance of Christ as their Saviour. Their emotional nature has not been greatly stirred. They have not been down into Gethsemane, nor up upon the heights of Tabor. They have simply been made to see their need of redemption, and simply accepted the offered Redeemer. They have been found of the "still small voice," and have bowed their heads to His utterances. Then comes a larger class on whom the earthquake, and wind and fire have done their work. Their moral nature has been convulsed to its lowest depths. They have been rent and torn with the consciousness of sin. They have looked into the open doors of hell. Their faces have grown white with fear. And when relief came, the ecstasy has been as extravagant as the depression. Their ideal of religious life is a life lifted on the flood-tide of blissful emotion. They are contented only so long as the New Jerusalem is in full view. They are in the strict sense of the term *emotional* Christians. And then there is a third class in whom the law-work has been thoroughly done, but in whom the gospel-work has been feebly done. They see their sins much more clearly than they see their Saviour. Sinai is an overhanging reality – Calvary a dim outline on the far horizon. Faith is timid, hope weak, assurance a thing that comes and goes with shift of circumstances and varying moods of thought. Now it is evident, that between these several classes of converts there is a wide margin of difference, and equally evident that if left to themselves, they will drift wider and wider apart. The real problem which the church has to solve is – how best to *assimilate* all these varieties of spiritual life, so that the defects of each shall be remedied, and what is vital in each shall accrue to the benefit of all the rest.

It must be admitted that this involves no small amount of work. It requires time and thought, and prayer and effort. But it is work that can be done, and that *ought* to be done. The intellectual Christian may and ought to be lifted up to a level where he will feel more of the inspiration of the great hopes of the gospel, and have the experience of the heart added to the conviction of the will. The emotional Christian may and ought to be led to the apprehension that *principle* is a more important factor in religious life than mere feeling; and without diminishing his ardour, be shown how to put more substance into his piety. And the timid and doubting ones may and ought to be braced with strength – taught a larger trust, and be shown the way to serener experiences. The effort necessary in order to reach these several results is arduous, but it is rewarding. No Christian work pays better. If rightly managed, no other is so sure of success.

The methods of this work will vary somewhat with localities and circumstances. There is no rigid rule of procedure that will fit every case. Each pastor must decide for himself what plan of operations will accomplish the most in his particular community. And yet, as in processes of general education certain data have been determined by experiment, and the proper order of instruction for producing the most satisfactory results defined, so in this training of converts. While the utmost flexibility of *method* is allowable, observation has shown that there is a sort of natural order in the steps to be successively taken in endeavouring to build up a symmetrical Christian character. Without attempting to sweep exhaustively over so wide a field, it may not be amiss to indicate the general outlines of a plan of procedure that has been found to work successfully.

The training of converts naturally begins with *an examination of the real evidences of conversion.* The foundation must be fixed before we commence to build the house. Experience shows, that the views of young converts on this point are as vague as they are varied. Some put the standard too high, others too low. One man is in the heaven of assurance because of a certain glow of feeling which he experiences; another is desponding because his emotions do not match with those of some he has read or heard of. The only way of reconciling these diversities, is to press the Scripture test upon each man's notice. Judicious training will have it for its endeavour to set aside everything else offered in evidence, and line out, barely and sharply, repentance and faith as the only conditions and proofs of conversion. Such a test strongly pressed will be found a sword of double edge that cuts both ways. It will lead the over-confident to a more serious self examination, while it will give the doubting a ground of assurance. Time cannot be better spent with young converts, than in helping them to intelligent views on this point. Half the weaknesses of Christian life root back into false ideas of what constitutes a child of God. Let that question be settled at the beginning, and once for all. If the matter is properly managed it may be. It certainly ought to be. It is indispensable to the success of the voyage that we should know at the start that the vessel is seaworthy. No pastor should grudge the time, and patience, and tenderness that may be found necessary for perfecting this work. If it is done thoroughly at the outset, it is done for all time, and men and women who are able to give to themselves and others "a reason for the hope that is in them," are in a condition to grow strongly and continuously.

Next in order comes a *proper understanding of the helps to Christian growth.* In regard to this matter there is commonly great ignorance. Certain traditional views of the efficacy of prayer, and the usefulness of Bible study, held previous to conversion, are very apt to pass over into superstitions after conversion. A searching inquiry into the real form in which these matters lie in the minds of young converts, will usually disclose the fact that their conceptions are crude and faulty. Men very largely need to be schooled into the right use of these instruments of spiritual growth. How to read the Bible to the best advantage, how to pray, how to secure answers to prayer, are questions covering points in which a great deal of instruction is wanted. And almost every case will be found to be special in some particulars, requiring special treatment. It is never safe to take anything for granted in this department. Those men who are counted wisest are often the most ignorant. Beginners in the Christian life need the assistance of maturer Christian experience to help them out of the practical difficulties with which they find themselves face to face. Haphazard prayer and scripture study have little efficacy. There is an *art* of using these means which intuition seldom if ever masters. It is to be taught by experts, and careful explanation and instruction on this point, suiting the teaching to individual exigencies, will be abundantly rewarded.

Then let there follow a *consideration of the scope of the Christian doctrines, and their relations to practical life.* Here again experience shows that a very common misapprehension exists. There is an almost universal tendency in the minds of young converts to dwell too exclusively on what they have *felt.* A system of truth is something to which they are called to intellectually assent, but which is not recognised as having vital relations to spiritual growth. The creed is held to be something ecclesiastical rather than Christian. It is of the first importance that this false impression should be corrected. The great doctrines of the faith should be simply stated, and their bearing upon religious life unfolded. The creed should be emphasised as doing, in its way, just what prayer does in its way. And especially in this day when the drift of popular thought is so strongly towards a contempt of doctrine, and piety is so feebly differentiated from some things that pass for it, is it imperative that we insist upon the vital influence of Christian believing upon Christian living. Converts should be trained into the conviction that the great truths of Scripture are the "trees of the Lord that are full of sap," and their "leaves for the healing of the nations." Intelligent piety is the great want of the times, and the best way to secure it, is to show men in the beginning that belief and life are inseparably linked together.

And finally, and in fact all along in this process of training, an effort should be made to *create the sense of personal responsibility for Christian work.* Piety needs air and exercise. Give every convert from the start something to do, suiting the work to the talents and opportunities of the individual. Insist upon it that no drones can live in the Christian hive; that anything that is not working piety is worthless piety. The importance of developing this sense of responsibility at the outset cannot be too strongly stated. The beginning of the Christian life is the hopeful time. The soul always carries its birth-marks. Give piety something to do in the cradle, and you secure at least the probability of permanent religious activity. Our churches are suffering from a dearth of Christian workers. New responsibilities are continually rolling up, and there is nobody to meet them. The fault lies in the early training of the membership. They are allowed a honeymoon of inaction, which is liable to be indefinitely prolonged. The inertia of first experiences is hard to overcome, and the loss is individual as well as general. It reports itself in the type of piety as well as in the aggregate of work. An active Christianity is the ideal of the gospel. The religion that does not subsidise all the energies of the soul, can never be satisfactory to its possessor. It should be specially impressed upon the new-born child of God, that his future happiness as well as usefulness is conditioned upon his fidelity as a Christian *worker*.

And how are all the ends contemplated in this process of training best reached? That, so far as *methods* are concerned, must be left to the judgment of the individual pastor. But this much may be said, whatever the methods selected, they must be discriminating, specific, personal in their character. Preaching will do something, the freer form of lecture-room address will do more, but neither are adequate to the exigencies of the case. As a general rule, no expedient has proved more efficient than the plan of *convert classes*, meeting week by week, and following the Socratic method of question and answer. Personal views are thus elicited, and personal misapprehensions corrected, while each secures the benefit of the experience of all the rest. Until experience shows some better method to be practicable, this must stand as the most serviceable, the fullest of promise, and ordinarily the richest in results of any that has yet been tried.

And now, if any overworked pastor objects that this training process lays too heavy a tax upon his time and energies, it may be answered, that inspiration sufficient to attempt and carry it out to success may be gathered from the consideration of the certain results of work like this. It is written in the annals of art, that sculptors have spent months in wandering from quarry to quarry in search of a block fleckless and crystalline enough to worthily embody their ideal; and then have given months and years to the slow shaping of the crudeness of the stone into the grace of outline and loveliness of feature, that reproduced in the imperishable whiteness of the marble the dream of beauty which filled their thought. And surely this work of shaping immortal souls into the symmetry of Christ-likeness has its greater inspirations. The hope of at last presenting those whom we have in charge "perfect and complete, without spot or wrinkle, before the face of the Father," is enough to encourage us to weariness and toil however prolonged. And if, in the perplexity of difficulties, and in the infirmity of human nature, we often find ourselves asking, "Who is sufficient for these things?" – close upon the question of self-distrust, follows the sweet assertion of Christian assurance, "I can do all things through Christ which strengtheneth me."

Trusting that the *Handbook* may be a great success, and help the church of God to a better understanding of the philosophy of revivals, I am

Very truly yours,
E S Atwood.

From Rev Dr Cutting, Brooklyn, New York

My Dear Dr Fish – I have strong convictions as to the instruction to be given to converts preparatory to their coming into the communion of the church; and I am not unwilling to urge these convictions, whether by my example or in any other way, upon all who are charged with the care of souls.

I was ordained at West Boylston, Massachusetts, in March, 1836. During my brief pastorate there, (for I went to Southbridge at the end of the summer of 1837), I had the pleasure of baptising a considerable number, a large part of whom were young. It seemed to me that before I took the responsibility of bringing them into the church, I should know for myself that they were instructed concerning the nature, the objects, and the ends of Christian profession. I did not expect them to be theologians, I did not suppose them to be Christians ripened by experience, I did not imagine that all which is embodied in the articles of faith of evangelical churches could be comprehended by them. I did suppose, however, that a beginning could be made in indoctrination, that the breadth and force of Christian experience could be better understood by contemplating it, and that it was not becoming to ask the assent of young converts to articles of which they knew nothing.

I began, therefore, with the Articles, and grouped all which I had to say to them around instruction on these. I met them, and taught them on the basis of these Articles, that they might know, as well as possible, what they were professing, how much was implied, and the duties to which they were binding themselves by the most solemn of obligations. Imperfectly as the service was performed, I am certain that I was not mistaken in attempting it, and if I am pastor again, I shall not content myself with even this. I would begin earlier. I would have in part the instruction of the young under my personal care from the beginning, meeting the children of my congregation at least once a month, in some simple service, rendered as attractive as possible consistently with its ends, in which I would make myself *certain* that the foundations of Christian knowledge were properly laid in their youthful minds.

I have great respect for catechetical instruction, and do not doubt that, accompanied with wise illustrative teaching, it may be made most captivating to the young, and as permanent as the mind itself in its happy influences. The Sunday School, excellent and important as it is, should never replace parental instruction on the one hand, nor pastoral instruction on the other.

In the Cathedral of Notre Dame at Paris, I saw a large number of young girls who were engaged in a responsive service. I did not approach very near them, but I judged them to be receiving instruction preparatory to Confirmation. In such matters, Rome will never fail. Why should we fail who teach that which we hold to be so much nearer the truth as it is in Jesus?

Yours very truly,
S S Cutting.

We commend the above thoughts, and this whole subject of *convert-culture*, to the most earnest heed of all winners of souls. Leave not the work half done! Truly, it is a great thing to save men, even though it be only "as by fire." But is it not also a great thing to have them "rooted and grounded in the truth," instead of being "children, tossed to and fro, and carried about with every wind of doctrine?" Surely it is of inconceivable importance that converts come unto "perfect men, unto the measure of the stature of the fulness of Christ – from whom the whole body fitly joined together and compacted by that which every joint supplieth, according to the effectual working in the measure of every part, maketh increase of the body unto the edifying of itself in love." (*Ephesians 4:13, 16*).

"O Lord, Revive Thy Work!"

18

Revivals the Hope of the World

HOW this world is soonest to be given to Christ, is a question that should concern every one of his followers. Our object is to show that it will not be done apart from extensive and frequent revivals of religion.

The argument from the past is in place. Coleridge has likened *experience* to the stern-light of a ship, which illumines the track it has passed over. And Sir Philip Sydney affirmed that all is lip-wisdom which wants experience. The lessons of the thousands of gone-by years are here before us for instruction.

What we are today is attributable to revivals. This is a strong assertion; and yet the pages of this book abundantly confirm it. Let anyone read but the two chapters, *Historical View of Revivals*, and *What we owe to Revivals*, and our language will not be deemed extravagant. Nor is there the least ground for believing that God will essentially change the methods of His operations in the time to come. As He has hitherto carried forward His work by revivals, we may expect that He will continue to do the same, only on a much grander scale.

The present slow progress of religion comes in as an argument. There appeared some years ago in a leading religious paper, the following: "From the statistical report of the American Congregational Orthodox churches for 1862, it is seen that out of the fourteen hundred and eighteen churches of New England, seven hundred and thirty-eight, or more than one half, had not a single conversion, or addition by profession, during the year. One hundred and eighty-two other churches had but one conversion each. And only sixty-six churches had as many as ten each. Excepting the churches with which evangelists had laboured, there was an average of less than two conversions to a minister for the year; and for all the United States and Canada, probably not over two. The results for the last four years do not vary greatly from these numbers. Many of these churches have not been blessed with a revival for periods of fifteen, twenty, and even thirty years together; and some of them not with a single conversion. It further appears that the whole number of converts gathered at home and abroad, under the entire auspices of the American Congregational Orthodox churches, over the number of deaths and excommunications, was but two thousand and sixteen; which, divided among the three thousand and fifty-six churches of the denomination, gives an average gain of less than three-fourths of one to a church for the year. Or, otherwise stated, two thousand and sixteen churches had a net gain of one soul each for the year, and one thousand and forty churches had not one addition."

The article, no doubt, was based upon facts and statistics taken from the *Congregational Quarterly*, and published in a tract form in 1867. We give that part of the statement bearing on the point before us.

"There are about one thousand four hundred and twenty Orthodox Congregational churches in New England. The number of conversions, or additions by profession over losses by death and excommunication, reported by them for the year –

1860 was 385, or about one-fourth of one to each church.
1861 was 117, or about one-twelfth of one to each church.
1862 a loss of 284 over all additions.
1863 a gain of 318, or less than one-fourth of one to each church.
1864 a gain of 1,412, or nearly one to each church.
1865 a gain of 2,416, or nearly two to each church.
1866 about 1,257, or nearly one to each church.

"Nearly one-half of these churches reported, in each of these seven years, not a *single conversion*, or addition by profession.

"About two hundred other churches reported, in each of these seven years, only one addition each. A majority of the remaining churches reported little over two additions each. Nearly all the larger gains were made by those few churches that have made 'extra efforts,' for the conversion of men.

"Such is New England's record for the last seven years, and probably for the last thirty years it has been little or no better.

"The average number of the Orthodox Congregational Churches of the United States and Canada for these seven years was about two thousand eight hundred. Their gain over losses for the year –

1860 was less than one-half of one to each church.
1861 was less than two-thirds of one to each church.
1862 was less than one and one-twenty-seventh to each church.
1863 was less than one and one-half to each church.
1864 was less than one and one-third to each church.
1865 was about two and one-tenth to each church.
1866 about the same as last year.

"So far as can be gathered from their statistical reports, *the churches of the other denominations, have not been more successful* in gathering converts from the world during this period than the Congregational Churches have been.

"As the churches average less than one hundred members, and make a net gain of less than one member a year, at this rate of increase it will take *one hundred years* for them to double the present membership. While the population of the country will probably double *four* times in this period, and become one hundred and fifty million, the churches will be only about eight million. Without more general and powerful revivals than ever have been, how soon the churches will be overwhelmed and lost in the world!"

In view of such considerations, the remarks of Dr Noah Porter, [1] are worthy of the deepest thought. "At our present rate of march, we can scarcely keep in sight of the army of aliens whom we would subdue to Christ. I see the cause of human salvation to *be altogether hopeless* without the *special* interposition of the Holy Spirit. Should this interposition be granted only to one individual in ten, (which has been, perhaps, about the average of saving conversions in our evangelical congregations), *nine-tenths* of the population, even in New England would remain 'aliens from the commonwealth of Israel.' Darker still is the prospect in those sections of our country where scarcely one in fifty exhibits any evidence, or makes any

1. See also facts of the same nature under *Revival Means and Methods*.

profession, of piety. The hope of the church, then, is in revivals of religion – *continued, powerful, general revivals.*"

The *moral condition of society at large* strengthens this view. It is easy to boast of a great country; of a good government; of a common language; of Christian churches and religious liberty; of rapid inter-communication; of unbounded wealth; of numerical growth, and the like. But no one pretends that all this can ensure a people's welfare. With all this society may be corrupt from the crown of the head to the sole of the foot. And few intelligent Christians will claim that the mass of the population, with all we are doing, is being thoroughly leavened with saving truth. It were pleasant to think so; but such is not the case, even in the most favoured communities.

The old processes of Christian education are a laughing-stock to the present generation. Catechising, exact definitions of doctrines, creed-statements – these are scouted as things fit only for a "Puritanical" age. As someone has it, that charity which believeth all things *but God's truth*, has opened the doors to a fatal religious literature, in which, by a sort of universal solvent, all the doctrinal bones of theology are reduced to a gelatinous mass of ambiguous sentiment. And the consequence is, that the people are losing all sense of the diversities of creeds, become looser and more ignorant as falsehood grows familiar, and are led off to scepticism and universalism on one side, and to popery on the other; or not less degrading and ruinous, to Socinus, Swedenborg, familiar spirits, and the Mormons.

Even Christian teachers, and those claiming to be orthodox, from their pulpits and editorial chairs join in the cry against "the stringency of formulated creeds," and are so much more *liberal* than *loyal* as to forget that truth makes no compromises. Perceiving diversities of doctrines and opinions and beliefs would help the people out of their difficulties by knowing what to hold, by telling them that all beliefs are equally valid – that some doctrines are not essential, even admitting that they are truths! – and that "it does not matter what the creed is if the practice be right!" Dr Guthrie once said, "The more that 'works' are preached up instead of 'faith,' the worse are the 'works' that men do." Might it not be claimed with equal force, that the more men clamour for "life" in place of "doctrine," the more corrupt are the lives of many who subsist on such preaching?

Further: are the numerous evangelical churches positively putting forth their power upon the communities? Forms and ceremonies, yea, and sound doctrines, *may* exist, where the church is spiritually prostrate. Indeed it often occurs that the "*ability*" of churches lead to extravagance and indolence; so that a body boasting that she "is rich, and increased with goods, and has need of nothing," is really "wretched, and miserable, and poor, and blind, and naked." And what do the above facts and figures show as to the actual power of the churches upon the communities?

Nothing so impresses the thoughtful mind as the *possibilities* of influence on the part of the churches. But it is like the power of steam before it was evoked and applied to man's service; like that of electricity before science climbed the height of the skies, and seized the spirit of thunder, and chained it to the chariot of human progress. It is *latent* power.

Capital that is unused is called *dead* capital; and a man might have a shop or storehouse full of it and still not get ahead. Oh, the amount of dead capital in the churches! Oh, what numbers of them are dying of inertia – dying of the dry-rot of formalism! dying of decency and respectability!

Now it is specifically the effect of revivals to increase church-power. This is not a thing of *organism*. Undoubtedly Christianity would be advantaged by consolidating her resources. But will a grand, imposing organisation furnish the power that converts bad men into good ones? Will it enable them, when converted, to lead holy and spotless lives? Will "a strong Church," in popular acceptation, give greater effect to sermons, more unction to exhortations, more success to the instruction of the young, and richer answers to prayer? Will it make Christians more humble, more contented, more charitable? Will it make the covetous liberal, and bring the Lord's portion into his treasury? *This* is not the solution of the problem of church-power! It is the "*power of the Highest*" that we need!

Consider what revivals would do for the *rural districts*. In 1802 Rev Jesse Edson wrote from Halifax, Vermont, thus: "The Holy Spirit seemed to come down like a rushing, mighty wind, to melt the souls of God's children, to cause sinners to tremble, stubborn wills to bow, and hard hearts to relent. Numbers flocked to Christ as a cloud, and as doves to their windows. Fifteen were received the next communion, twenty-one the communion following; about sixty, in the whole." In later years, and especially under the labours of Rev Samuel Fish, frequent and blessed revivals were experienced in that town, among the fruits of which were not less than twelve or fifteen missionaries and ministers of the gospel, besides great numbers of efficient Christian workers; most of whom, however, have either deceased, or removed to places of greater social or business advantages.

Years ago the church of Mr Edson, (Congregational), died out. That of Mr Fish, (Baptist), barely survives, (in two localities), to keep the gospel banner flying on those hills. The extinct church lived for fifty years by virtue of the revival referred to; and on account of the later awakenings the surviving society has not expired. Now, one powerful revival in that town would put the feeble interest on its feet for another whole generation, and save the community from being given over to religious indifferentism and social barbarism. We see no hope for the cause, whatever, except in such a special awakening. And this is but a picture of thousands of rural districts, especially in the inland parts of New England, where the population is depreciating. Will anyone tell us what is to save such places from godlessness except gracious revivals?

Consider, too, what revivals would do for the *cities*. In the absence of strong remedial agencies, great cities are great sores. *With* such influences they are centres of gracious influence. Our Lord, and after him the apostles, bestowed effort chiefly upon cities, "beginning at Jerusalem," the capital of the nation. They acted on the principle on which Alexander and Caesar, and all the great conquerors of all times act, that of seizing upon the strong places of power, and holding them in subjection, with the assurance that all other places will then become an easy conquest. For in cities are accumulated wealth, and talent, and energy and enterprise; and if this be consecrated it is a mighty gain. Besides, men are in masses there, and therefore ought to be more readily reached and moved; and carrying these, the surrounding villages and all parts of the country are reached.

Now there is no way of doing it but by powerful revivals. Look at things as they exist. City churches are not really reaching the dense masses of population. Strong in their wealth and social position, they are too much like polished shafts whirling on their bearings, but without cogs interlocking them into anything. They are not linked with society, and moving it with a magnificent influence. Even with all their appliances of Sunday Schools, city missions, tract operations, ragged schools and the like, the churches only touch the rim of the surrounding wickedness. Not one quarter part of the population of the great cities ever hear the gospel! A large proportion of the people are practically heathens – as much so as are the dwellers in absolutely pagan lands.

By present processes, then, these masses of immortals will never be reached and rescued. Multitudes of them have no Bible; or if they had, they could not read it, or would immediately pawn it. They spurn a tract, or if they do not, it would be useless to them. Multitudes of them study concealment; practise crimes which cannot be exposed to the light of day; and alike shrink away from police officers and friends of religion. Here and there some Christian effort picks off *one* soul from the godless mass; but nothing is making anything like an inroad upon it.

What is wanted is an awakening that would shake the dry bones in even the lowest stratum of society, rousing them from filth and drunkenness, and raising them into a great army to fight the battles of the Lord. What is needed are mighty *revival* impulses, urging them toward inquiry, and urging godly men and women to carry the heavenly light to those who will not come to it, and to compel the wanderers to come in that the divine guest-chamber may be full. And what short of powerful revivals can accomplish this? Is there any conceivable way except that by which God thus suddenly arouses the churches, and moves simultaneously the hearts of great multitudes?

A succession of such revivals as have occasionally been witnessed, sweeping all through the great cities of Christendom, would secure every condition of the moral elevation of these myriads of inhabitants. And without them the case appears hopeless indeed.

Again: *the relation of the ministry to revivals* is to be taken into account. As we have seen in a previous chapter, *What we Owe to Revivals*, the large part of good ministers of Jesus Christ have hitherto come from revivals; and in the mere point of numerical supply, whence but from this source can they be expected in the future? Without revivals, the hosts of young men necessary for home and foreign work, glowing with love to Christ, and ready to sacrifice for

His cause, cannot be expected to come forward, but will continue to be drawn into business and the other professions.

Besides: those converted in revivals may be expected to be the most efficient winners of souls. They possess the same revival spirit, and adopt the same style of preaching, and substantially the same means, as they had felt and witnessed to be mighty through God to the pulling down of strongholds.

Moreover, actual contact with revival work wonderfully intensifies a preacher's power. In a revival a pastor is thrown upon his own resources. His energies and ingenuity are taxed to the utmost. And thus new ideas are created, and new methods of illustrating and applying divine truth are acquired. His soul is aflame; and his words go blazing from his lips, and falling like fire upon the consciences of men, and onlookers are amazed at his added pathos, energy and power. For the *ministry's* sake, then, we must have revivals.

Again: the *great benevolent movements of the age* cannot progress without revivals. Every outpouring of the Spirit raises up new friends to the cause of missions, increases the amount of funds devoted to that cause, and wafts to heaven more numerous and fervent desires that the kingdom of God may come. Let but revivals cease, and what would become of the great enterprises for converting mankind to God? What would become of our benevolent associations, of various kinds at home? And how could our foreign work go forward? A general and lasting declension of religion would dry up all the sources of supply, both of men and money, upon which such operations depend.

We forget that each generation of the modern world consists of 30,000,000 of children; so that to christianise this added population alone there must be *one million conversions per year!* In this view of the case, what a prodigious work is before us! And how can it be accomplished without remarkable and wonderful and sudden effusions of the Spirit of God?

Revivals, then, are emphatically the hope of the world. From every estimate we can form on this subject, it would seem clear beyond a doubt that we must have them, and of a still more powerful character than we have hitherto had, or else the work of this world's conversion to God can never be consummated. It is impossible to see how 800,000,000 souls, or any considerable part of this number, can be washed from their sins, within the most distant time to which the millennium can be deferred, by the single drops of converting grace falling as now. Mighty revivals must become yet more and more frequent, until there shall cease to be intervals between them, and they shall run into each other, and flow together in one long and still spreading river of salvation.

And why not have such revivals? We do not see why they are not to be looked for – those of far greater power and wider extent than have hitherto been experienced. Where is the improbability of supposing that whole nations, the largest associated bodies of men on the globe, are to feel the power of the Spirit in one general and simultaneous effusion, and to show that they feel it by a general and simultaneous turning to God – even as the whole army of dry bones in the prophet's vision were re-animated and stood upon their feet at once, when the Spirit from the four winds came upon them?

Not less apposite than animating, just in this connection, are some words of the late Dr J W Alexander, of New York. "Imagine a shower of grace in this single city; every house filled with worshippers, every place of business made solemn or joyful by the presence of religious emotion. Think of seasons during which religion should be the great matter of interest with every young person. Think of the effect on ministers, on professing Christians, on sinners. Imagine, if you can, a universal work over the whole country and world! My brethren, what visions arise before the eye of faith in the expectation of such a blessing! Oh that I could impress, and be possessed myself with a due sense of the loveliness, the glory, the indispensableness of such a gift! If I judge aright, all other pursuits are nothing to the pursuit of this! Here is the great work of philanthropy, the *only* thing worth living for!"

"O Lord, Revive Thy Work!"

19

Are You Revived?

UNDER the pressure of deep feelings we pen these last lines. It arises, particularly, from the attempt to say a few things to the official teachers of God's Word. Ministers and Revivals! What a conjunction of terms! *Ministers*, how weighty their obligations! *Revivals*, how fraught with the mightiest consequences!

Is it not lamentable that *students for the ministry* are not more instructed upon the all-important subject of revivals? In what Theological Seminary does this hold even a subordinate place in the course of study, or the classroom exercise? Were it not well, among other provisions, to establish a Revival Professorship, or a Chair on Soul-Saving? Says Dr Noah Porter: "I deem it all-important that ministers, and those who are preparing to become ministers, should be *revival men*. I mean, men who understand the subject of revivals, who enter into it with a warm and decided interest, and whose preaching and influence in all respects shall be adapted to promote revivals. To cherish the spirit of revivals, then, in our Theological Seminaries, is the direct way to *multiply* revival ministers."

Precisely at this point is to be found a radical defect. The evil lies in the process of training. In the absorbing attention given to the science of theology, that which should be the chief aim in all ministerial preparation is comparatively lost sight of; and the young preachers do not enter upon their pastorates as *proselytisers of men*. They are skilled, it may be, in sermon-writing, and in the niceties of metaphysical and theological distinctions; but they are not skilled in the holy art of winning souls – if, indeed, they have any right appreciation of this as their work. We earnestly commend the thought to the leaders of the Lord's hosts.

If in any one thing more than in others the proverb, "Like priest like people," holds true, it is in respect to revivals of religion. Rarely, perhaps never, is the standard of piety in a church higher than that of its ministry, while the fruitage of a lifeless ministry is almost invariably a dead or lukewarm church. On the other hand, it is a rare fact to find a dead church under a living ministry. Look at all those great revivals whose records gild the page of church history with its brightest glory. Were not the ministry the first to receive the hallowed quickening in every instance? Was not Pentecost preceded by a baptism of fire on the apostles? Did not the Reformation owe its existence to the spiritual power of Luther in Germany, and Zwingli in Switzerland? So in America and in Great Britain, Edwards and Tennent, Whitefield and Wesley, were the first to be filled with quickening power. And thus it has continued to our day.

How evident, therefore, the fact that it is not the getting of men for the ministry that is the question now. Nor is it, 'How may we secure learned, able, eloquent, polished, educated men?' These may be very needful matters; but they are of the second grade. They are not the essentials; they are not indispensable. The question now is, 'How may we secure men full of the Holy Ghost and of faith?' 'How shall we bring forward a great army of *soul-savers?*' It is high time that a different standard and different balances came into use – the standard – not of literature and eloquence – but of the *apostles*, the *balances of the sanctuary*.

What an impressive lesson, too, does this teach us who are now the ministers of Christ. If the pulpit first receives, and then conveys, the quickening flame, is not an inert church largely due to ourselves? We cannot shun responsibility. It always goes with privilege, with leadership. Responsibility is measured by opportunity. God holds every man accountable for the use he makes of the power committed to his trust; and if one fail of fulfilling his obligations, he must answer both for that failure and for all the evil ensuing therefrom. Surely, then, the thought of our responsibility is enough to make us tremble! For with us is lodged a measureless power of good or evil.

Just here the question is in place: Do we not often attempt to shirk responsibility by casting it upon God? Thus one has written – "The language we have been accustomed to adopt is this; we must use the means, and leave the event to God; we can do no more than employ the means; this is our duty, and having done this, we must entrust the rest to Him who is the disposer of all things." Now such language sounds well, for it seems to be an acknowledgment of our own nothingness, and to savour of submission to God's sovereignty; but it is often *only* sound. It has not really any substance in it. Though there is truth stamped on *the face* of it, there is falsehood at *the root* of it. For it is only an attempt to cover our indolence. It is a way we have of blinking responsibility. We may be altogether *too* resigned in seeing no souls converted. Our orthodoxy may be a shield for our inactivity. Instead of acquiescing in the low state of Zion, it were better if, like the good Payson, we were in a "constant fever" over it.

Are we not rebuked by some of the great examples set before us in the preceding pages? Do we know a *prayerfulness* like that of Luther, who once said, "I have so much business to do today that I shall not be able to get through it with less than three hours' prayer." It is John Angel James who said, "We are weak in the pulpit because weak in the closet." Edward Payson thus writes to a brother minister: "Prayer is the first thing, the second thing, and the third thing necessary for a minister, especially if he have revivals. Pray, then, my dear brother, pray, pray, pray."

And Rev William Reid, in his admirable *Words to Winners of Souls*, speaks thus to his brethren: "Why is there so little anxiety to get time to pray? Why is there so little forethought in the laying out of time and employments, so as to secure a large portion of each day for prayer? Why is there so much speaking, yet so little prayer? Why is there so much running to and fro, yet so little prayer? Why so much bustle and business, yet so little prayer? Why so many meetings with our fellow-men, yet so few meetings with God? Why so little being alone, so little thirsting of the soul for the calm, sweet hours of unbroken solitude, when God and His child hold fellowship together, as if they could never part? It is this want that not only injures our own growth in grace, but makes us such unprofitable servants of Christ."

Do we know a *tireless industry* like that of Whitefield, who, true to the symbol on his seal – a winged heart and the inscription "Astra Petimus," "We seek the stars," – preached 18,000 sermons in his 34 years' ministry – over ten per week: or like that of Wesley, who preached 42,400 – over fifteen per week – in the 53 years of his ministry?

Do we know an engrossment in the master's business like that of Brainerd? – who could say of himself, on more than one occasion, "I cared not where or how I lived, or what hardships I went through, so I could but gain souls to Christ. While I was asleep, I dreamed of these things; and when I waked, the first thing I thought of was this great work."

Do we know a *travail of soul* for the ungodly like that of Paul? – who could affirm, "I say the truth in Christ, my conscience also bearing me witness in the Holy Ghost, that I have *great heaviness* and *continual sorrow* in my heart. For I could wish that myself were accursed from Christ for my brethren, my kinsmen according to the flesh." (*Romans 9:1-3*).

Do we know a singleness of purpose like that to which the sainted Brown, of Haddington, exhorted his sons? – "O labour, labour, to win souls to Christ!" Can we satisfactorily answer the question, "Is this my aim in *every sermon* I preach, in every visit I pay? Is it under the influence of this feeling that I continually live and walk and speak? Is it for this I pray and toil and fast and weep? Is it for this I spend and am spent, counting it, next to the salvation of my own soul, my chiefest joy to be the instrument of saving others? Is it for this that I exist? And to accomplish this would I gladly die?"

Do we know a *sincerity and engagedness* like that of Mr Shepherd? – who declared on his death-bed that the studying every sermon cost him prayers with strong crying and tears; that before he preached any sermon he got good from it himself; and that he always went up into his pulpit as if he were going to give up his account to his God.

Do we know a *reverent and earnest study of the Word* like that of Whitefield, who read the whole of Henry's *Exposition of the Bible* on his knees?

Of Richard Baxter it was said by one of his contemporaries, that when he spoke of the soul's weighty concerns, "his spirit was *drenched therein.*" And yet he confesses, "I seldom come out of the pulpit but my conscience smiteth me that I have been no more serious and fervent in such a case. It accuseth me, not so much for want of ornaments and elegancy, nor for letting fall an unhandsome word; but it asketh me: 'How couldst thou speak of life and death with such a heart? How couldst thou preach of heaven and hell in such a careless, sleepy manner? Dost thou believe what thou sayest? Art thou in earnest, or in jest? How canst thou tell people that sin is such a thing, and that so much misery is upon them and before them, and be no more affected with it?' " If *he* could say that, what might *our* confession be?

And, now, can we really say that while we admire the character of such men as we have referred to, and are ready to exclaim, "Would that I were such a minister; that such a grace might dwell, and rule, and shine in me; and make me thus faithful, and bring me to such blessedness," – while we are ready to say this – are we willing to *use the means* which they used for obtaining such holiness? Edwards says, "Often I have had very affecting views of my own sinfulness and vileness; very frequently to such a degree as to hold me in a kind of loud weeping, sometimes for a considerable time together, so that I have often been forced to shut myself up." And Archbishop Usher used, at one period of his life, on Saturday afternoon, to go alone to a riverside, and there recount his sins, and confess and bewail them to the Lord with floods of tears? Are we willing to live up to the Scripture precepts for the ministry as they did? Are we willing to watch and pray, and fast, and study, and keep our hearts, and fight with our sins – willing to deny ourselves, take up the cross, daily, and follow Christ – as they did? The Lord knoweth!

Let us admit it: if we who are ministers were nearer right, the churches and the world would be nearer right. If we were properly revived, the people around us would not long remain dull. We say *properly revived*, for all attempts to promote a revival till our own hearts are right, is mere beating the air. With a fervent state in our own mind, how full of unction will be our prayers, how deep the sincerity of our exhortations, how earnest and powerful the pleadings of our sermons! But in the absence of this all our effort will be empty and vain.

Alas, it is but too true that while we may not be chargeable with unsoundness in faith, nor outward negligence of duty, nor inconsistency of life, yet we may be the most grievous obstructions to revivals. As William Reid says, "One may be a dry and empty cistern, notwithstanding his orthodoxy; he may be freezing up and blasting life at the very time that he is speaking of the way of life. He may be repelling men from the cross even when he is in words proclaiming it: he may be standing between his flock and the blessing, even when he is calling it down from heaven!" These are terrible considerations, but they are only too true.

And how true also, these other words from the same source: "It is easier to speak or write about a revival than to set about it. There is so much rubbish to be swept out; so many self-raised hindrances to be dealt with; so many old habits to be overcome; so much sloth and easy-mindedness to be contended with; so much of ministerial routine to be broken through; and so much crucifixion, both of self and of the world, to be undergone, that we recoil from it. As Christ said of the unclean spirit which the disciples could not cast out, so we say here: This kind goeth not out but by prayer and fasting."

Certainly, dear brethren, we are feeble as preachers because we are feeble as *Christians*. And our very *profession* exposes us to this shallowness of piety. Because we are engaged in holy things, the people may think, and *we* may think, that we are holy – *forgetting* that a holy office does not make one holy – *forgetting* that he may be spiritual in his pulpit and not in his closet – *forgetting* that he may be the keeper of others' vineyards, without keeping his own – *forgetting* that it is easier to declaim against sins in others than to mortify them in himself – aye *forgetting* that he may be the instrument of grace to others, and yet himself be *lost!*

O, let us take heed to these things. Let the startling language of John Owen ring in our ears: "He that would go down to the pit in peace, let him obtain a great repute for religion; let him preach and labour to make others better than he is himself, and in the meantime neglect to humble his heart, to walk with God in a manifest holiness and usefulness." And equally startling are the words of Swinnock: "It is a doleful thing to fall into hell from under the pulpit; but Oh how dreadful a thing to drop thither out of the pulpit!"

Nor let us attempt to shun *our responsibility for revivals*. Again we say: If the churches are not revived, it is largely our fault. There is no question of it. And *what* a thought, that we are chargeable with the absence of revivals! – that *because we* do not act, no revival commences! Who is expected to be first in a reformation if not ourselves? Whose *duty* is it to lead the way *but* ours? God forbid that we lack either the requisite courage or consecration! God forbid that the blood of the impenitent be found on our garments!

And of the *churches* we would ask each one, How long is it since you have been refreshed from on high? How long have you been mourning the Saviour's absence? And are you now waiting anxiously, prayerfully, for His return? – showing, also, by your works, that you desire His return speedily.

It is a great question for each church to ask, Are we doing our part towards the world's conversion? Are we "daily adding" to us such as shall be saved? And it is a poor reflection if you are *barren* that other churches around you are so likewise. If a drought were consuming your crops, and the same were the case with the region around, would it give you comfort to know that you were no worse off than your neighbours? Or, if the showers were refreshing their parched fields, would it not awaken and increase your anxiety for equally copious rains? If others are dormant, surely that is a greater reason why *you* should be active.

Nor forget, that it is a fearful thing to be *merely* maintaining the proper and decorous service of God's house. Christianity is not simply a power of conservation, but of aggression. It must not merely live, but increase and cover the earth. It is not an outpost garrison, fixed and stationary in its defences, but an army burning for conquest, and going on by rapid marches and increasing victories. Indeed, if a church be not thus aggressive, it must dwindle and spiritually die. Staid and wealthy, but indolent churches, would do well to heed what Mr Spurgeon says: "While a church is not bringing others in, her own heart is becoming weak in its pulsations, and her entire constitution is becoming a prey to decline. The church must either bring forth children unto God, or die of consumption; she has no alternative but that. A church must either be fruitful or rot; and of all things a rotting church is the most offensive. Would God we could bury our dead churches out of our sight, as Abraham buried Sarah – for above ground they breed a pestilence of scepticism and moral death!"

To *individual Christians* we would say, Have you apprehended the fact that formalism – the having "a name to live while you are dead," – is your greatest peril? "I am not afraid," said one, "so much for my children that they fall into open vice – that they should become drunkards, thieves, or extortioners – as I am afraid that they shall get into that formal state which speaks about religion, professes it, and is yet destitute of it: if this should be their state, I would indeed fear for their eternal salvation." Well might one most dread this state; and yet perhaps in that very state may *you* at this moment be found!

When you consecrated yourself to Christ, you laid yourself on His altar. You presented your being a *living*, not a *dead* sacrifice. You declared yourself to be Christ's; having no right or title to your body, soul, property, time or talent. You professed to be dead unto sin, and alive unto God. And you set out with the inquiry, "Lord, what wilt thou have me to do?"

How has your life corresponded with that profession? How, in the matter of *separateness from sin?* Time was, in the days of the martyrs, when a female trained in the refinements of the Roman capital, would not throw a grain of incense on a pagan altar to save herself from the flames. Are you ready thus to resist every form of evil – if need be, even unto blood?

How has your life been in the matter of *Christ-like devotion to others' good?* There are many professing Christians who have never in their lives been the means of converting one soul! But who might not rationally hope, by humble, prayerful, faithful prosecution of every opening and opportunity for personal Christian influence, to be the means of leading to Christ at least *one soul every year?* Now consider what will be the result whenever this shall be the earnest aim of every Christian – taking their present number as the basis. The church would be doubled annually; and in less than three years, this whole nation, or an equivalent population, would be gathered into the fold of the Good Shepherd! – prepared to go out and unfurl the gospel banner in every nation, town and hamlet under heaven, proclaiming in every tongue the wonders of redeeming grace! And if but the same ratio of increase were continued for *nine years*, the whole world would be converted to God!

How entirely practicable, therefore, the world's conversion, if but individual Christians were alive to their duty. All that is wanted is a real absorption, a genuine enthusiasm, in this work of soul-saving. Said Mr Moody, of Chicago, when in England, and addressing a large crowd, with scholars and noblemen in it: "We want enthusiasm in God's work. We find it in the world. Men are desperately in earnest in business circles. Hell is earnest. Why should we not be? We talk about infidelity, and all the *isms* that are creeping over the world; but I am more afraid of a cold formal*ism* than anything else. One thing I admire in Garibaldi – his enthusiasm. In 1867, when on his way to Rome, he was told that if he got there he would be imprisoned. Said he, 'If fifty Garibaldis are imprisoned, let Rome be free!' And when the cause of Christ is buried so deep in our hearts that we do not think of ourselves, and are willing to die for it, then we will reach our fellow-men!"

This was well and nobly said. For an engagedness like that would transform one's whole being into a living power for good. The whole depends, under God, upon whether we will act, henceforth, under the constant presence of a high purpose to live, not unto ourselves, but *unto the Lord*. From a thousand wires welded into one they forge the Damascus blade, that can divide the gossamer, or cut an iron bar asunder. So only let the manifold energies of one's being be molten into a single force, by the potent heat of a mighty purpose to serve God always and in all, and that holy and steady resolve will shape a life invincible by anything except almightiness itself.

And is not the single consideration of the peril of men's souls, of a dying race, enough to produce such engagedness? A heathen king once put on sackcloth over the sin and ruin of a single city. Another heathen monarch, at the head of two million men, sat down and wept because in a hundred years all that host would be dead. And still other heathens cried out to one of God's unfaithful servants, "What meanest thou, O sleeper? arise! call upon thy God!" Would that a louder cry of perishing millions would wake *our* guilty slumbers! Oh, where will they all soon be? Dead! dead! And yet where are our tears and loud weeping, both for ourselves and for our fellows? Alas! that we can see thousands perish around us, and our sleep never be disturbed! – no vision of their awful doom ever scaring us! – no cry from their lost souls ever turning our peace into bitterness!

Was Dr Arnot *too* enthusiastic when he exclaimed: "I see men and women perishing. The number is so great that it overwhelms me. My brain is burning; my heart is breaking. The church is asleep, and the world, too, and they are hugging each other. I am weary with holding in. I must cry out; and I would rather be counted singular in the judgment of man than be unfaithful in the judgment of God!"

Dear reader; bring all this home to your own conscience. *You are neglecting souls!* And can you let another day pass without an effort to save at least *one?* Choose whom you will try to influence; and then go to your closet and cry mightily to God for His blessing upon your endeavour; and next go to that soul, with tract, or book, or loving epistle, or broken sobs, and tears – and it may prove to be an arrow in God's bow to bring down one of his enemies.

Then try to stir up a revival spirit in the church to which you belong. Do not wait for a *large number* to move. What evidence can be drawn, either directly or indirectly from the Scriptures, that a great many must unite in prayer before God will hear and answer? We do verily believe it to be a device of the enemy of revivals, to persuade Christians who begin to feel anxious for their return, that there is no use in the prayers and efforts of a few, as long as there is no general waking up of the church. Instead of this, ask, "Am I right in this matter?" "Do not I need in this respect a great revival?" "Have I felt and acted on these points as I ought to have done?" And when *you are truly revived,* unite with the few others of like feeling and resolve *never to give up without a blessing.* Go to your pastor with that feeling, and tell him of it. Ministers are greatly influenced by their members. The writer has often been stirred to thought and effort by someone in his flock saying, "Pastor, is it not time that we had a revival?" Speak to *others,* also, of your feelings, and mention it in the prayer meetings, and so work on; and *you will be the means of a great awakening.*

Who, in laying down this volume, will not join in these "*reasons why I desire a revival?*"

God loves revivals. A revival is not a questionable good. It bears the superscription of heaven.

There is great need of a revival. Zion languishes. Christians are asleep. Iniquity is coming in like a flood. Sinners are perishing. Christ is dishonoured.

God comes near in a revival. Our sins have hid his face from us. He seems far distant. If He deign to revive His work He will return. He will hover near. He will cause His face to shine, and we shall be saved.

I wish my own spirit to be refreshed. "As the hart panteth after the water-brooks, so panteth my soul after thee, O God."

A revival of religion would be a precious evidence that God accepts my poor endeavours. Often am I ready to cry out, "Who is sufficient for these things? Am I in the way of God's working here? Oh for some tokens of my Master's favour!"

A revival would be a great blessing to this church. Why are these followers of Christ so negligent in prayer, so worldly, so barren? I long to see Zion put on strength. O Lord, quicken thy people, and make Jerusalem a praise!

In granting a revival, God would glorify Himself. He manifests His glory more especially in revivals of religion. He glorifies His sovereignty, His power, His truth, and His grace. If He pour out on us a Pentecostal blessing, how would men and angels praise Him!

A revival would add glory to the crown of Christ. Souls are Christ's choicest jewels. They are "the joy set before Him." I faint to see His kingdom come. The bowing of sinners at the foot of His cross is the rumbling of His chariot wheels. Come, Lord Jesus, come quickly!

"O Lord, Revive Thy Work!"

Made in the USA
Monee, IL
18 October 2026

66035059R00155